THE
NAMES
OF
DEAD
GIRLS

Also by Eric Rickstad

Lie in Wait
The Silent Girls
Reap

Praise for
The Names of Dead Girls

"Beautifully written with original language and imagery, *The Names of Dead Girls* is a chilling page-turner. The superb cast of characters rings so very true, from the conflicted mom police detective to the troubled Rachel Rath to the anthropomorphic, wet fog. Atmospheric, empathetic, and addictive."

—James W. Ziskin, Edgar-nominated
author of the Ellie Stone Mysteries

"Eric Rickstad is the rare writer who can wrap a dark, gritty story in smooth, poetic prose. If you haven't discovered his work yet, *The Names of Dead Girls* is the place to start. It's a taut, masterful thriller and a terrific read."

—Alafair Burke, *New York Times* bestselling
author of *The Ex*

"A tour de force of unstoppable suspense drives readers deep into Rickstad's dark and haunting world. An out-and-out bone chiller. Impossible to put down."

—Gregg Olsen, #1 *New York Times* bestselling author

"Eric Rickstad has handed us a diamond of a thriller in *The Names of Dead Girls*. […] Rickstad is a seriously gifted writer, and trust me when I say that this book, from its explosive beginning to its startling ending, will grab you by the throat and not let go. You have been warned."

—Mark Pryor, author of *The Paris Librarian*

"A complex and emotional thriller—Rickstad blurs the lines of good and evil as a detective's desperate need to protect his daughter from a depraved killer, and his hunger for justice, distorts his obligation to the law."

—Wendy Walker, bestselling author of
Emma in the Night and *All Is Not Forgotten*

"*The Names of Dead Girls* is that brilliant, rare literary thriller: captivating in character, told with precision, and fueled by relentless, mounting terror. A compulsive page-turner that will have you racing to the end even as you dread what's coming."

—Steve Weddle, author of *Country Hardball*

"*The Names of Dead Girls* is a taut, slick thriller that absolutely races out of the gate. Eric Rickstad has a special talent for writing scenes that are almost unbearably tense. Warning: Once you start this one, you won't be able to stop."

—Brad Parks, author of *Say Nothing*

THE
NAMES
OF
DEAD
GIRLS

A Canaan Crime Novel

ERIC
RICKSTAD

wm

WILLIAM MORROW
An Imprint of HarperCollins*Publishers*

HarperCollins
PUBLISHERS
Since 1817

HarperCollins books may be purchased for educational, business, or sales promotional use. For information, please e-mail the Special Markets Department at SPsales@harpercollins.com.

FIRST EDITION

Designed by Diahann Sturge

Library of Congress Cataloging-in-Publication Data has been applied for.

ISBN 978-0-06-267280-3

17 18 19 20 21   LSC   10 9 8 7 6 5 4 3 2 1

For Meridith, Samantha, and Ethan

PART I

The winter of imprisonment is over, freedom his again after years of forced dormancy.

Freedom.

The taste bright and metallic, like a drop of virgin's blood on the tip of the tongue.

Freedom.

The sight irresistible, like the first flourish of pale, young female flesh in spring.

Freedom.

The sound musical, like the simper of the meek begging release from the mighty.

Freedom.

The odor intoxicating, like that of sweat shimmering off the skin of the terrified.

Freedom.

The feel intimate, like fingernails of the desperate raking runnels in the flesh of his face.

He watches, his head bowed, hat pulled tight to his brow, cracks his back and stretches his arms above his head taking in the expanse of his domain. Emperor. Lord.

He radiates with freedom, exalted.

Saliva pools in the fleshy pockets at the back of his mouth, where once he extracted wisdom teeth with pliers for the sole, sweet, ex-cruciating ecstasy of it.

He reaches a hand into his trousers, feels himself, dreaming of what is to come.

Freedom unleashed.

1

Thursday, November 3, 2011

Rachel Rath's flesh knew before her mind did that she was being watched.

Her face flashed hot, and the skin on her back prickled, terror trickling down her spine as if her backbone were being traced with the crooked, grimy finger of a letch, one single vertebrae at a time.

This was not the creepy sensation she and girlfriends endured when ogled by middle-aged but decidedly milquetoast men. This was an instinctive caution the body signaled for its survival.

Be aware.

Beware.

Rachel turned, incrementally, as if in a nightmare, her arm slipping from her boyfriend Felix's arm as she pivoted.

The sensation of being violated scurried over her skin and sank in her belly, leaving her exposed.

She saw no one, yet she shivered, as attuned to her surroundings as a rabbit hidden in a screen of brush.

She reached to tug Felix's sleeve as he busied himself with a bag of birdseed for his canaries—and stopped.

Seized with terror.

There.

There he was: the one whose gaze drained her blood.

2

Canaries.

Frank Rath stared at the disconnected landline phone in his hand.

Ned Preacher had just hung up on him, the echo of his strained breathing and lecherous laugh echoing in Rath's bones.

And another sound, too.

Canaries.

Where had Rath heard canaries? He pounded a fist against his forehead, tried to remember.

Had to remember.

It was imperative. Where—

It struck him like a blow. He'd heard canaries in his daughter Rachel's new place, the apartment she'd moved into just days ago to live with her gangly boyfriend, Felix.

Felix owned two canaries.

Preacher must have called from Rachel's place; he must have been hiding and watching Rachel in her place, called to torment

Rath who was an hour away and would never reach Rachel's apartment before Preacher—

Rath tried not to imagine what Preacher might do. Did not have to imagine. He had seen it firsthand, Preacher's *work*.

Sixteen years ago, Rath had been first on the scene to his sister Laura's murder; not as the young state police detective he'd been at the time, but as Laura's younger brother. He'd been an hour late. Instead of showing up on time to help Laura with the birthday dinner she'd planned for him, he'd been with a woman in a motel room. He was allowed, he'd reasoned. It was his birthday. As he'd parked in Laura's driveway he'd rehearsed the lie he'd tell his sister for being late: he'd been working on the Connecticut River Valley Killer case.

Her front door had been open and he'd stepped inside, calling out: "Sorry, I was—"

Her body had lain at the bottom of the stairs, legs pinned abnormally beneath her torso, her lacerated face turned to the side as if in shame, the once white carpet now so drenched with her blood it squished underfoot. Clots and strings of blood slopped on the walls. Her neck had been broken and she'd been rudely violated with objects other than the male anatomy, though that would prove to have been used too. Her husband Daniel's body had lain draped over her as if trying to protect her even in death. He'd been viciously and repeatedly stabbed.

This was Ned Preacher's work.

Preacher: Laura and Daniel's former handyman who'd skipped town sixteen months earlier. Preacher, now just paroled after serving only sixteen years of his twenty-five-to-life sentence for the murders. Preacher, who now claimed on the phone *he* was Rachel's father, claimed he'd had an affair with Laura before leaving town. Preacher who'd exulted: *Your sister couldn't stay away from the bad boys any more than you could from the bad girls. Well, she picked the wrong bad boy, wouldn't you say, playing with her handyman while her pretty boy husband was away? Then, I came back through town to give her some more. And she gave me holier than thou, Holly fucking Hobby bullshit. A mask. I fucking knew. What I didn't know was about the baby upstairs. Until later, when I read about it in the papers. She should have let me take her one last time. Given in to her nature. I'd have gone off none the wiser. Instead she had to play Good Girl.* Agitate. His voice had sounded distorted. Demonic. *I can do simple fucking math. Rachel. She's mine. How is she, Rath,* your *daughter? She seems fine. From what I see.*

Rath's brain crackled with violent thoughts.

He had to get to Rachel's place.

The caller ID showed PRIVATE. Rath pressed *69. A mechanical voice droned: "This number cannot be reached by . . ."

Rath slammed the phone receiver down so hard it cracked.

On his cell phone, he dialed Rachel's number. He should have called her first. He wasn't thinking clearly.

Rachel's phone kicked to voice mail.

"Call me!" Rath shouted.

He dialed 911.

A woman's measured voice inquired: "911. What's—"

"I need to report a break-in."

"What's the address, sir?"

"I don't know the exact address."

"The break-in isn't taking place where you're calling from?"

"No."

"And you don't have the address?"

Rath's heartbeat accelerated.

"How do you know someone is breaking in if you don't know where it is occurring, sir?" the woman said.

"I— It's in Johnson. Up a hill by a—" He had to think. His brain fritzed with adrenaline. "I know where it's happening. My daughter's apartment. I got a call."

"From your daughter?"

How could he say he got a call from the person who had broken in and have this woman believe he wasn't a lunatic?

"Sir? If this isn't a serious call—"

"My daughter is in danger," Rath barked. He took a deep breath. Whether Preacher planned to harm Rachel physically or not, whatever he had in mind was meant to cause pain. "I'm a retired detective, my name is Frank Rath, and my daughter is in trouble. Someone is at her apartment. Right now. Someone who intends to hurt her. A man who—" Raped and murdered her mother, and now claims he's . . .

"But you don't know where your daughter lives?" The woman's voice was bright with suspicion.

"She *just* moved there. I don't know the exact *address*. It's off— I'm trying to remember the road, it goes up a hill in Johnson, near where the post office is—" His mind careened. He needed to slow his thoughts. The microwave clock showed five minutes had elapsed. What Preacher could do in five minutes— "Forget it."

"Sir. If you hang up we have to—"

He killed the call and charged out the kitchen door, no time for a jacket. No time for anything. He'd lost too much time already.

A bitter rain battered him. The clear skies had fouled in the time he'd been home, the deep snow starting to melt as fog reached its tentacles across the old farmyard.

In his '74 Scout, Rath took his .22 revolver from the glove box, checked that it was loaded, cranked the ignition key.

The engine sputtered.

He cranked the key again, worked the choke.

The engine caught.

The Scout juddered down his sloppy, muddied dirt road. Rath tried to dial Sonja Test, the Canaan Police detective he'd recently worked with as a consultant on what the media called the *Mad Doctor* case, macabre murders involving teenage girls. Test could call ahead to colleagues in Johnson for him, except Rath's nerves were too splintered and the Scout shaking too hard for him to work the phone.

At the end of his dirt road, he dialed.

Test's phone went to voice mail.

"Call me," Rath said.

He speed-dialed another number, Harland Grout, a friend and former Canaan Police senior detective who'd quit his post following the Mad Doctor case.

The phone rang and rang.

A logging truck hurtled out of the forming fog, rocking the Scout on its aged springs, strafing it with road grit.

"Rath?" said Grout. "If you shot another deer and called to beg for help hanging it—"

"Call the sheriff's department in Johnson. Soon as we hang up. Someone you know personally, have them get to a— There's, um, a red house. It's on a dirt road. I think the one that that winds up past the post office. Whichever one runs along Gihon Stream."

Rath pulled onto the road and hit the gas, much to the Scout's protest. "Get a car there ASAP."

"What is this?" Grout said.

"Preacher, he called me," Rath said. "He's at Rachel's."

Silence bled on the line.

"On it." Grout hung up.

Rath pinned the gas pedal. The Scout bucked so hard it felt like it would fly apart. Still, it managed just 53 mph.

Not fast enough.

Not nearly.

3

Harland Grout could not concentrate on the White Mountain Mall's security camera feeds in the mall security office. He had never heard fear or panic in Frank Rath's voice in all the years he'd known him. Going back to seventeen years ago when Rath had served as Grout's mentor as a state police detective in the '90s, Rath had always been stoic and composed in the face of any atrocity. Yet in their phone call just now Rath's voice was cut through with both fear and panic. It unnerved Grout so much he'd called the deputy in Johnson and told him to get up to the house Rath had described, like yesterday.

Ned Preacher meant Rath's daughter harm. Preacher: serial rapist who'd gamed the system and served a third of the time he should have for multiple rapes and murders by pleading to lesser crimes and being the golden boy saint while inside prison to reduce his time served for *good behavior*. Preacher: slippery, evil con man and murderer of Rath's sister and her husband while their baby, Rachel, had slept upstairs. Rachel left for Rath to raise alone, the reason he'd quit as state police detective sixteen years ago.

Preacher: paroled early from prison. Preacher: in Rachel's apartment, and calling Rath to torment him.

When Rath had said those two names together—*Preacher* and *Rachel*—Grout's initial fear had been replaced by disgust and the need to act. Then, futility. Because Grout was stuck here, unable to act. Stuck in a mall in northwestern New Hampshire watching the camera feeds until a rogue form of OCD compelled some poor woman to take a five-finger discount on a tchotchke from the Hallmark store, so Grout could bust the poor soul as if she'd committed infanticide.

Grout was stuck wearing a uniform that made him look and feel like a Webelo. No sidearm. No cuffs. All the legal authority of a dormitory monitor. No ability to do what was in his nature, what he was good at, being a detective. He'd quit his position as the Canaan Police senior detective following the Mad Doctor case and taken this gig to do what he believed was best for his wife and two kids, all for an extra $75 a week. He'd known it was a mistake his first day on the job. He might as well have lopped off his own nuts with pruning shears.

How could he just stand here, rooted like a potted plant?

How could he—

A voice spoke to him.

Grout blinked.

"Sir." The newest and most earnest of the young recruits from Granite Private Security addressed Grout from his CCTV station that covered the C Quadrant of Spencer Gifts.

"What?" Grout said.

"We've got a live one, sir." The newbie could hardly contain his prideful and slippery grin. "A red hander."

On the monitor, a teenage boy slipped an item in his hoodie's front pocket. The item looked like a pet rock.

"That's the second one he's put in his pocket," Newbie said, his voice trilling. He was all but drooling. "He's making his way out, sir!" He stabbed a finger at the screen as if Grout couldn't see the shoplifter. Newbie's body coiled. "Soon as perp exits premises! And . . ." His body coiled tighter. "We got 'im DTR."

"DTR?"

"Dead to rights, sir."

"Go get 'im."

"Really, sir?" Newbie's eyes gleamed.

Grout nodded.

Newbie broke for the door and exited in a blur.

Grout looked at his car keys on his desk. *Do it,* a voice said. The voice of the detective he'd once been, still was. *Do it. Just go.*

Instead he sagged in Newbie's abandoned chair and moaned for Frank Rath and for his daughter, Rachel, who in all likelihood was dead by now.

Or worse.

4

Rath drove the Scout as fast as he could without crashing into the cedars along the desolate stretch of road known as Moose Alley that wound through thirty miles of remote bog and boreal forest. The rain was not as violent here, the fog just starting to crawl out of the ditch.

Rath hoped the police were at Rachel's and had prevented whatever cruelty Preacher had in store; but hope was as useful as an unloaded gun.

The Scout's temperature gauge climbed perilously into the red. If the engine overheated, Rath would be stuck out here, miles from nowhere, cut off from contact. In this remote country, cell service was like the eastern mountain lion: its existence rumored, but never proven.

Finally, Rath reached the bridge that spanned the Lamoille River into the town of Johnson, his relief to be near Rachel crushed by fear of what he might find.

At the red light where Route 15 met Main Street, he waited,

stuck behind a school bus full of kids likely coming from a sporting event.

He needed to get around the bus, run the light, but a Winnebago swayed through the intersection.

The light turned green.

Rath tromped on the gas pedal. The Scout lurched through the light. On the other side of the intersection, Rath jammed the brake pedal to avoid ramming into the back of the braking bus, the bus's red lights flashing.

A woman on the sidewalk glared at Rath as she cupped the back of the head of a boy who jumped off the bus. She fixed the boy's knit cap and flashed Rath a last scalding look as she hustled the boy into a liquor store.

The bus crept forward.

No vehicles approached from the opposing lane.

Rath passed the bus and ran the next two red lights.

The rain was a mist here, and the low afternoon sun broke briefly through western clouds, a silvery brilliance mirroring off the damp asphalt, nearly blinding Rath.

Rachel's road lay just ahead.

Rath swerved onto it and sped up the steep hill.

A state police cruiser and a sheriff's sedan were parked at hurried angles in front of Felix and Rachel's place.

He feared what was inside that apartment. Feared what Preacher had done to Rachel.

Sixteen years ago, standing at the feet of his sister's body, Rath had heard a whine, like that of a wet finger traced on the rim of a crystal glass, piercing his brain. He'd charged upstairs into the bedroom, to the crib. There she'd lain, tiny legs and arms pumping as if she'd been set afire, that shrill escape of air rising from the back of her throat.

Rachel.

In the moment Rath had picked Rachel up, he'd felt a permanent upheaval, like one plate of the earth's lithosphere slipping beneath another; his selfish past life subducting beneath a selfless future life; a niece transformed into a daughter by acts of violent cruelty.

For months, Rath had kept Rachel's crib beside his bed and lain sleepless as he'd listened to her every frayed breath at night. He'd panicked when she'd fallen quiet, shaken her lightly to make certain she was alive, been flooded with relief when she'd wriggled. He'd picked her up and cradled her, promised to keep her safe. Thinking, If we just get through this phase, I won't ever have to worry like this again.

But peril pressed in at the edges of a girl's life, and worry planted roots in Rath's heart and bloomed wild and reckless. As Rachel had grown, Rath's worry had grown, and he'd kept vigilant for the lone man who stood with his hands jammed in his trouser pockets behind the playground fence. In public, he'd gripped Rachel's hand, his love ferocious and animal. If anyone *ever* harmed her.

Rath yanked the Scout over a bank of plowed snow onto a spit of dead lawn.

He jumped out, tucked his .22 revolver into the back waistband of his jeans, and ran for the stairs that led up the side of the old house to the attic apartment.

He hoped he wasn't too late.

5

Dusk leached what pale gray light remained of the winter afternoon. Fog curled.

A trooper and a deputy sheriff stood at the top of the apartment's stair landing, the trooper's hands cupped to his eyes as he peered into the apartment door's window, lit by a light from inside.

Rath bounded up the stairs as his revolver dug into his lower back. The lawmen turned to him, hands going to their sidearms.

"I'm her father!" Rath shouted, winded.

The two men's hands remained on the butts of their weapons as Rath stood just below the landing. "I called this in," he said. "Frank Rath." The deputy's eyes brightened with recognition and he removed his hand from his sidearm. His coarse mustache was black as shoe polish. The trooper, Rath's age with an impeccably trimmed ginger goatee flecked with silver, kept his hand on his weapon.

"She's in there with him," Rath said, his voice cracking.

"You called this in, sir?" the trooper said. Being a step above

Rath, the trooper stood a good foot taller, his position of command undeniable. "No one inside called 911?"

Rath stepped onto the landing, forcing the trooper to take a step back. The trooper recognized Rath now. Preacher's recent early parole had caused a hum of outrage in regional law enforcement, and the Mandy Wilks and Mad Doctor cases Rath had helped solve had made headlines. Photos of Rath had been part of several stories.

Rath's revolver jabbed into his lower spine. He needed to keep at an angle so the revolver remained concealed. It was legal, but being armed would escalate the situation.

"If *you* called, we can't just break in," the trooper said. "We need probable for a locked building."

"You *have* probable. *And* you needed to be inside an hour ago." Rath tried to shoulder between the two men, but the trooper stepped in his way. "I pay the damned rent," Rath lied. "Break it down. She's in there with Preacher."

"*Preacher?*" the trooper said. "You think he's in there? Preacher?"

"I know he is. Didn't Grout tell—"

"Get it," the trooper said to the deputy.

The deputy hurried down the stairs to pop his cruiser's trunk, hustled back up with a door ram.

"Stay outside," the trooper said.

Rath wanted to break the door down and rush in there himself, but he understood his need to stand down, for now.

"Out of the way." The trooper drew his sidearm as the deputy rammed the door just below its knob, the weakest part of the structure.

The door splintered; the deputy rammed it again.

The door's lock broke, and the door swung open.

Canaries shrieked.

The trooper charged inside, shouting: "State police!"

The deputy strode in behind the trooper, weapon drawn.

The canaries flapped and fussed as the two cops swept to the kitchen, then down the hallway.

Rath reached for his revolver and stepped into the apartment.

"Police!" the trooper shouted from the back.

Rath looked around. A laptop computer sat open on the scarred pine trunk in front of a flea-market futon. The screen saver faded in and out with photos of Rachel and Felix.

The trooper said from the back, "What the hell."

Rath grasped his revolver, took a shooter's stance.

The air grew brittle with the tension of imminent violence.

Rath eyed the crawl-space door set in the wall beside the futon. It was open, a crack. Just enough for someone to see out from inside.

Rath licked his dry lips.

He stepped toward the door, revolver trained on it.

The canaries chittered frantically.

A feather floated in the air.

Rath reached for the crawl-space door.

A voice behind him demanded, "Stop."

Rath didn't move, eyes locked on the crawl-space door.

The deputy stepped into Rath's line of vision, shook his head fiercely, his sidearm drawn but its muzzle aimed at the floor at Rath's feet.

"Depart the premises." The deputy wagged his sidearm toward the door. "And holster the firearm. Understand? Don't make me arrest you."

Rath eased the .22 down. He could not know if his revolver or something the deputy had witnessed in the back room spurred the deputy's grave bearing.

"Until you tell me what's back there," Rath said, "I'm not moving." His lower back, along the *erecta spinae*, ignited with a cauterizing pain he'd thought he'd left in the past.

From the rear of the place, the state trooper appeared. His face was all wrong.

Exasperated.

He holstered his weapon, stared Rath dead. "You sure your daughter was here?"

Rath raised an eyebrow at the crawl-space door, to indicate the door was open a crack.

"The place is cleared," the trooper said as he nodded to Rath that he understood, trained his weapon at the crawl-space door. He nodded to the deputy, counted three on his fingers.

The deputy threw open the door and swung his weapon on it. He peered inside the space.

"Shit." He turned to Rath. "Nothing. Boxes."

"I heard the birds," Rath said. He needed to get out of there. But to where? He took his phone out and tried Rachel's cell. Voice mail. "Call me," he pleaded, "now. Please."

"Birds?" the trooper said.

Rath waved a hand at the caged canaries. "When Preacher called, I heard those goddamned things."

"What is this about, sir?" the deputy asked.

Rath apprised them of Preacher's call, leaving out Preacher's sickening lie about Rachel.

"Didn't Grout *tell* you?" Rath said.

"Dispatch just said a break-in was in process. Grout couldn't reach me. But there was no evidence of such when we showed. You sure it was those birds?" the trooper said.

When Preacher had implied he was watching Rachel, intimated he would hurt her with his ugly lie, Rath had heard birds. He'd assumed they were Felix's canaries. Who wouldn't have? Maybe he'd been right, Rachel and Preacher *had* been here, except Rath was too late.

"Sir?" the trooper said. "You sure you heard these birds?"

"No," Rath said. "But—"

The trooper gazed at the apartment's ruined door, his concern now clearly whether he'd get his ass chewed for busting down a door he had no legal right to bust down.

Rath's cell phone rang, startling the canaries into discordant birdsong.

PRIVATE.

Preacher's ID.

Rath stared at it, his muscles locked with the grim certainty of whose cold voice would greet him.

"Answer that, sir," the trooper said.

PRIVATE.

"Answer it."

The phone would kick to voice mail in another ring.

"Answer it. Or I will."

Rath answered.

6

From the other side of the birdcage, the man appeared again.

He'd disappeared so quickly earlier that Rachel had begun to believe she'd imagined him, the threat of him. Now, he stared at Rachel, just long enough to lock eyes for half a heartbeat, only his eyes visible to her, his face obscured by the bars of the birdcage.

He turned away, as if satisfied his message had been received. But what message? Who was he?

"What do you want?" Rachel said, her voice too loud, a cry.

Birds squawked, a dog barked.

The pet shop patrons gawked at Rachel: the girl who cried out.

"What is it?" Felix took her icy hand in his warm one.

"Nothing." She tried to swallow. Couldn't. Her throat dry as bone dust.

"*Nothing?* You're shouting and shaking. Your hand is freezing. Are you sick?"

"No." She'd be damned if she'd let Felix know some guy glimpsing her for a blink had traumatized her. She didn't need him thinking she'd gone berserk. She'd been distraught enough since learning just days ago that her birth parents had been murdered when she was a baby, that they had not been killed in a car wreck as her adoptive father had told her years ago. She was *still* freaked out. Who wouldn't be? But she didn't need Felix to think she believed every creep who eyed her was going to kill her. Even if she did feel that way now, about this man.

Truth was, since learning of her parents' murders she'd felt altered. Alien. And angry. *Infuriated*. Not at the truth of her parents' deaths so much as how she'd heard it—from a stranger, a weirdo girl with purple hair at a Family Matters meeting for young women trying to decide what to do about their unplanned pregnancies. Rachel hadn't been pregnant, thank God. She'd gone to figure out if a predator was using the meetings to select victims. Since she was a little girl she'd helped her father with his mundane private investigation cases, and recently she'd had a fixation with deviant violent criminals and serial killers; so when her father had told her a dead girl might be linked to the meetings, Rachel had investigated, despite her father insisting otherwise. Purple Hair had mentioned Rachel's parents' murder in passing, assuming Rachel had known. Shaken, Rachel had holed up in a motel and googled the murders on her phone. She'd not found much, the crimes old. But she'd read a headline and enough to know it was true. Enough to know she did not want to know any more about it.

What galled her was that her dad had thought she was too weak to hear the truth. What bunk. He'd raised her to be, if not tough, then resilient. If she were a boy, he probably would have had a "man-to-man" when she was thirteen. It maddened her. And wounded her, too, that he believed she had so little brass.

And now? If she told Felix some freak staring at her in a pet shop with other people around skeeved her out, she'd look even weaker. She wouldn't stand for it.

Besides, the man was gone again now.

Vanished.

Where was he?

Felix was speaking, his voice white noise. Rachel pushed past a boy tapping a finger on an aquarium to taunt a tarantula and came to the other side of the birdcages. The man was gone, and Rachel was left with a need to ask him just what the fuck he meant with his leer. Her heart pumped hard. She felt like her old self for a second. Defiant. Able. She felt like her dad's daughter.

She spun in a circle to try to locate the man, knocking Tarantula Boy. The boy shrieked.

Again, all eyes on Rachel.

Mortified, she slunk out of the store, Felix trailing.

Outside, the dying sun had broken through rain clouds, its reflection mirroring off the dark, wet street, shimmering in the fog and backlighting the rain so it streaked down as flashes of liquid silver.

She did not see the man.

"What's going on?" Felix said.

"Nothing." In the few months she'd known Felix, Rachel had never lied to him, not even about nonsense, and questioned why she lied now and in the store to hide her fear. Who cared if she was afraid? It felt ridiculous now anyway, her fear, out here in the open air.

That feeling died quickly.

As she and Felix entered the Lovin' Cup coffee shop next door,

Rachel felt the stranger's eyes on her again, her face warming, the sensation of that grimy fingertip snaking down her spine again, down and down and down as she sneaked a look back over her shoulder, afraid of what she might see; afraid more to see nothing to explain her terror.

7

As she and Felix sat on a bench under the Lovin' Cup's awning, Rachel turned on her phone to find messages from her father, each more urgent than the last.

Back in September, when she'd come here to attend Johnson State, she'd often put off returning her father's calls, even when she'd missed him; especially when she'd missed him. She'd wanted to prove to herself she could be on her own. All she'd proven was she could choke back her homesickness and wound her father with unnecessary worry. In not getting back to him she'd denied herself and her father a chance to share in her transition, and she had come to regret it.

Now she wanted to hear her father's voice as much as he apparently wanted to hear hers, perhaps more.

"Hey," Felix said.

Rachel pressed her fingertips to Felix's lips.

Her father picked up first ring.

"Where *are* you?" His voice was all wrong, aggrieved.

"School. Well. In town."

Water dripped from the awning above Rachel.

Felix got up and stood at the edge of the sidewalk.

"Get home," her father said.

"I can't, I have my evening English Lit in an hour. My Civic's dead. And—"

"Not *home* home. Your apartment. Get over here now. Meet me here."

His severe manner scared her. She'd had enough of fear. "What are you *doing* there?" she said.

Felix was looking across the street.

"Get here as soon as you can," Rachel's father stressed.

Water dripped from the awning, spattered the toe of her boot. It was tinged red, like thinned blood.

Felix crossed the street and looked back at her, though Rachel could not make out the look on his face. The rain and fog, and the strange glow of the wet pavement cast that entire side of the street in a silvery halo.

"Fast as you can," her father said.

"OK. Hang up. Everything's OK."

"Right."

Felix stared at her. No. Not at her. At the awning?

The bloodred water dripped.

What the hell was going on?

Rachel stepped out onto the curb and shielded her eyes against the rain and the disappearing sun to look up at the awning. What was Felix staring at? She saw nothing, except the red water, trickling from rusted nails' heads in the tin roofing.

She suddenly felt a presence behind her, at her neck. Heard breathing. Too close.

She spun around.

Felix.

"Damn it. What are you doing sneaking up on me," Rachel said.

"I wasn't sneaking. *You* were spacing."

"We gotta go see my dad. He's at our place. Why are you acting so sketchy?" Rachel said.

"Trying to figure out what that guy was looking at."

"What guy?" Rachel's pulse fluttered at her temple.

Felix pointed across the street. "Some guy was over there. I tried to tell you, but you shut me up. I swore he was looking at you. Like. Weird."

"What did he look like?"

"Hard to tell. And he had his hood pulled up over his head. But he just stood there. I don't know how to describe it. I went over to see what was up, but he was gone. I looked to see what else he might have been staring at." He tipped his chin up toward the balcony a story above the awning, where patrons of the Lovin' Cup sat in warm weather. There was no one there. "I thought maybe someone was up there." Felix frowned. "No one was."

"We need to see my dad," Rachel said. "Something weird is going on."

Water dripped from the awning into Rachel's pixie cut she'd bleached platinum for kicks, and now wished she hadn't. Her sprouting roots looked moronic; soon she'd sport a reverse skunk stripe for her middle part. She wiped at the water on her cheek. Rubbed it between her fingers.

In the fast-falling dark, she'd have bet her life it was blood.

8

Rath spotted the pale glow of the cell-phone flashlights in the fog as Rachel and Felix hiked up the dark road toward him. He wanted to run to Rachel, but feared he would alarm her more than he already had. Alarm was fine—it sharpened focus—panic was not. Whatever came next would require cool heads.

Rath's phone rang. Harland Grout. Grout had been the one to call Rath earlier in the apartment, his mall work number showing PRIVATE. He'd asked how things went. Rath had berated him for not reaching the deputy personally to give the specifics about Preacher, and told him to call back. Rath let this new call go to voice mail.

A car crept up the hill behind Felix and Rachel, headlight beams swimming in the fog, illuminating the couple's silhouettes as Felix helped Rachel over the slags of plowed snow on the roadside, got her safely up against a scrub of alders to make room for the car.

The car, an '80s rust heap, slowed as it came alongside them.

Its muffler growled. Rath tensed. The two cops hurried down the stairs from the landing.

The vehicle's license plate was crusted with road salt, the number obliterated.

The car stopped.

Rachel and Felix, arms locked at the elbow like Dorothy and the Scarecrow, leaned toward it.

"No!" Rath shouted, a hand going to his revolver.

Rachel looked up at Rath.

The car's tires spun as the car slung past Rath. He drew his revolver and stooped to get a look inside the vehicle. But the windows were fogged, and the car dark inside as it climbed around the bend. *Was it Preacher?* Or were fear and paranoia distorting reality?

The couple picked their way along the road toward Rath.

"Who was in that car?" he asked.

"Someone asking directions. What's going on?" Rachel eyed the cops. "Why are *they* here?"

"Let's get inside," Rath said.

He let the kids get by him and go up the stairs, Rachel pausing on the landing in the fog lit beneath the floodlight: "What happened to our door? What's *going* on?"

"Inside," Rath said.

"Stay out here, if you would, miss," the trooper said.

"I'm not staying out here. I'm freezing and it's dark. I'm going inside my home."

"Then don't disturb anything."

"I just want to be inside my place. Our place." Rachel glanced at Felix.

Inside, the canaries piped up.

Rath despised the birds more with each chirp.

He shut the door as best as it would shut. Rachel leaned with her back against the counter dividing the living room from the kitchen. Felix moved next to her, but her look—*give me space*—halted him, and he sat on an arm of the futon, stooped to accommodate the pitched ceiling.

The deputy brandished his notepad as the trooper clasped his hands behind his back.

There were too many people in the cramped space. It made Rath itchy and claustrophobic. He took a breath and told Rachel only what he felt she absolutely needed to know about Preacher's phone call.

"I heard the canaries, birds," he finished. "So I thought Preacher was here, with you and—"

"Canaries?" Rachel looked at Felix.

They both looked at Rath.

"We were at the pet shop," Felix said.

Rachel's fingers worried the buttons on her coat. "Browsing, comforting puppies, and getting birdseed."

The cops eyed each other.

"And?" Rath said.

"There was this guy, looking at me," Rachel said.

"What guy?" Felix said just as Rath said it: "What guy?"

"The creep outside Lovin' Cup?" Felix said.

"You saw him, too?" Rath said.

"I didn't get a close look. And Rachel didn't *tell* me about a guy in the shop. So I don't know if it was the same guy."

"Stop," Rachel said, her voice measured, calm. "Please. Stop talking. I didn't say anything because I'm used to weird looks, all women are *used* to it. *And* I *barely* glimpsed his eyes, really, through the birdcages."

Rath knew she was downplaying the encounter. The more reasonable her tone, the more emotion she hid. She'd done it all her life. And in this case the emotion she tried to hide was fear. It grieved, but did not surprise, Rath to see her hide it, try to battle it alone. She was just like him, a true case for nurture over nature.

She glanced at Felix to invite him back to her side. He knew to smother her would drive her away, being by her side was enough. Smart kid.

While it irked Rath that Rachel and Felix could not describe the man, it didn't matter. He knew who it was.

"You need to interview the pet shop's employees, check CCTV footage," Rath said to the trooper.

"Let's go outside." The trooper nodded at the deputy. "Have the kids look around the place, see if anything's out of place. Besides the door."

9

Outside, the trooper stood with his back to the broken door. His voice was low and authoritative. "I understand from what I read in the paper, a lot of stress was put on you. But I can't be going to pet shops asking about Preacher."

Rath didn't want to hear the legal, procedural rationale, not while Preacher was following Rachel. For now, Rachel needed to leave this apartment. She could live back home, for a while; Felix, too. If they slept in separate rooms. Rath was not naive, but he wasn't prepared for Rachel to share a bed with her boyfriend under his roof just yet.

Even if she came to live with him for a spell, she would need to get to campus daily for class, do her work-study at the library, be in public, visible.

"Well, did he?" the trooper was saying.

Rath forced himself to attention. "Did who what?"

"Preacher. Did he explicitly threaten your daughter?"

"*Mentioning* her name is a threat. He *murdered* her parents. But he's too clever for a direct threat. He was saying sick shit."

"What sick shit?"

"Lies. Meant to unnerve me." Rath was not going to tell this trooper, or anyone else, especially not Rachel, that Preacher had claimed to have slept with Rachel's mother several times while working as a handyman at her home, claimed he was Rachel's father, and was going tell Rachel that. Tell Rachel how if her mother had just been with him one more time that day he'd stopped by, instead of rejecting him, she'd never have been raped or killed. She'd made him do it. Pushed him. It was her fault.

"If he made no threat, there's no need for action," the trooper said.

"I don't take chances with my daughter."

"If you're concerned for your daughter's well-being—"

"*If*," Rath said.

"—then do what you feel best. But unless something is out of place in their apartment, I can't extend resources to this episode."

Episode. The trooper made it sound as if Rath had suffered a breakdown.

"Let's go see," the trooper said. "Honestly, part of me wants there to be no reason to help, that this guy, sick as he is, was toying with you, but is harmless."

"You have no idea who this guy is," Rath said.

Inside, the deputy said, "The two young persons have noted nothing of concern in the apartment."

"Is that accurate?" Rath asked Rachel.

Rachel nodded, her fingertips peeking out from her coat sleeves. Her face showed bewilderment. Her lips seemed to tremble, but Rath knew she was whispering to herself, preparing questions for him as soon as the officers left.

"I'm sorry about the door, miss," the deputy said. "I'm glad everything is OK otherwise."

The trooper surveyed the room a last time. "Do what you feel you need to keep her safe," he said, and Rath understood the trooper believed Rachel was in danger, but was straitjacketed by the law. Unlike Rath.

10

As soon as Rath shut the door, Rachel found a hairband on the counter and shoved back her platinum-dyed pixie cut. Her new style was an about-face to the long, natural dark hair she'd always worn, and which Rath thought had perfectly reflected her personality. He did not know the young woman this style reflected, but was certain Rachel knew her. Rachel had always known herself; it was Rath, as Rachel's role of adopted daughter diminished and her many roles to the outside world expanded, who knew her less as she became more of a stranger to him.

Rath braced himself for her blitz of questions, but her lips persisted in moving silently, as they had when she slept as a child and murmured dialogues with her unconscious self, her face alternating from frowns to grins.

There were no grins now.

And the blitz did not arrive.

Her eyes searched the room deliberately, her head and body remaining still, just as Rath had taught her the one autumn she'd shown interest in deer hunting. Rath had taken her into the woods on the backside of Ice Pond, hiked up Mount Monadnock to the high ridges in search of a good buck's track to follow. He'd taught her to *look*. Use just her eyes. *Look*. Study the woods, her surroundings. Learn it. But don't give yourself away to your prey through movement. She'd practiced for weeks, enthused she was honing her peripheral vision.

Then, one morning, she woke up and her interest in deer hunting was gone.

Now, she charted the room, predator assessing her landscape. "What does he want?" she said and seemed almost in a trance. She locked eyes with Rath. Except for the radical hair color and the bobbed locks, she might have been her mother's twin when her mother was her age. No. It was not quite her mother's face. There was the subtle bend at the end of her nose that mimicked someone else's DNA. Or did it?

"It was him in the shop, wasn't it? Preacher? The man who killed my parents. Feet from me." She yanked the hairband off and twisted its ends opposite each other, stressing the cheap plastic.

"I don't know who else it could have been," Rath said.

"Any old creep," Felix said.

Rachel turned on him. "Don't try to give me false comfort because you think it'll make it easier."

Felix flinched. "I'm not. There are lots of creeps, that's all."

"OK." Rachel softened her tone. "We were *both* freaked by some guy. And—" She faced her father. "Preacher called you to threaten me. So—" She twisted the hairband. "How can he do this? Get away with it? Why is he even out after what he did? Free to go wherever he wants and do whatever he wants, the same things we do, when we didn't hurt anyone and he's murdered and raped?" She bit down hard on her lower lip. "I'll claw his eyes out," she whispered. "If I ever see him. I *hope* I see him. I will claw his eyes out. Cut his heart out." She twisted the hairband until it seemed it would break in half. "What are we going to do?" she said.

11

The fog was ungodly, and all the headlights of Dana Clark's '73 Bug did was light it up so intensely in the dark that it felt to Dana as if she were about to vanish in it forever.

And the rain. The merciless, tyrannical rain. It was biblical, is what it was.

The Bug's wipers slapped at it in vain.

There was no way Dana was going to make it to her daughter's home before 7 P.M., forget 6 P.M., which in itself was an hour later than usual. Dana was driving 13 mph on a road she usually took at 50, even at night, for pity's sake.

She needed to pull over to call Tammy, let her know how late she was running, and grab a snack, too. My word, her stomach was as empty as an upside-down bucket.

She turned up the volume on her CD player and sang along to Susan Boyle's cover of "Don't Dream It's Over," a favorite song of hers back in the day. Her teenage self would have mocked her for liking this version, but she preferred it; familiarity had long ago bled the original of its magic, and whenever she sang to pop songs from her youth these days, she felt asinine. She was a grandmother after all, like Boyle. A young grandmother, let's be very clear about that, but a grandmother nonetheless. Whenever she told expectant mothers on the Valley Hospital maternity ward that she had a ten-year-old granddaughter, Dana got the same reaction—You're kidding!—implying Dana must be old but looked fantastic for her age. Dana was not old; let's be very clear about that, too. Still, she didn't bother explaining that she'd given birth to Tammy at seventeen, and Tammy had given birth to her own daughter at seventeen. *Maybe I'll be a great-grandmother at fifty-one,* Dana mused. Why not? Babies were blessings.

Up ahead, a red glow leaked through the fog like blood through gauze.

Dana crept the Bug into the parking lot of the Wayside Country Store, pulled up close to the porch, beneath a lighted Pepsi sign so ancient it sported the slogan A NICKEL DRINK—WORTH A DIME!

Dana got out and dashed for the covered porch, yanking her hood around her face to keep the rain off her glasses.

The Pepsi sign creaked on its rusted chain.

Rain roared on the porch's tin roof as a nearby downspout belched a torrent of rainwater.

Except for one light in the window's hodgepodge display of ice melt, chain saws, and holiday cookbooks, the store was dark inside. Not a soul lurked. The place had shuttered early.

The fog dampened her face and seeped through her jacket, under her scrubs, to chill her.

Dana's new glasses were fogged from the heat of her breath on the cold lenses. She took them off and wiped them with her coat sleeve, dialed Tammy on her cell phone, and gazed in the store window. She needed to get ice melt for the steps at home. Once this rain froze—and it would, count on it—the world would be glazed with ice. Martin was supposed pick up ice melt before he headed to deer camp, but Dana knew he'd forget. She was better off performing errands herself during hunting season.

In the window's reflection, her car, just feet away, was lost in the fog. Gone. Beyond the smudged light from the window and the Pepsi sign, the world was nightmare black. You'd think it was 3 A.M., not 5 P.M., it was so blessed dark.

Tammy's phone rang as Dana admired her new glasses in the window reflection. On her lunch hour, when the day had still been sunny and bright, Dana had waffled between two frame styles at LensCrafters in the White Mountain Mall, finally buying both pairs, even though it put her way over her budget. 25% Off a Second Pair! was no great shakes—she wasn't dim—but it had lured her into forking over a hundred bucks extra, anyway. The pair she wore now was a butterfly frame, Conch Shell Pink. She liked them. They suited her.

The phone on the other end of the line rang.

Behind Dana, milky headlights leaked through the dense fog, creeping closer.

Tammy answered the phone: "Ha! I told you! You were dreaming if you thought you'd ever make it here by six." Tammy wasn't upset, merely stating a fact that proved her right, a trait she'd had since she was four. "You were too optimistic, as usual."

"It's not possible to be too optimistic," Dana said.

"Tell that to the idjits who built the *Titanic*."

Dana heard her daughter draw a deep breath. Cigarettes. The

habit upset Dana to no end, all the more because Tammy had picked it up from Dana herself. It bothered Dana to have passed the deadly habit on to the person she loved most.

In the window's reflection, the smear of headlights encroached as the vehicle—truck, car, or SUV, Dana could not tell in this unearthly fog; it may as well have been a UFO—edged past on the road.

"Just go straight home if you want. I'm not going out now in this mess anyway," Tammy said. "It's just a bowling league, it's not like it's Black Friday Midnight Madness."

Dana laughed. For years, she and Tammy had gone to the Black Friday Christmas sale at the White Mountain Mall. At first just for the savings, but over the years it had become a tradition, an excuse for mother and daughter and granddaughter to spend time together, just the girls. They'd shop from midnight till 4 A.M., eat an early-bird breakfast in the food court, then hit the outlets. Around two in the afternoon they'd drag themselves home to wrap presents while they indulged in a cooking-show marathon. The first year, the men had protested that the day after Thanksgiving was their day to hunt deer, one of very few nonholiday weekdays they took off all year from their construction business. Dana told them if they hadn't shot a deer after two full weekends of rifle season, they were out of luck.

Red brake lights glowed like demon eyes in the fog as the passing vehicle slowed with a plaint of brakes. The red lights blinked out, replaced with brighter white lights that seemed to throb in the fog. Reverse lights.

"Mom," Tammy was saying, "you there? Where are you?"

"I'm here. At the Wayside."

The vehicle eased backward into the store's dirt lot and idled behind Dana's Bug, blocking her. Eddying fog settled back to conceal the vehicle before Dana could see what it was.

"I'll try to get there by seven," Dana said.

A vehicle door opened and closed in the fog.

In the window's reflection the fog coiled around the figure of a man who walked toward the porch behind Dana.

Dana could not make out the man's face; her glasses were so misted, and the man, like Dana, kept his head tucked against the rain, and the snorkel hood of his jacket pulled up around his face.

Dana shivered.

She told herself it was the fog and the darkness that caused the trickle of fear. Why be afraid of a man who'd stopped at a store he couldn't tell was closed until he stepped up onto the porch?

Which the stranger did now, stepped up on the porch behind her, quite close.

Dana had kept a can of pepper spray in her handbag ever since, well, for a long, long time. For years, she'd replaced the canister regularly, just as she'd replaced the fire extinguishers and the batteries in the smoke detectors at home. What good was it to have something meant to protect you if it didn't work when you needed it most?

Except, she couldn't remember the last time she'd replaced the pepper spray. Too long. The old canister sat at the bottom of her handbag, lost among tissues and loose mints and minibottles of hand lotions. Whether it would work or not, she did not know. And she needed to know.

"Don't hurry in this weather," Tammy said now on the phone. "Be safe."

"Right," Dana said.

Why was the man just standing there, looking down, his face hidden.

Get a grip, Dana told herself.

Over the din of the rain, Dana believed she heard another sound. Breathing. Deep and low. The breathing of someone trying hard to calm and control himself.

The breathing of the man behind her.

Dana wedged a hand down into her bag, trying to act casually, naturally. Except now nothing felt natural. Her throat squeezed down on itself. She had to will herself to breathe, feared any quick movement would provoke the man behind her.

Provoke him into what? She didn't know. But she knew what men, some men, were capable of doing to women.

She knew.

The porch floor seemed to buckle beneath her as she became aware of an odor coming off the man. A funk that reminded her of a time she'd been working the emergency room midnight shift and tended to an old farmer's gashed foot, septic with gangrene; its hot, putrid odor of seeping flesh mixed with the bright metallic bite of blood.

Dana cupped her hand around her phone. "Don't hang up," she whispered into the phone to her daughter. She dug her other hand deeper into her bag, fingers crawling like a spider around the bottom, searching for that damned pepper spray.

"What?" Tammy said.

"Someone's behind me," Dana whispered.

"What?" Tammy said again.

The man did not say a word, did not move, kept his head down, not lifting it to face her image in the window. Hiding it. Just standing there in his putrid stink, the air vibrating.

Dana's fingers crept along the bottom of her bag. Where was that damned pepper spray?

"There's a man behind me," Dana whispered, mustering all of her willpower not to scream *Help! Get help!*

"What?" Tammy said.

There. Dana's fingers seized the pepper spray.

The Pepsi sign screeched on its corroded metal chains.

"There's a man and he won't lift his head, he won't—"

As if he'd heard Dana, the man lifted his head, but her damned glasses were too fogged, and the man's face too hidden in the dark shadows of his hood for her to see his face. Where his face ought to have been was a dark hole that seemed to glow an eerie swamp-gas green, the vague hint of what should have been the white of his eyes the same ghastly green.

Dana tried to speak, but her voice was gone.

The man lifted his arm.

Dana spun around, clutched the pepper spray, tried to extract it from her bag and wield it. She would not let what had happened so long ago ever happen again.

She would die first.

Her hand was stuck at an odd angle in her bag, elbow trapped under the strap. It slowed her. Just enough.

The man held up his hand. An object glowed in the dark.

A cell phone. That was what had made his face seem to glow so eerily, not some spooky aura. And the funky smell . . . Was it coming off the farm fields nearby, simply the familiar, sour fermented scent of manure churned up by rain?

There was nothing remarkable about the stranger's face, certainly nothing threatening, at least from what little Dana could make out through her misted glasses and the shadows that shrouded his face. But it was clear the man was not intentionally hiding his face.

Dana let out a sob of relief. A distant voice called to her. Tammy's voice, from the cell phone dangling in Dana's hand. Dana put the phone to her ear. "Lost you for a sec," she said to Tammy.

"What the hell is going on, Ma? Are you all right? Did you say something about a man? Do you need help?"

"I'm sorry," the man said, his voice calm and natural, almost familiar. "Sorry I frightened you."

"Ma?" Tammy said, "are you all right? Did you say something about a man?"

The stranger slipped his hood back off his head. He looked to be in his fifties. A handsome fifties. He smiled and stepped away to stand by himself on the top step, clearly, courteously permitting Dana her privacy as he looked off into the night as though debating whether he wanted to make a break in the rain for his vehicle just yet.

"I—" Dana said into her phone. "It's nothing."

"You sure?" Tammy said.

Dana sighed again. This damned storm. It had triggered her darkest imagination. After so many years, she was still so easily put on edge.

What had happened once could happen again.

Now though, she relaxed, the slightest. All she wanted was to see her daughter and granddaughter. Have a mug of Sleepytime tea and maybe stay the night, get under the covers and read a chapter of *The Wizard of OZ* to her granddaughter. The sooner she put the phone away to protect it from this monsoon and got in her dry, safe car, the better. "I'm sure," she said. "Really."

"OK, drive safe, see you soon," Tammy said and was gone.

The man smiled, and a sense of déjà vu slipped like a silver-fish through Dana's bloodstream. Did she know him? He seemed vaguely familiar. Someone from the hospital maybe.

The fog whorled around him.

"Again," the man said. "I apologize for scaring you."

"You didn't really."

"I did, I can see it," the stranger said.

Dana emitted a nervous, embarrassed grunt. The man smiled.

"Maybe just a little," Dana admitted.

"Well, then, I'm doubly sorry."

"Please, don't be."

"I should have scared you a lot more than a little. Out here in the fog and dark and no one around. A woman would be justified being more than a little scared."

"I really have to go." Dana drew a deep breath and moved to edge past him. He stepped cleanly out of her way, granting more than enough room as he nodded with graciousness and played with his phone, muttered as he likely tried to figure out where on earth he was on this godforsaken night. *This man is no threat,* Dana thought. *Just lost.*

As she was about to step into the fog, Dana said, "Where are you trying to get?"

The man swiped a finger on his cell-phone's screen. "You may not want to know." The man held up his phone.

Dana could not make out the screen, her glasses so clouded. She'd have to return them. No two ways about it. She took off her glasses, her vision worsening. She wiped the lenses on her sleeve and put the glasses back on.

Leaned in for a better look.

Fear sliced its icy finger into her heart.

She wanted to back away. Couldn't. Couldn't peel her eyes from the image on the screen. An impossible, insane, nightmare image. An image of an old Polaroid.

Impossible for anyone to have.

Anyone except one person.

HIM.

The man who'd—

No.

HE was dead.

You don't have to worry. He's dead. That's what she'd been told so long ago. *Promised* a lifetime ago. That's what she'd *believed*.

Except now HE was standing before her. She'd never seen his face clearly all those years ago, but it had to be HIM before her now, all these years later, with no one else around for miles, her pepper spray lost again at the bottom of her purse as HE took a step closer, her daughter at home awaiting her safe return, HIS breathing deep and slow, as if HE were trying not to pant and drool.

HE was not dead.

HE was alive.

She'd been lied to, all those years ago.

Lied to by the one person she'd trusted.

And now Frank Rath's lie would cost her.

12

Detective Sonja Test needed to hurry.

She browsed the Kids Attik of the Canaan General Store, rummaging through racks of snowsuits for Elizabeth, and had just been told by the owner that the place would close early, in twenty minutes. The torrential rain the past two hours had prompted severe flood warnings and threatened to wash out roads and knock out the power. High winds were predicted, and when the temperature plunged, the town was in for an icy hell.

Claude had driven his Jeep separately from home to haul back the generator Test insisted they rent if the power went out, *when* it went out.

Twice, the lights in the store had flickered out and left Test standing in the dark wondering if the power was out for the night.

She cursed herself. She should never have wasted her afternoon at the White Mountain Mall across the river, in search of a *bargain* snowsuit. She knew better. The snowsuits in the mall fit the family budget, but the suits were no bargain. They were cheap, poorly insulated, with cuffs and collars that let in the snow and wind; and the flimsy zippers had broken on two of Elizabeth's previous *bargain* suits. Yet the prices at the ski shops for quality snowsuits were absurd, especially since the snowsuits were good for a season, if that, with how fast the kids grew.

So now here Test was, shopping where she should have come first instead of at home getting the kids ready for bed at a reasonable hour so tomorrow morning wouldn't be a total catastrophe of overtired kids who resisted getting out of bed with the ferocity of one being dragged to a vat of boiling grease.

Test hurried now while Claude occupied the kids downstairs in the Toy Korner, once a wonderland of local wooden handmade toys before kids' sections everywhere were conquered by Melissa & Doug.

God, she was frayed, not the least due to this mad weather, this climatic bubonic plague; twice on the way from New Hampshire to the house to get the Jeep, visibility had been so poor Claude had needed to pull over.

As Test checked a price on a snowsuit her work cell phone rang in her coat pocket.

Today was supposed to be her day off, though a cop, especially the temporary, sole detective and forensics-team-of-one for the Canaan Police, never had a day off. Test would have it no other way.

She dug around in her coat pockets, retrieving her phone.

Chief Barrons. Test's spirits were buoyed, believing the chief had decided to promote her to the senior detective position vacated by Detective Grout.

"Chief," Test said.

"Where are you?" he said, skipping the pleasantries.

This was not a call about a promotion. Bad news was coming.

Then again, when did a chief of police call an officer bearing good news?

"The Kids Attik," Test said.

"The what?"

"Canaan General Store."

"I need you over at the home of Tammy Gates."

"Who? What's going on?"

"I'm not sure. She called dispatch, frantic. Something about her mother. She fears something's happened."

"An Alzheimer's thing?" Test imagined an elderly woman lost in this fog. It happened too often, the aged wandering off. A dangerous scenario that could prove fatal fast in this weather.

"If that were the case, I'd get Larkin on it and not bother you. Dispatch said the daughter was talking about a strange man."

"What man?"

"I'm sending Frank Rath out there to help."

"Rath?" Test stared at the phone as if it had spoken in place of Barrons. She put the phone back to her ear. "Why?"

Barrons did not answer. The chief did not have to justify his decisions.

Test respected Frank Rath. His consultant work had broken two recent, horrific cases, but he'd done it ad hoc while investigating a missing girl as a favor to Detective Grout. In the end, Rath, taciturn as he was, had handed Test the arrest of the girl's killer when he could just as easily, and more understandably, handed it to Grout. A friend. A man.

Test owed Rath.

But Rath wasn't on the payroll, consultant or otherwise, as far as Test knew—and she *should* have known.

"Why Rath?" Test pressed. If Barrons was even considering Rath for the senior detective position, Test deserved—

"I'll call Rath and get him over," he said and hung up.

Test aborted her shopping mission; hopefully Elizabeth wouldn't need a snowsuit for a while if this crazy rain kept up.

Test took the stairs down from the Kids Attik, ducked under the beam at the bottom. Canaan General was housed in an 1800s converted barn, the Kids Attik the old haymow, the stairs' risers hand-painted with "Caution, steep stairs" and "Watch your head."

Test found Claude and the kids in the Toy Korner, Elizabeth playing with plush stuffies on a turnstile rack, George sacked out on a beanbag chair in the corner, a *Great Brain* book splayed on his lap, his open mouth drooling.

"Why'd you let George doze?" Test said. "He's going to be a nightmare when he wakes up and never go down tonight."

Claude glanced at George. "He must have just fallen asleep."

Test rolled her eyes. "With that drool? Well, he'll be your nightmare. We have to go."

"We just got here!" Elizabeth complained.

"*Mama* has to go, OK?" Test knelt and kissed her daughter's forehead. "The store is going to close in ten minutes and you'll have to leave then. Leave nicely. Be good for Daddy."

She stood, kissed Claude on the cheek.

"What is it, car wreck, flooded roads?" Claude asked.

"Not sure. Nothing good."

"I don't know how you do it."

"It's not how. It's *why*."

"What time do you expect to be back?" Claude said, though he knew estimates were pointless when Test was called out.

"Could be an hour, could be all night," she said.

"I've *got* to be on the road by five A.M. tomorrow to make it to Burlington on time in this weather."

Test had forgotten about Claude's interview for a two-week visiting artist position the next spring at the University of Vermont in Burlington. Not because it wasn't important. It was. It would give Claude clout, and the stipend was generous, though the two weeks would be a slog for Test alone with the kids. Test had forgotten because it had created no conflict until now. It was possible she wouldn't make it home in time for Claude to hit the road, and there was nothing she could do about it.

She had to see events to their conclusion if she wanted the vacant senior detective position. Especially as a female detective. A mother.

"I *have* to be there," Claude said.

"I'll do my best. Give me the Jeep keys? By the time I get done, I'll probably need four-wheel drive to get home."

13

She did not belong here. Not anymore.

Yet, here she was. Forced back. Feeling foreign in her childhood bedroom, as if she'd been gone decades instead of days.

She couldn't be here. Couldn't stay. She had midterms to cram for before Thanksgiving break, and she needed to be around the buzz of her friends, fueled by the chaos of all-nighters to kick herself into gear; *and* she *had* to have access to campus Wi-Fi, not the sketchy DSL here in the boonies. Campus was nearly an hour drive, *if* the roads were good. With this damned fog, it could mean she missed exams; her GPA would plummet.

Her dad and Felix had countered each valid point with one argument: her safety was the priority. Forget grades. Forget everything else. Forget living her life. Her father had even proposed she put her studies on hold and *take a break* to some place sunny, like Florida, until the situation was cleared.

Florida? Seriously? And, the *situation*? *How,* exactly, was the *situation* supposed to be *cleared*? By divine intervention?

Preacher wasn't *going* anywhere. Just how long was Rachel supposed to *take a break someplace sunny* or lock herself in her old bedroom, caged like one of Felix's canaries?

And hadn't her father tried to protect her throughout her childhood by not telling her the truth about her parents' murders? How had that worked out? There was no way to guarantee her, or anyone's, safety.

Rachel shut her bedroom door, cutting off the low yet urgent voices of Felix and her father in the kitchen, no doubt discussing the *situation*. As if it didn't concern her, as if she needed to be protected by high walls and knights in armor, unable to fend or to know what was best for herself. She did not want to be here. Yet, here she was.

She sat on the edge of her old twin bed, seething.

The air of the room was as fusty as a summer camp after being shuttered for the winter.

What was she going to do? What could she do?

She fell back on the mattress, arms out as if to make a snow angel. A part of her wished she were still the little girl who made snow angels with her father, got swept up on his shoulders afterward as he tromped through the snow, her face buzzing with cold, back to the warm house to make hot chocolate.

But the part of her that longed for such days was a small part, smaller each day. The more the future tugged her forward, and the more exhilarated she became by the unknown life awaiting her, the sharper the stab of melancholy was for the girl she was leaving behind, as if she were mourning her own death. Her fingertips fiddled with the satin edge of her blanket. The cool slippery feel of the silky material gliding between her fingertips had always soothed her. Felix found it cute, and a tad disturbing, that she bought coats with satin-lined pockets so when she got uptight or nervous she could work the satin for solace; yet what was once relief was now more of a way to reconnect with that girl fading away within her.

She let go of the blanket and stared at the walls. She'd picked the color years ago when lilacs had been her favorite flower. Now it made her queasy. Pepto pink more than lilac; yet her father had gladly painted the room the exact color she'd wanted.

A pink prison now.

It was unjust. A sick, violent man could follow her, yet *she* was the one imprisoned. She radiated with hatred at the thought of what he'd done to her parents. Who was this man? This Ned Preacher?

Rachel had not wanted to know anything about him when that weirdo at Family Matters had told her of her parents' murders. Now, she wanted to know everything. Had to know. About the murders. And the murderer. Had to know the orchestrator of her imprisonment.

She opened her laptop. She had a LexisNexis account, through the college. It would give her access to the old print articles about the murders.

The browser loaded with all the speed of a hibernating toad's heartbeat. Finally, she brought up the LexisNexis interface and entered her password. Typed in Laura Pritchard, murder, Ned Preacher, Vermont. May 3, 1995. She rubbed a fingertip on the track pad, stared at the Search button.

She rose and opened her door a crack, peered out to see her dad at the kitchen stove, staring out the window.

She did not see Felix, but as she made to shut the door, she heard the shower going on in the bathroom next door.

Rachel could use a good shower too. After what she was about to research online, she was sure she'd need one.

She eased the door shut and sat at her childhood desk, her back to the door but ears keen for the sound of the shower.

She stared at laptop screen, took a deep breath, and clicked Search.

14

Rachel felt ill as she stared at the image on her laptop screen. Not just sick to her stomach; sick in her blood, as if she were infected with malaria, her face sticky and feverish with cold sweat, limbs weak and ponderous, fingertips numb.

She glanced at the shut door behind her, listened for the shower running.

The photo on the laptop showed Ned Preacher being escorted from the courthouse in shackles following his arrest for the murder of Rachel's parents.

Rachel zoomed in on his face. His look was smug—satisfied. It said: *I did it. So what? She had it coming. They all have it coming.*

Rachel leaned in closer.

Was this the man from the pet shop? Yes, her gut told her. It was Preacher. She'd only seen his eyes, but that was enough. His eyes alone had chilled her, but it wasn't the photo of Preacher that sickened her most. It was the headline: SUSPECT IN VICIOUS DOUBLE SLAYING PLEADS TO LESSER CHARGES.

She read how Preacher had "sexually assaulted" her mother.

Sexually assaulted? She despised the weak euphemism for rape. Why did the press and judicial system insist on not calling rape *rape*? Why did they sanitize it, to make it more palatable, less brutal, less real?

In many articles *the baby*, Rachel, was mentioned, though never by name.

There was mention of Preacher's previous murders and *sexual assault* convictions. His entire life, he'd preyed on women and girls, then gamed the system, over and over, serving less time by pleading to lesser charges to save the state time and money, to gain him a freedom he did not deserve.

He never should have breathed fresh air again after his first rape and murder of a girl barely in her teens, let alone been free to kill Rachel's parents. Now, he was out *again*.

Free.

The idea was lunacy.

The reality incomprehensible.

The old newspaper articles glossed over Preacher's atrocities. Rachel needed to know details. Real details. She did not want to know just that her mother and father had been stabbed; she suddenly wanted to know everything as it had *actually* happened. She wanted to know exactly how many times her parents were stabbed, the type of knife used, the precise location of their wounds, how deep or shallow they were. How hard her parents had fought against Preacher. How long they had suffered. Had they even been given a chance? She wanted the unvarnished version. She wanted the truth.

There was only one place to get the information.

She got up and put her ear to the door. The shower was still running.

She picked up her old landline phone and dialed.

A woman answered: "Canaan Police."

"Detective Sonja Test, please."

"She's just gone out on a call."

The sound of the shower fell quieter. Rachel listened intently. She couldn't have Felix overhearing her. She did not want to share this with him. It was too private. Too sensitive. Family.

Rachel gave the woman her name and number. "Can you tell her it's important, that I want my parents' murder file?"

Rachel hung up and sat back with the article about her mother's rape and murder.

That was the worst of it: the rape. The word tore at her, a cruel onomatopoeia for the violation through force that it represented— *rape: to seize prey, abduct, force.* The initial *R*: a ripping sound. The *A*: long, prolonged, like a scream; like the *A* in *pain*. The *P*: abrupt and final. The *E*: as silent as so many victims.

The word awakened an ache in Rachel's belly in a way the word *murder* did not. To murder was inhuman, irreversible. But murder could be instantaneous, even painless, done without the victim ever knowing. And no matter how it was done, when it was over, it was over.

Rape was never painless. Rape *was* pain. Cruelty. The victim made to endure the anguish of the act at the mercy of another. There was no end to it; even after it happened, no end to the trauma.

How awful it must have been for her mother, made to suffer that way, knowing her own baby was upstairs, alone.

Rachel sobbed to think of it. And of Preacher. The man who just hours earlier had stood a few feet from her, leering, making her skin feel flayed. She tried to push the thought from her mind. She looked up at the glow-in-the-dark stars on the ceiling. How many nights had she gazed up at these stars, fantasizing about becoming the Big Girl and of all the freedom that would come with it?

She thought about the boxes hidden beneath her bed: boxes of DVDs and books about appalling murders and the fiends who'd committed them. She felt ashamed now for ever having enjoyed them. Not just enjoyed them, but been titillated by them. Tales of depravity had been an opiate for her: intoxicated and damaged her.

How could she ever have been drawn to it?

Why?

She had been an infant in a crib upstairs when her parents were stabbed to death, her mother raped. Had she heard the sounds of their last moments? Had they remained with her, germinated inside her and manifested themselves as a prurient interest in acts macabre and violent?

Since grade school, she'd helped her father with his private investigation into tame, nonviolent local crimes of town treasurer embezzlement and the like. She'd helped him sift through evidence and form theories. It was a way, she realized, for him to share time with her, keep her close, safe. When she'd asked why the town treasurer had humiliated himself and his family, risked jail to steal money he didn't need, her father had put forth a theory. He believed people who committed crimes were not addicted to the act, or to the money or the power, but to the secrecy. The deeper and darker the secret—the more individuals had to protect their secret crimes, their secret lives, at all costs—the more singular and exceptional those people felt. In the mind of the criminal, secrets sharpened the edge of dull lives, elevated the common to significance.

Her fascination with violent crime, however, had not taken root until she'd found a disturbing case hidden in her father's files. A seventy-eight-year-old farmer, Leonard Stikes, had killed his granddaughter's boyfriend with a shovel and hidden the corpse in a manure pile. When the boy's body was found, the old man had broken down and confessed he'd done it in a fit of rage to protect his granddaughter from the boy's abuse. *I didn't know what else to do!* he'd cried. His despair was believed to bring on the stroke that slayed him in his holding cell. The boyfriend had a record of abuse, and many witnesses, including his mother, attested to their fear of the boy, his cruelty, and his threats to kill them for the slightest insult.

The incident was seen as a tragedy all around, until a year later when the old man's barn was razed by his two surviving sons, and the remains of eleven boys were found in various stages of decomposition, one skeleton having been beneath the barn for forty years, that of the old man's first son who had disappeared in 1967, when he was ten. Each skull had been busted by a shovel. The same shovel.

Rachel had wondered about that farmer ever since. How he'd done what he'd done, hidden his savagery from family and friends for five decades. A man so dark he'd murdered his own son, yet so devious he'd kept his lust for murder a secret until almost the very last. Everyone had believed the old man had killed his granddaughter's boyfriend because he feared for his granddaughter and "didn't know what else to do!" They had felt pity and empathy for him.

He had tricked them all.

He had gotten away with murder.

Had he been driven by an addiction to secrecy?

Ever since she'd learned of that farmer, she'd been fascinated with sordid murders that left her blood cold but her heart hot, snared in a warren of madness and bloodlust. Her addiction had crept up on her with a slow yet steady and unrelenting progression. She'd kept it secret.

Now her obsession with murder felt dirty, criminal in its disrespect toward her parents' memories, and all victims.

She pushed herself up off the mattress and peered under the bed at the boxes of books and DVDs. She'd burn them first chance she got. Purge by way of fire.

She stood.

She had to get out of here. She should never have let her father and Felix talk her into coming here, against her will, let herself be hidden away.

I can't be the one imprisoned, she thought. *I won't be. I refuse.*

She'd meant what she'd said about Preacher back at their apartment: she'd cut out Preacher's heart if she got the chance. And, she realized, even after reading the articles, she wanted that chance. Welcomed it. The violence in her surprised and emboldened her. If she were back at her apartment, she could wait for him. Make him pay. She'd get a big knife. Or better, a gun. This was Vermont, she could buy a gun anywhere. She'd get a gun and she'd wait for him. She'd let him come, lure him even. And when he took the bait—

Her blood sang with the idea of exacting pain from him.

Staying here at home accomplished nothing.

This place was no secret compound. This address could be found in two seconds on the Internet.

There was no way Preacher didn't know its location.

For all she knew, Preacher was out there now in the fields or woods, watching.

Biding his time.

Waiting for the heart of night when they were all asleep, so he could slink in through a window.

Just who did Ned Preacher think he was?

Rachel jumped when her old landline rang.

The shower next door had fallen silent. Felix was whistling in the bathroom.

The phone rang again. It could only be Detective Test calling.

Rachel answered.

"This is Detective Test," a woman's harried voice, clearly on speakerphone, said. "You left—"

"I'd like to have my parents' murder files," Rachel said.

"I don't understand."

There was nothing to *understand*. The files were public record. "I want to know what happened," Rachel said. "*Exactly what happened.*"

The detective sighed, and Rachel heard the slap of windshield wipers in the background. "Honestly, I don't think you do," the detective said.

"That's not up to you. All due respect," Rachel said.

"I still don't understand—"

"Do you need to understand?" Rachel said, riled. "Is that a prerequisite for a citizen getting public records? You understanding?" It was not Rachel's nature to be so stony, but the detective had no right to know her motivation, was treating her like a juvenile in need of protection. Rachel was sick of being sheltered from the truth by others who "knew best."

"Of course I don't need to understand," Detective Test said. "I never could. But a murder file, it's ugly, unimaginable stuff."

For a moment Rachel almost hung up, didn't want to know

the details. "I was *there,*" she finally said. "I was a baby, but I was there. I *need* to know. It sounds morbid, but it will bring me closer to my parents if I face their murders, prove there is no shame in their deaths."

The detective sighed again, more deeply. "If that's what you want."

"It is."

"Normally, a citizen wanting copies has to fill out forms and come in for the public records themselves. But, look, since I know who you are, know your father, I'll have an officer locate the files. Get copies made, mail them. Unless you plan to come into the station."

"My car's kaput. Copies work."

"You're sure about this?"

Rachel wasn't sure. She was crazy scared. But she needed to know. Not for the reason she'd given Test. That was a lie. She needed to know everything she could about Preacher and what made him tick. *Know thy enemy.*

"You can't mail them here," Rachel said. "I'll text you the address of wherever I end up temporarily. And. You have to promise. If you ever run into my dad, you can't say a word about this."

The detective hesitated. "Of course," she said.

Rachel hung up, startled to find Felix standing behind her, a towel wrapped around his waist as he brushed his teeth. He extracted the toothbrush from his mouth, lips foamed with spent toothpaste.

"Who was that?" he said.

"The police," Rachel blurted, unable to think of a lie fast enough. "I wanted to know about restraining orders."

"Why not ask your dad?"

"I can do stuff on my own behalf. I don't need to ask him for everything."

"I know." Felix stuck the toothbrush back in his mouth.

"You better get dressed, speaking of dads," Rachel said. "I'll be right out."

With Felix gone, Rachel rubbed her cold arms and opened the door to her room to find her father outside it, yanking on his coat, a manic look on his face.

15

I have to go out," Rachel's father said.

"Why? What's happened?" However emboldened Rachel had been in her bedroom, however defiant and capable she'd felt, and knew she was, her father's news that he had to leave the house knocked the breath out of her.

"I have to meet Detective Test," he said.

What? Rachel thought. Had Test already betrayed her confidence, turned around and called her father? "I can't believe she would—"

"Chief Barrons called and asked me to go out to a call. I told him absolutely not. He pressed. Said he'd send Officer Larkin to park outside, lights flashing, for as long as I was gone. Larkin should be here any minute."

Rachel sighed, relieved Test had not violated her privacy. "It has to do with him? Preacher?"

"I don't know. I hope so. We need to catch him breaking parole, put him away, so you're safe."

"What's the call about? What's he done?"

"A woman's worried about her mom being late, worried she's in trouble." He looked toward the window as headlights lit the darkness outside. "Larkin's here. But lock up anyway. Keep all the lights on. You've got Felix."

Rachel saw her opportunity to speak her mind. Her father needed to do what he needed to do, even if it left him conflicted. Rachel did too.

"I'm not staying here. This isn't my home. Campus is," she said, proud to speak it but saddened to see pain shadow her father's face. "With Felix. We'll get a motel tonight, find a different apartment, but I'm safer on campus, with all my friends around."

"No. I—"

"You can't be around twenty-four seven. Obviously."

Her father winced.

"I didn't mean that," Rachel said. "Not like that. You need to go out. I want you to go, especially if it's about him. On campus I'll be around people all the time. Friends, students, teachers, Felix. I didn't want to come here. I don't want to be here." The more she spoke, the deeper she cut her father. She knew, because she was cutting herself, too.

"I'm sorry you're scared and hurt, and—"

"I'm *not* scared, or hurt. I'm *furious*. I want to fucking kill him."

"You let me handle that." He tried a laugh, but it faltered. "How about this? I'll help you and Felix find a new place. First thing. But you stay here tonight. Doors locked. Lights on. Officer Larkin outside. Please, give your dad peace of mind. You can watch movies with my shotgun across your lap." Again, his laugh, forced and desperate. "Drink hot chocolate. Relax. Felix can stay in your room." His face reddened. "Try to get a good night's sleep you'd never get in a motel. You can't operate from rage."

"Why not? You do."

"I don't work from rage."

"Anger *drives* you. At least when you're after anyone who hurts other people."

"That's different. After I found your mom and dad like that—"

"You found them?" Rachel had not known this. And, selfishly, since finding out about her parents' murders, she'd thought of them *only* as *her* parents. *Her* mother. *Her* father. *Her* loss. Except, her mother was his sister. His only sibling. His loss. He'd known her all his life until she'd been murdered. Rachel had never known her parents at all. They remained abstract figures to which she could not connect emotionally, as much as she willed it. "I didn't know," she said.

"I didn't want you to know." He exhaled a long breath. "Let me help you find you a new place. But, please. Stay here until then. Give me peace of mind. Besides, this fog. No one wants to be out in that mess unless they absolutely have to be. I'll find you a room or—"

"OK. OK. I'll stay," Rachel said.

"Follow me and lock up?"

At the kitchen doorway, Rachel hugged her father and wanted to tell him to keep safe, but he slipped out the door before she could say it.

She locked up and stood at the kitchen door window and watched her father get in his old heap.

As soon as the Scout disappeared into the fog, she wanted him back.

16

I t's strange," Tammy Gates, the daughter of the missing woman, said.

Rath wondered if the daughter were speaking about the thought he'd had since he'd first arrived: *I know this woman, I've met her in the past, spoken at length with her.* Yet, he knew this wasn't true; he did not know this woman. Had never laid eyes on her, let alone spoken with her.

The woman stood from the couch, unable to stay in one place. Rath couldn't fault her. Her mother had vanished, as if dissolved by the fog.

The woman scuffed like a sleepwalker to the window. She battled with the strings of the Venetian blind, finally drawing the blinds up enough, crooked, to stare out the window; or stare *at* it. The black night transformed the window into a dark mirror.

Test readied to ask the daughter a question, but Rath begged her off with a look, wanting to let the daughter reveal in her own time whatever she was hiding, because she was hiding something. Rath knew the look.

The daughter reached down and pinched out the flame of a purple drip candle squatting on the coffee table. A tendril of smoke spiraled from the wick.

The wind shrieked and rattled the windows, in each of which hung a dream catcher. The dream catchers appeared homemade: rough, asymmetrical hoops constructed of birch twigs strung with a spiderweb of beaded wool thread decorated with crow feathers.

Rath understood from his layman's knowledge that most people had dream catchers wrong; the dream catcher did not catch dreams, it caught nightmares. The crisscrossed wool thread, originally dried gut string, was a spider's web. The Ojibwe of western Quebec believed *Asibikaashi,* a spider woman, oversaw the safety of women and children; so mothers wove the webs to catch their children's nightmares and leave pure thoughts when the children awoke.

These dream catchers had failed. Whatever nightmare might be unfolding had not been snagged.

Why do I think this is a nightmare unfolding? Rath thought. Tammy's mother had only been out of contact for a few hours. Likely, she was creeping her car along in this fog or pulled over with no cell service. Yet, the fact that Barrons ordered Test to come out here, in this storm, let alone Rath himself, disturbed Rath, made him believe this was indeed a nightmare unfolding.

Tammy Gates eyed Rath, and again Rath sensed he had met her, long ago.

What is going on here? he wondered.

Perhaps, he was just exhausted. The day's events had left him wiped long before he'd driven here. And now it was approaching midnight.

"What's strange?" Test said.

Tammy Gates spoke without looking at Rath or Test. "That's what my ma said. *It's strange.* Or something like that. About the man."

"What man?" Test said.

"I don't know. I couldn't make out much of what Ma said."

She's stunned, Rath thought. *Her understanding of her world has lost its context.*

"Sorry," Tammy said. "I'm out of it. All Ma said was a man, she couldn't see his face, was standing close to her. But then she calmed down and said it was nothing. So—I thought the fog had rattled her. I mean she was on the steps of the Wayside General, with people inside working so what was some guy going to do?"

"The store is closed," Test said.

Rath cringed. He would not have divulged this information. It set the daughter more on edge, caused her to focus less and worry more. Worry's uselessness was an enemy. Just as hope was.

"Closed?" Tammy Gates said.

"We sent a trooper to look for your mother's car. The place closed early," Test said.

"My mother's car? Was it *there*?"

"I don't know," Test said. "Waiting to hear." The car wasn't there, Rath sensed. Which meant what? Surely this strengthened the possibility that the mother was simply very late because of the weather and was out of cell service or had her phone off while driving.

"My mother was out there *alone*, with *him*," the woman said. She said *him* as if she knew who the man was.

She looked at Rath. Recognition in her eyes. Fear, too. She was nearly catatonic with fear.

"Why are you so scared?" Rath said. "I understand being worried in weather like this, about your mom driving and being late, as far as maybe an accident, and the incident on the phone doesn't help. But she could easily be late due to the weather, or out of cell service. Why are you so scared—"

"Because of who my mom *is*."

"Is she a public figure or—" Test said.

"It's not like that. She's a nurse on the maternity floor at Valley Hospital."

A nurse? Rath thought. *At Valley Hospital.*

"It's because of what was done *to* her. Not what *she's* done." The daughter stared at Rath, as if she expected Rath to know what she was talking about.

Rain raged against the windows. Rath wondered if the wooden bridge he'd taken across a creek to get here would be swept away, cut him off from Rachel.

"She's *dead*," the daughter said. "We can at least admit that. My mom's dead. He got her this time. I have to *face* it. I won't be one of those people who cling to delusional false hope year after year until I see a body. I won't torture myself on top of everything else, waiting for someone to come back who is never coming back."

"I understand your concern, but you can't think—" Rath said.

"Of course *you* understand."

"Why? Why does he understand?" Test said, sounding as perplexed as Rath felt.

"Because *he* was there. When I was six and I found my mother in our garden."

No, Rath thought. *No.*

"Stabbed so many times. There was *so much* blood," the daughter said. "Like she'd been dunked in a vat of blood. She was facedown. I couldn't see yet that it was blood, that her face was covered in blood too. I thought she'd changed out of her pale yellow sundress she liked to wear gardening, and into a red dress I'd never seen."

No, Rath thought. *It can't be.*

"I thought she'd fallen and hurt herself," the daughter continued. "Or was sleeping. I was only *six*. Sometimes she fell asleep out on the lawn by the garden. I didn't know what to think when I saw her *red dress* was blood soaked through her yellow dress, and the dress was torn at the neck and at one sleeve. And her underwear was— Nineteen times, she was stabbed. It was— I was in shock. And now. This. You understand. Now this. She's not late. She's not out of cell service. My mother is dead."

Holy Christ, Rath thought. *It's her.*

Rath knelt before the daughter where she sat on the edge of the couch and laid his hands on her wrists. He felt Test watching him.

"Your maiden name is Clark. You're Tammy Clark. Your mom is Dana Clark," Rath said. "I didn't know."

That's why Barrons called me out, Rath thought. *Barrons thought I knew who Tammy was, knew her married name.* But why hadn't Barrons mentioned that the missing woman was Dana Clark?

Test looked bewildered, as if she'd just walked in late on a movie with no context or perspective to understand the drama unfolding.

Tammy clasped her hands over Rath's hands.

"I didn't recognize you," Rath said.

"What is this?" Test said.

Tammy nodded at Rath. "I'm not six anymore. And if it weren't for you being in the news recently for those murder cases, I would never have recognized you, either," she said. "As you said, I don't have the same last name anymore. How could you recognize me, if the chief didn't make it clear. I assumed he had."

He should have, Rath thought.

"I *sensed* I knew you," Rath said. "You look like your mom, but I haven't seen her in—far too long."

Rath took Tammy Clark's hands and looked into her eyes as if about to propose. He sensed Test's embarrassment now competed with her confusion.

"She's dead," Tammy said. "I know it. *You* know it."

Rath looked her in the eye. "We don't know any such thing. The troopers will look for her and her car and she'll be back tonight."

"The man she was talking about, it's him, isn't it?"

"We don't know that," Rath said, lying. He patted her knee and stood, glanced at Test and back to Tammy.

"Will you give us a moment?" Rath said.

Tammy nodded.

Rath motioned for Test to join him in the kitchen.

The kitchen smelled of onions and burned toast.

"What the hell is this?" Test said. "Were you and her mother involved?"

"In a way."

"I need context. If it has any impact on the investigation—"

"It was years ago."

"You meant something to her."

"It goes both ways."

"I see."

"You don't," Rath said. "Her mother was the only woman to survive an attack from the Connecticut River Valley Killer. At least that's who we thought it was. As the lead detective, I was the first person she shared the heinous details of her attack with. Sharing like that can create a sort of macabre intimacy. It forged a bond between us."

Test nodded. It was a nod to encourage Rath to continue, not one of understanding.

"I kept in touch," Rath said. "We did. For years, long after I left the state police, after my sister's murder."

"That's why Tammy said you *understand*."

Rath nodded. "Occasionally, Dana and I met for coffee and I had to explain nothing had developed in the case. Eventually, I lost touch. The CRVK murders stopped after Dana's attack. Which made us all the more certain her attacker was the CRVK, that Dana being the only victim to survive to even vaguely, partially describe him had scared him out of the region. Or into hiding."

"And Tammy was six when she discovered her mother like that?" Test said.

"It was hideous."

"What were the other theories about who had attacked her, and the connection with the CRVK?" Test said.

"That the CRVK had moved or stopped for other reasons. Got sick or died. Went to jail for another crime. Something happened. Changed." Rath sighed, glanced out at Tammy who sat with her face in her hands, an unlit cigarette dangling between two fingers. "There was a suspect we had in custody, about a year later, for a short time. A Vern Johnson fit Dana's very loose, practically useless, description and had been in the area for certain for two CRVK strangulations. After questioning, he was released. He drove from jail to Pennsylvania where he tied up his estranged wife and their son, lit the house on fire, and burned them all alive."

Rath looked out again at Tammy, to make certain she was not listening.

Rath lowered his voice. "I told Dana that this suspect, Vern Johnson, was our man. I wanted to give her peace. She was suffering extreme PTSD. Nightmares, depression, anxiety, paranoia. She had her daughter to raise, her husband had been laid off. She needed to feel safe again, and nearly all regional cops believed Johnson—the CRVK—had died in that fire. I was the odd man out. Barrons and I. So—. Who was I to dissent?"

"You didn't believe he was the CRVK?"

"Dana needed to heal. She was dying. The injuries alone had nearly killed her, left her in a coma for weeks. And in the hospital for months after she awoke. It was as if she were dying a long slow death believing he was out there. Could come back and harm her. Or worse, harm her daughter. But. No. I never fully believed it. And I still don't."

"And now this."

"Now this."

"But Dana Clark's car *isn't* at the Wayside. If a lone stranger pulled up in his own car and did something to her, where's her car? The odds of two predators working together is astronomically low," Test said.

"But possible. Maybe the person moved her car just down the road, off into the woods," Rath said. "In the crap out there you wouldn't see a car pulled off the road, even in daylight."

"She's only been missing a short time. We don't even usually look into a possible missing person for seventy-two hours."

"This isn't a usual case. It's a priority. Seventy-two hours is out the window on this one. Barrons knew who she was. Tammy.

But I can't figure why he didn't tell me the missing woman was Dana Clark. It bothers me. But that's why he made it a priority. Because the missing woman is Dana. The CRVK case plagues him to this day."

"What is it you're not telling me?" Test said.

Tammy moaned. Rath and Test looked, but Tammy still sat, rocking now, cigarette unlit.

Test shook her head. "Six years old, and she finds her mother like that."

"And she had to walk two miles to her neighbors, carrying a Polaroid of her bloodied mother the whole way so they would believe her, know she wasn't joking around."

"She took a *picture* of her mother like that?"

"*She* didn't take it. The last sounds Dana Clark heard before she fell into a coma were the click and whir of a Polaroid camera. Over and over and over. Click. Whir. Click. When she awoke weeks later, it was the first thing she remembered. The click and whir of that Polaroid camera, as her attacker took photos of her. And the attacker accidentally left one photo behind. But with no useful print on it."

"You're still not telling me something."

"There was one other theory." Rath scratched his jaw. "The CRVK killings stopped after Dana's attack, but also coincided with Preacher's arrest for the murder of my sister. We, Barrons and I, thought the CRVK might be Preacher but could never prove it. But there were no CRVK killings after his arrest."

"And now he's out."

"And now he's out."

17

Friday, November 4, 2011

Fuck, Rath thought. That *fuck.*

Preacher. Weeks out of prison and Preacher was at it again. Who knew what he'd done to Dana Clark; but no doubt he was behind it. He had to be. Didn't he? *Fuck.*

The microwave clock pulsed in the kitchen's darkness.

3:12 A.M.

Rath had returned home an hour ago and insisted Officer Larkin remain on his detail in the farmyard until dawn. Rachel and Felix had been asleep, and Rath had been sitting here at the kitchen table ever since.

Rath wanted to believe Dana Clark's car had broken down or she'd been forced to pull over in the fog and would reveal herself come morning or be found and helped by a state trooper or a fellow citizen.

He wanted to believe that if he found his daughter a temporary place in Johnson, close to her friends and campus, a place Preacher would not know about, she'd be safe.

He wanted to believe that Preacher had nothing to do with Dana Clark going missing.

He wanted to believe all of this.

But he couldn't.

He'd be fooling himself, and he knew it.

It was said among cops that when it came to casework, there were no coincidences. This wasn't true; meaningless coincidences happened all the time, and to believe otherwise was to believe everything was connected and everything had meaning and equal weight. It was a detective's job to discern between coincidence and true connections in a case.

Was it a coincidence or a connection that the CRVK murders stopped after Vern Johnson had killed himself? Or after Dana Clark's attack left her as possibly the sole living witness?

Was it coincidence or connection that the CRVK killings stopped after Preacher was arrested for the murder of Rath's sister a week after Dana Clark was similarly attacked?

Coincidence or a connection that the day Preacher called Rath and stalked Rachel, Dana Clark went missing?

Since the different theories pointed to two separate killers—Preacher or Vern Johnson—some had to be meaningless coincidences.

The microwave clock changed to 3:15.

Rath crept down the hall to Rachel's bedroom door, opened it a crack, and peeked in. She lay sound asleep on her back, snoring, a forearm tossed over her face. Felix lay beside her, asleep yet still clothed atop the bedspread, his head on her stomach, arms wrapped around her waist.

Rath needed fresh air.

Outside, he glanced at Larkin's cruiser, lurking in the fog, invisible save for its blue flashing lights illuminating the fog.

The rain fell as a drizzle, for now.

Knowing his way blind, Rath picked his way across the back field to sit on a stump beside Ice Pond where he often sat to unkink his knotted thoughts. Out here, the night was so black the fog was rendered invisible

Until recently, Rath would have brought a bottle of scotch with him to help, and fail, to allay the back pain he'd suffered; however, a steroid shot had sent his back pain into hibernation, his thirst for drink along with it. He lit a cigarette and drew in a deep drag, smoke searing his lungs. Immediately, he crushed the cigarette on the bottom of his boot; it seemed he'd lost the taste for self-destruction and was glad for it.

In the distant northwest horizon, a pale yellow glow throbbed, even the dark night and fog unable to keep at bay the distant lights of Montreal, ninety miles away. A trout splashed near the shoreline of Ice Pond. Big wild brookies dwelled in there. Carnivores. They crashed baitfish and crayfish against the shore, stunned them, then fed on them ravenously. Rath had caught brookies up to seventeen inches in there, but suspected some bettered twenty inches, weighed up to five pounds. Nocturnal predators. One night, Rath would venture out here with his old Scott fly rod and strip a mouse pattern across the surface to discover what monster he could trick into attacking.

Thoughts of Preacher and Rachel and Dana possessed him. There was no forcing Rachel to stay here or to abandon her studies and leave the state. She was right: even in the short term she could not maintain her grades from here. Yet what purpose did good

grades serve if she were harmed? For the first time, Rath regretted living so far out in the country that cell-phone and Internet
service were as trustworthy as a politician's campaign promises.
His remoteness was costing him. If he lived where the twenty-first
century reached him, where Rachel could Skype into her classes
and research efficiently online, it would be easier to coax her to
stay here, keep an eye on her.

*If you can't keep an eye on her at all times, keep an eye on
Preacher.* The thought sprang into Rath's mind.

He needed to know where Preacher had landed after his parole,
into what hole he'd slithered. Preacher would be listed online any
day now as a registered, violent sex offender.

Rath couldn't waste another hour.

He needed to know where Preacher lived now. He'd stick to
Preacher like bluing on a gun. Whatever Preacher did, or tried
to do, Rath would be there. And when Preacher committed the
slightest violation of parole, and he would, he'd be put back behind bars, Rachel safe again, from a serial rapist and murderer,
who, despite lack of hard evidence, may well have attacked Dana
Clark and been the CRVK, too; and never paid for it.

Rachel was all that mattered. She was also the reason Rath had
to be careful, resist his urge to hurt Preacher, or worse. If he succumbed, he'd be suspect number one. Caught and convicted. He
would not shame Rachel like that, nor risk sabotaging a case to
put Preacher away again, this time for good. He had to let the law
run its course. Unless Preacher tried to harm Rachel, which he
couldn't do if Rath watched him.

Rath needed Preacher's address. Test would have access to it.
She'd want to know why he needed it. He had an angle worked
out. Rath pulled his cell phone from his pocket. It was close to

4:30 A.M. Test had young kids. While she may not be up yet, she would be soon.

Test answered on the second ring, her voice hoarse, beleaguered. "You can't sleep either, huh? I haven't heard anything; Dana's still missing." She thought he was calling about Dana. Good. She was dedicated. Obsessive. Sleepless nights were status quo for a successful detective. Rath didn't know how she managed it with two kids. A spouse helped, Rath imagined, and Test's husband struck Rath as a solid guy.

"You've heard nothing at all?" Rath said, playing along.

"Not a thing."

"Where's he living?"

"Who?"

"Preacher."

"Why?"

"He's clearly a person of interest. If not the primary."

"I know. I looked into it. He's out at the end of Forgotten Gorge Road."

"Way out there."

"It is odd. It's not so far from the Wayside Country Store, either. In the fog, thirty minutes tops. I want to speak to him, but, right now, Clark isn't even officially missing. So we can't. *You can't.*"

Rath knew Forgotten Gorge Wilderness well. He'd deer hunted and foraged for morel mushrooms in those woods numerous times. It was equidistant to Johnson to the west and the Wayside to the east. Preacher could have easily been at the Wayside after leaving the pet shop in Johnson. But how would he know Dana would be there? Had he been watching her? Had he patterned her travel after work?

"Let me know if you get news about Dana."

"First chance."

They hung up.

A brook trout whirled on top of the water, devouring baitfish at the surface. Monsters lurked here, in the deep cold pond, waiting for the precise moment to strike as they took advantage of the cloak of darkness.

PART II

The fog is an accomplice as the girl appears from it like an apparition, as if she is already half gone from this world, scuffing her boots on her way to the mailbox across the road from the driveway; the mailbox, the only one for miles on this lost country road, hidden from the house by the fog.

Look at her, oblivious. The stupid, betraying child.

She looks both ways at the roadside; there is nothing to see or hear approaching in the fog. No vehicle is coming. No one is coming. Not that she knows.

Look at her.

Did she think she would not be found out? That she could keep it a secret?

She crosses the road, toward the mailbox. Toward the trees behind it. Toward the end of her.

Closer.

That's it.

That's it.

Closer.

Come, stupid child. Come.

She does not see me. I am engulfed in wrath's flames. If she were to look up, she would see a hot, white, incandescent light illuminating the fog around me.

But, the fool, she does not look up.

She crosses to the mailbox and opens it.

So close.

The melting rags of snow are wet and slippery. But oh so quiet. Steps soundless in the chorus of rain in the trees.

She turns.

Away from the mailbox.

She drops an envelope and stoops to pick it up from the muddy road.

She stands upright again, brushing the soiled envelope against her fleece jacket.

The heart is a wild panther lunging at the bars of its cage.

She is in reach.

She looks one way down the road she cannot see in the fog, listening.

Looks the other way, listening.

No vehicle is coming.

No one is coming.

Nothing is coming.

Except her end.

Her end is coming.

Her end is here.

The loop swings over her head and is pulled tight to her throat.

The envelopes drop to the snow as her legs drum.

She is no match.

She is easy.

Now, she will confess what she knows, what she has done.

Now, she will confess her sins.

18

The Gihon River Inn stood in the center of Johnson, between Sheer Deelite Hair Salon and a stationery shop whose window display of Crane résumé paper and fountain pens made the establishment seem like it had not been touched since CDs rendered vinyl obsolete. It made Rath wonder if the place was a front.

The inn was not ideal, but all except the seediest apartments in town had been rented back in August, before the start of school. At least the inn was on Main Street, and people would be around at all times.

Carrying the birdcage with the two canaries, Rath followed Felix and Rachel up the narrow stairs and down a hall to room 217, the birds quiet under the cloth draped over the cage.

Rath noted there was no peephole in the door to Rachel's room, no way for her to peer out into the hall. He'd insist one be installed, or put one in himself.

Rachel worked the key in the door.

The caustic bite of creosote tainted the stale air; the odor likely from the fireplace, charred black with soot. The spacious room was otherwise clean. Floor-to-ceiling windows overlooked the street, facing south to allow sunlight to stream in, if the fog outside ever abated for the sun to show itself again.

A poster bed with a quilt of geometric patterns took up the center of the room. Rath averted his eyes from the bed where his daughter would sleep with Felix. A counter beside him spared just enough room for a tray of drinking glasses which were turned upside down, a minifridge, and a microwave the size of a toaster. "Not much of a kitchen," Rath said.

"I use my meal card most of the time," Rachel said.

"I'll grab more of your clothes first chance," Rath said.

"I hate all those clothes," Rachel said. "And this stupid haircut and dye job. I look like an idiot."

"I love your new look," Felix said.

"I'm trying too hard. I feel desperate. Not myself." She looked at Rath. "I never told you. I loved the jumper you bought me from that shop in Canaan. It was sweet. And. It was me."

It warmed Rath to hear Rachel say she liked what he'd picked out for her; or rather, what the store clerk had picked out for her based on Rath's input. He'd been the one who'd felt desperate, buying Rachel the jumper on the spur of the moment a couple weeks back; desperate for a connection with her. Any connection. He'd thought she'd hated the damned thing. Now, he didn't dare say anything, afraid his voice would falter.

"I can buy you some new clothes from there, if you want?" he said.

"Would you? Really?" Rachel said. "I'll pay you back."

"*Pay me back.* I'm your father."

"I know."

Rath did not want to return to the Dress Shoppe. He'd first gone there to interview clerks who'd waited on Mandy Wilks the afternoon prior to the night she'd disappeared. He'd ended up on a date with Madeline, a clerk he'd interviewed, his first date in the sixteen years since adopting Rachel. A debacle of a date. He was as inclined to go into the store as much he was inclined to go vegan. For Rachel, though, he would risk the embarrassment.

He offered Rachel a hug. She stepped into his arms and hugged him back, pulled away.

"It's clean, anyway, the room," Rath said.

"And right on the main drag, got a cool claw-foot tub," Felix said, peering into the bathroom near him.

Rath didn't need to hear about a tub any more than he needed the bed on display, but he admired Felix's enthusiasm under the circumstances.

"It'll do," Rachel said, "until we get back to normal in our place."

There was only one way to get Rachel back to her place, back to normal, and as soon as Rath left here, he was going to set in motion a plan to see to just that.

19

Rath inched the Scout up Forgotten Gorge Road in LOW I 4WD. At this higher elevation the rain mixed with sleet and snow. The road was a treacherous track of frozen and thawing muck edging a ravine that fell steeply away to the gorge below, no guardrails to keep a vehicle from plummeting. With Preacher's place a half mile ahead, Rath stopped the Scout, idling in the road. He was tempted to go to Preacher's door and face him, warn him if he ever spoke to Rachel, or came near her again, Rath would see he was arrested, or worse. But he couldn't do it. Preacher would bask in Rath's anger, feed on it. Rath could not afford to bait him.

He turned the Scout onto a logging road and drove out of sight of Forgotten Gorge Road. At a clearing, he got out of the Scout and took a deep breath, letting the cold, clean air fill his lungs. He put on a knit cap and a camouflage waist pack, slung his climber tree stand over his camouflage jacket, and pulled a head net on over his face. The head net made him feel invisible, and he nearly was; it would be difficult for anyone to see him in the trees from even a few feet away, especially in the gathering fog.

A half hour later, winded and sweating, he descended the other side of the ridge until he came to a grove of ash trees where he foraged morel mushrooms in May. The tree trunks stood straight and true and branchless for many feet, ideal for his climbing stand, and just a couple hundred feet up the ridge from Preacher's place, granting Rath an ideal, concealed vantage.

He strapped his tree stand to the base of a tree and cursed himself for forgetting his safety harness. With a rope from his pack he jury-rigged a harness around his torso and under his arms, and ratcheted the stand up into the tree, thirty feet, much higher than he would climb to bow hunt.

He removed his pack, worked his makeshift harness around the tree trunk, tied it off, minding his footing on the stand's platform. One slip without a harness and he'd plunge three stories to the rocks below. He sat on the stand's padded seat, his heart pounding. Now that he was seated he realized how bone-tired he was. The past two nights he'd slept all of a few fitful hours. If he closed his eyes, he'd be asleep in an instant.

The air stirred near his ear as a chickadee lighted on his shoulder, hopped onto his knee. The bird peered into his eyes with its own glassy black eyes, cocked its head, and flitted away on a breeze. Down the ridge two hundred feet, a 1970s duplex sat just visible amid dark hemlocks. Preacher's lair. Dark vertical boards faced the bottom half of the place, the upper floor horizontal Masonite clapboard, both painted a deep forest green. If Preacher left the house, Rath would have to hike back to his Scout, giving Preacher a head start. But Rath would catch up. He knew the road well, far better than Preacher, and could drive it at a speed Preacher couldn't.

Two vehicles sat parked on the plowed area of yard; a dented, gray Subaru Impreza and a late '90s Ford Ranger pickup. Rath wondered which vehicle belonged to Preacher and which to the tenant in the adjacent unit. If he were still a cop, he'd have run the plates. Instead, he'd observe. Sooner or later, someone had to leave the premises.

He took his binoculars from his pack and focused them on Preacher's entrance—number 1, on the left. He zoomed the binoculars to a meticulous clarity able to make out rust flakes on the nail on which Preacher's mailbox hung by the door. The dark green was not paint. It was moss. The house was diseased with a dark, fungal moss.

Rain pattered the dead leaves. Rath yawned and stretched, his mind turgid with thoughts of Dana Clark, the CRVK, Preacher, and Rachel. The duplex sat quiet.

Snow melted, slipped free of the branches above, cascaded in clots to stamp protozoan imprints into the soggy snow below. Rath pulled his collar up against the strengthening rain. From his pack, he took out one of the cheddar cheese sandwiches he'd made, ate it in a few bites, washed it down with black coffee from his thermos. He'd spent many days bow hunting from a tree stand, from dark to dark, watching the woods and waiting for a good whitetail buck to appear, a creature far more cautious than any man could hope to be.

He pulled his coat collar tighter to his neck and hunched against the rain, fatigue settling deeper into his bones. The sandwich had done more to tire him than the coffee had to waken him. A door to the duplex opened. Not Preacher's door. Rath trained his binoculars on the person on the porch. A woman, a dark ski cap pulled down so low it framed her face, her dark hair peeking out at the edges. Her black satin parka, the back emblazoned with a Harley Davidson logo, was unzipped and hung to her knees. She took a shovel from where it leaned against the duplex on the porch and scraped at the slush that had fallen from the branches of the overhanging trees.

Rath wondered if the woman knew that just one thin wall separated her from a man who had raped and murdered girls and women. *She has a right to know. To be warned,* Rath thought. The woman set the shovel back against the duplex and tromped across the slushy snow to get into the Subaru.

The Ford Ranger belonged to Preacher.

The faint sound of the Subaru engine turning over was followed by the loud thump of bass music playing inside the car as the car drove away.

The shovel slid and fell to the porch.

The house remained still as the dead.

Rath leaned back, worked his jaw and rubbed his face to ward off sleep, closed his eyes.

20

On the steps of Willey Library, Rachel glanced at her phone to check a text message from Detective Test. Finally, the detective had gotten back after Rachel had sent several texts with her new mailing address, so Test could send the reports.

"What is it?" Felix said.

"My dad, checking in," Rachel lied.

"He's a good dad." Felix kissed Rachel's cheek, then pulled the hood of his duster over his head. "Meet me back here after we're done with work-study?"

Rachel nodded. Felix made a mad dash in the fog and rain toward the Dibden Center for the Arts where he helped catalog the college's art archives.

When the fog finally claimed Felix, Rachel reread Detective Test's text: Had an officer drop your "material" at the desk at the inn on his way to a training seminar. Good luck. Rachel broke for the off-campus shuttle, leaping onto it just as the doors sucked shut behind her. The rain fell ludicrous. It sounded like the drumbeat of the apocalypse on the shuttle roof.

In town, Rachel rushed down the block from the shuttle to the inn, her peacoat drenched by the rain. Here in town, the fog grew worse, thick as steam from a hot shower in a winter cold bathroom. She could see all of ten feet. If that. The fog seemed alive, an amorphous and mindless protoplasm insinuating itself into every crevice, strangling lampposts and pedestrians, eating away at reality.

In the inn's lobby, Rachel asked the manager for her package. He held up three manila envelopes. "These?" he said, as if he had heaps of manila envelopes back there to dole out.

Rachel snatched the envelopes and bounded up the stairs.

In her room, she locked the door, tossed the envelopes on the window table. She dumped her soaked peacoat and hat in a plastic laundry basket and sat at the window table. She had fewer than forty-five minutes to get back to campus and meet Felix without raising his suspicions. She did not want to worry him. And she did not want him to find out about the murder files.

The envelopes were so stuffed they seemed about to burst, as if unwilling to contain the contents forced inside them. Rachel thumbed the brass clasp on the top envelope, opened the seal, and took a deep breath.

She got up and paced, trying to calm herself. She opened the minifridge, stared at amber beer bottles: Felix's beer. He bought it at a local brewery anointed *Best Brewery in the World* by some geek site, attracting pilgrims worldwide in search of beers with hipster names like Uncle Floyd and Peace & Understanding. Rachel didn't like beer. Felix was a fiend for it. He and his buddies poured it into special glasses, into which they stuck their noses like pigs rooting truffles. They commented on frothiness of head, stickiness of legs, creaminess of mouthfeel. It was all vaguely pornographic and farcical. Felix wanted so badly for Rachel to *appreciate* beer that when he prodded her to take a sip and give her opinion, he'd await her reaction as if he'd just proposed marriage. "Looks like beer. Smells like beer. Tastes like beer. Diagnosis: beer," she'd say without enthusiasm, though the high alcohol content gave a cozy glow. Which she now needed.

She took a bottle from the fridge, a bottle with the kind of cork flip top that always managed to pinch her fingers.

She sat with the bottle, worked its cork free, pinching her fingers. She didn't use a glass. Her dad drank his beer from the bottle or can. *Why let a middleman spoil things?* he said. Why, indeed. She took a long sip, tasted none of the citrus and mango and biscuits and whatever the hell else Felix went on about. It tasted like bitter beer. But it calmed her.

She slid the documents from the envelope. There must have been thirty pages. The top pages were typed up by a state police detective named Barrons. Rachel wondered if this were the same Barrons who was now Canaan's chief of police.

She flipped to the transcript from a recorded interview with the first person on the scene. Frank Rath. He'd been a detective in those days, but never spoke of it beyond that fact. It still numbed Rachel to know he had discovered the bodies of her mother and father. His sister. It must have shattered him. Even in the cold, objective typeface of Detective Barrons's typewriter, her father's pain lay bared. His sentences not sentences. But fragments. Ellipses littered the transcript.

```
I was late . . . You see . . . I was late for—
Because. I was with someone. A woman. No one
important. A one-time thing. And . . . So . . .
```

I was late. To see my sister. She was putting
on a . . . birthday dinner, for me. I'd said
I'd be there to help . . . promised. She had
the baby . . . to tend to and all. Except. I
was late. I said that already. Instead of being on time. Instead of helping her. I . . .
found her. Her . . . body. It. At the bottom
of the stairs . . . on the white carpet . . .
just. Engulfed . . . by blood. An ocean. Blood.
Her blood . . . her husband's. I doubt there
was any blood left in them. He was draped over
her. She'd been . . . stabbed. Dozens of times.
Dozens. Her . . . neck. Broken. I didn't . . .
touch her. Them. I didn't want to contaminate
the scene. I did . . . touch her wrist. For a
pulse. Even though . . . I knew. I knew. Her
head. It was barely hanging on to her neck. And.
Then. I heard her. The baby. Upstairs. Rachel.
Their daughter. And I forgot . . . all about
my sister. She was dead. There . . . There is
nothing we can do. For the dead. But . . . she
was alive. We must do something for the living, if we can. She was what mattered. I don't
know . . . what is going to become of her? She's
a baby . . . my niece. I don't know what's going to become of her. What on earth is going to
become of her?

There were pages and pages of him speaking of the crime
scene, always returning back to the baby. To her. To Rachel.

Rachel took a drink. The beer had warmed some and warmed Rachel. She had to admit, it tasted pretty good. She picked up a cache of Xeroxed photos of her mother's and her father's bodies. There was more blood than she'd ever believed could be inside a person. And. The wounds. Shown in alarming close-ups, uglier and meaner than she'd imagined. If she'd imagined anything, she'd imagined slices, punctures, clean wounds. These were not that. The flesh was gouged and torn, flayed, as if her mother had been attacked by a prehistoric bird, a pterodactyl with fierce talons and a ragged beak. Her mother's head was cocked at a sick, macabre angle, head cranked around so it almost faced backward.

The profound and profane violence did not crush Rachel; the photo of her parents alive, beaming, coddling their swaddled baby between them, did. They were radiant. They were *young*. In their *twenties*. Scarcely older than Rachel.

Rachel forced herself to memorize the photos. She would never look at them again, but she wanted her blood to absorb and her mind to be tattooed with the images.

It wouldn't prove difficult. The images would never let her forget.

She stared. The body of her birth father—for how else could she think of him, a man she'd never known—lay draped over the body of her mother, a woman she'd never known, at the foot of the stairs of a house that held no memories. Her parents made strangers by murder.

The white carpet on which the bodies lay was black with their blood. An orgy of blood slung in furious strings across the walls and furniture. The bodies had been photographed from every conceivable angle and distance. From above and from each side, down low, so it appeared the photographer must have lain on her side on the bloody carpet with them, nearly nose to nose with the corpses. In most photos Rachel's mother's face was mercifully turned away, hidden from Rachel and the camera's eye.

Rachel's birth father's face was visible in most photos, the eyes wide open with what looked like amazement, the mouth hung open in grief or agony. His tongue lolled out of one corner of his mouth, cartoonish and mortifying. Rachel wanted to tuck his tongue back into his mouth, close his mouth and his eyes. Grant him dignity.

Rachel took another drink of beer.

It tasted bitter again.

She read the medical examiner's report. The clinical, scientific language that described her parents' wounds seemed cruel and uncaring.

The murder file told of Preacher's backstory. In 1989, he'd sodomized a twelve-year-old girl in upstate New York. Then, showing "a kindness," he released her naked and bleeding into the Adirondack wilderness, saying in the police interview: "If God wanted her to live, she would." He'd destroyed this girl for perverted pleasure, but "cooperated," pleaded down from aggravated first-degree rape and kidnapping to third-degree sexual assault. Five thousand dollars bail, which he'd jumped. Within months he'd kidnapped a fifteen-year-old girl in Maine; took her to a forest and raped her while he'd told her how he was going to kill her. The girl escaped while Preacher slept. He was caught. Pleaded. Again. Got a lesser sentence. Again. Served *five years,* minimum security, and underwent behavior modification. "Mr. Preacher," a social worker said in court documents, "*and society* will profit from behavior modification. He accepts blame for his role." As if someone else, his victims, had played a *role* in his savagery.

He was paroled. Again. Moved to Vermont to work as a handy-man for local residents, including . . . Rachel's parents.

He knew them? The revelation shocked Rachel. It made his crime more odious. More mystifying. The report showed that while he'd worked for them in Vermont, his time there had been short. He'd left abruptly to live back in Maine for nearly a year and a half, until he became a suspect in an attempted kidnapping of a mother and daughter.

When he'd fled to Vermont, he'd headed straight for Rachel's parents' home.

Rachel felt vomit churning and rising in her. She breathed deeply and put her head down between her knees, her arms wrapped behind it. After a spell, she sat up again. Why had Preacher killed her parents? And why a knife? Why had he sud-denly escalated to such a savage double murder? It was an act of outsized rage, almost personal. Was he jealous of them? Did he feel slighted? There had to be a reason, in his sick mind. Until the mother and daughter he was suspected of trying to kidnap in Maine, all his prior victims had been girls. He'd never chosen women, or a male of any age. He'd never used a knife, as he'd used on Rachel's parents. A knife he'd bought that morning at the local hardware store, knowing in less than an hour he'd butcher two people with it. The store cashier said there was "nothing out of the ordinary with his behavior. In fact, he'd seemed jovial."

Jovial.

And now he was out, because he'd *behaved* inside, found Jesus.

Rachel read another of Barrons's notes: *It appears the male vic-tim was not planned, but killed when he entered the house unex-pectedly.*

There was another note from Barrons: *Is he the CRVK?*

Rachel knew from her fixation with serial killers that violence was an addiction for them. The lust for the adrenaline rush often intensified, and more extreme acts were needed to reach the same endorphin high. Perhaps that explained the knife. The rage. But was there something else at work to explain the departure in his MO both in choice of victim and the acts?

Rachel's mind felt splintered into a thousand shards of broken glass. It hurt to think of what Preacher had done. Physically ached. Sorrow burrowed in her like an injured animal seeking a place to die. She'd read and watched dozens of biographies of sadistic killers, been sickened and disturbed and titillated. But she'd never felt sorrow.

She had ten minutes to catch the shuttle back to campus to meet Felix. If she missed it, she'd have to wait another twenty minutes or hike up the long hill. Felix would freak if she wasn't on time. He was letting fear get the best of him, too. Fear that emerged as concern and protectiveness, but fear nonetheless.

Preacher. What he'd done by following her at the pet store was seeping into her blood. Consuming her thoughts. It had to stop.

She understood now why her father had not told her the truth about her parents' murders. It was to spare her this anguish and confusion. What better reason was there to lie than to save a loved one pain? She'd have done the same, she realized, because she wished now she'd never laid eyes on these hideous files. It was too late. There was no undoing what she'd done any more than there was undoing what Preacher had done, had started, sixteen years ago.

She felt a deep compulsion to harm him. She could not let this man, this beast, who'd rewritten so many lives sixteen years ago with a knife, author her or her father's future. Could not allow it.

Or allow him to keep her trapped here, in need of a chaperone, her movement limited as she hid out in a musty inn with doilies and quilts, and do it in fear.

A plan formulated. Detestable. Abhorrent. Necessary.

A thump came at the window. Rachel let out a sharp cry. She was on the second floor. No one could reach the window; besides it was sealed so tight with decades of paint it might as well have been nailed shut.

Rain streaked the pane. Outside, the fog lent the day an aura of a failing silvery dusk, as if Rachel were looking at an antique negative gel plate of the town from an earlier era. Dark shapes scuttled in the fog, trailing swirls of mist as they retreated to warm, dry havens.

Except for one shape.

A dark figure under an awning across the street.

Still as stone.

Rachel could not tell if the figure—a man, by height and size—stood facing her or facing the shop window on his side of the street.

Even if he were staring up at her window, he couldn't possibly see her well enough to know who she was.

She considered drawing the curtain, but if it were him, she wanted him to know she saw him; she wasn't going to shrink from him.

Fuck him.

Her germinating plan was to do anything but shrink.

It was the opposite.

She'd go out there now, cross the street and—

The figure moved.

Was he pointing?

At her?

It was hard to tell.

Another figure approached him out of the fog.

The man lowered his arm and embraced the person, and the two figures walked away, though Rachel was nearly certain the figure looked back at her as it slipped into the fog.

She stuffed the papers in their envelope, crammed the envelopes in her backpack, and put on her coat and hat. God, her peacoat was soaked, heavy as a suit of armor. Cold.

As she unlocked the door's bolt and made to leave, the doorknob turned in her hand, from the other side.

21

Rachel grabbed the doorknob with both hands. She made to look out the peephole but there was no peephole.

The knob cranked in her hand.

She looked around wildly, for a knife, a solid object. Nothing presented itself, except the beer bottle, thick and heavy, on the window table.

She sprang for it, knocking the table and sending the bottle to the floor. Scrambling for the bottle, she heard the door open, then close, behind her. She clutched the bottle by its neck and stood wielding it.

"What are you doing?" Felix stood in the doorway, wet hair plastered to his face. "I've been texting for twenty minutes. I was going to call the police if you weren't here." Rainwater dripped from his duster jacket.

Rachel remained disoriented with panic. How long had she stared out the window at the figure?

She dug her phone from her coat pocket. "I turned my phone off in the library."

"What's going on? Why didn't you meet me? You're freaked, I can see that."

"I felt sick and didn't feel like waiting—"

"You should have texted me, with everything that's going on, you should have—"

Rachel cringed. *Should* did not sit well with her. It was presumptuous and condescending, even when it wasn't meant that way. Even from Felix.

"I just wanted to get home and not hurl on the shuttle," Rachel said.

She did not want to share details about her parents' murders with Felix, with anyone. Felix would want to know *everything*; that's how their relationship operated. They shared everything. Just, not this. This was hers alone. And if Felix knew everything she was planning, he'd want to change her mind, stop her.

"Smells like a brewery in here," Felix said, forcing a smile. "Not that I'm complaining."

He noticed the beer bottle in Rachel's hand. "You cracked open my Susan?"

"I wanted to relax."

"Susan will relax you. Good, huh?"

"It's beer."

Felix struggled out of his dripping wet coat and hung it in the closet. He was good at putting stuff where it belonged, keeping things neat. Rachel slung clothes over the nearest object or dropped them on the floor if the floor proved most handy.

Felix kissed her forehead. It was sweet, though she wished he'd kiss her in a way to distract her. Knowing Felix, he feared taking advantage of her emotional state. She wished he'd realize she wanted to be taken advantage of, distracted. If he could not help her forget, then who?

"You don't seem like yourself," Felix said. "Even with everything, with this weirdo, you seem. Off."

"I'm fine," she said.

"It's OK not to be fine."

Of course it's OK. Of course it is.

What was wrong with her. Normally she'd appreciate his questions and tender concern. Normally. Now, she felt poked and scrutinized.

"Let's get a pizza," she said, food always a good ploy to distract Felix.

"Let's get it delivered," Felix said. "It's the end of days out there."

22

Nothing. They had nothing. The state troopers had found nothing at the Wayside Country Store to shed light on Dana Clark's disappearance. They'd found no tire tracks in the parking lot because the lot was under five inches of water that was steadily rising.

They'd found no evidence of struggle.

They'd found nothing to indicate that Dana Clark had ever been on the porch, though it was assumed she was, unless she'd lied to her daughter.

They'd found no sign of Dana's car along the roadside for fifteen miles in either direction of the Wayside; however, the fog remained the chief hindrance to knowing outright if Dana's car was in the trees or a field near the road, whether due to an accident or foul play. Dana herself, her body, might be out there, too, along the road, in a ditch or in the trees or a shallow grave.

The fog put it all into question. It obscured the world. Test felt as though a fungus or a degenerative disease had left a film over her eyes, blurring her vision, and if she just put in enough eyedrops or wiped her eyes well enough, she'd see clearly again. Except, there was no seeing clearly again. She'd blink back the moist air, wipe at her eyes, and still the world remained milky. She was helpless against it; there was not a thing she, or anyone else, could do to see more clearly. It grated on her, the lack of vision that impeded her job, and her lack of control over it.

If the temperature was just a few degrees colder as it normally was in early November, there would be no fog, and perhaps Dana, or at least her car, would have been found by now.

The state troopers, driving ATVs, had reached the deer camp where Tammy Clark's husband and father were hunting. The two men had been shocked to learn Dana was missing and headed home without delay. Neither was a suspect.

Test sighed, the case stalled before it had begun.

She opened her laptop on the kitchen counter, which despite her having to prep dinner soon remained strewn with cereal boxes, dirty bowls, and scummed orange juice glasses from the kids' breakfast in the morning. Claude would see to cleaning up. Sonja could hear the floorboards above her head creak under Claude's feet now as he made his way to the bathroom to shower off a day of oil paints and thinner. The kids were miraculously playing peacefully in the living room.

Test browsed her laptop for Thanksgiving recipes. She needed to prepare ahead to find a fresh take on her staid, dry turkey that no one ate without drowning in her gravy, which was no great shakes, either. Claude claimed Test's turkey was delicious, the liar. Her turkey was sawdust. Did anyone even like turkey? Or green bean casserole or canned cranberry? On her laptop, a sweet potato casserole with condensed milk and a brown sugar topping caught her eye. Maybe she'd just serve a colossal sweet potato casserole on paper plates with plastic spoons. Call it a day.

Claude entered the kitchen, barefoot in jeans and a flannel shirt, wrapped his arms around her from behind. He felt good. Strong. Warm. Smelled good. Of soap. She wondered what he wanted to tell her. He always wrapped her arms around her like this, held her in a slightly less affectionate way when he needed to tell her something rather than be amorous.

"What is it?" she said.

"Giving my wife a hug."

"Mmm hmm. What is it?"

She could tell something weighed on his mind. She'd hardly seen him in two days as she'd worked the Clark case till past dinner. When she had come home, Claude seemed preoccupied and sequestered himself to tend to his portfolio in his studio until all hours of the night.

"It's been two days. You're still not curious?" he said.

"Oh, shit. Your interview." She'd forgotten his interview with UVM. "Why didn't you say something?"

"I didn't want to mention until we had time to get into it."

"So it went well? You think they'll offer the post?"

"The question is, do you think I should accept it?"

"You got it? Of *course* you did." She smiled. Breathed him in. Claude did not smile. At times, the more pleased he was by his success, the less he smiled, as if it would jinx the very reason he had to smile. His superstition was subtle, but there for his wife to notice. His detective wife. While he kept his mouth tight, he could not keep his eyes from smiling. He'd wanted this visiting artist post more than Sonja had realized.

"You didn't tell them yes?" she said.

"It has to work for both of us."

His two-week absence would make for an exhausting, acrobatic, but joyful two weeks alone with the kids. In some ways, when she was alone with the kids, it was easier to let go, spread out, and not worry about the dishes or state of the house, or scheduling that normally stressed her. It was as if she were on minivacation. She went with the flow. One less adult in the picture, accommodating and loving as Claude was, meant one less perspective or schedule or mood to accommodate when making meals or decisions on how to entertain the kids. She wondered what Claude would say if, upon returning home after being away, he asked how it had gone, and she told the truth: "It was so much *easier.*" It was a matter of practicality, not lack of appreciation. He'd probably laugh and confess he felt the same way when she was gone. Of course, if she had a case come up when he was gone, it would be a nightmare. Their babysitter was reserved for rare and random date nights, their anniversary, and Valentine's Day. Even if she and Claude could afford it, the sitter could not cover during the day or through the night, and Test, if she held the senior position by then, could not punt her work to an underling such as Larkin and expect to hold the position for long.

"It's good money," Claude said. "It would take me three months to finish a painting I could sell for as much, if I even sold the painting."

"Your paintings sell."

"Some."

"No one bats a hundred."

"A thousand. No one bats *a thousand.*"

"How can you bat a thousand percent?" Test said.

"It's not a percentage thing."

"That's crazy. Look. Call UVM. Tell them yes."

Claude paused. There was something he wasn't telling her.

"It would probably lead to a full-time gig, next fall," he said.

"What? How long have you known this?" A two-week visiting artist gig was one thing. A full-time position was another. UVM was in Burlington, two and a half hours away. That meant moving. That meant it was impossible.

"They just told me. Don't get upset."

If there was one thing that upset Test, it was being told not to get upset. "You don't want a full-time gig. You always said teaching is a time suck from your painting."

"It would pay well. Plus free tuition. Especially if we have a third."

As if on cue, George piped up from the other room to call into question the sanity of a third child: "Where'd you hide it!" George shrieked.

"Get off!" Elizabeth screamed.

"Stop it in there." Claude deepened his voice instead of shouting, trying for authoritative instead of pleading.

"She won't tell where she hid my race car!" George railed.

"And torturing her helps? Lizzy. Tell him where it is. *Now.*" Claude looked at Sonja. "Still want a third?"

She did. Or thought she did. The past several months she and Claude had been "trying," a term she disliked more than *don't get upset*. But the process was, well, *trying*. Monitoring her ovulation and having to *try* even when her and Claude's moods or bodies or schedules weren't in sync. She wondered if a third child would allow her to perform her current job, let alone act as senior detective. She and Claude were already strained to their limits of time, energy, and money.

"I just wonder how practical it is," she said.

"Practical? Having kids? It's *insane*."

"We can't just move to Burlington."

"Of course we can. Burlington has a big police department."

"I want more bureaucracy like you want the ivory tower. That's why we live *here*."

"We'd be more stable."

"We *are* stable."

"Not if we have a third."

Then maybe we shouldn't, Test thought.

"If I got the full-time gig, I'd have time with the kids," Claude said, "*and* summers and breaks to paint. *And* a steady income. Not the sporadic one I have now. And free tuition."

"You've really thought about this."

"It's a long drive back from Burlington in the fog."

"You're in a fog. I can't just quit. Move. We can't."

"We can do anything we want."

"I *won't*," Test said.

Claude bristled.

"We love this house," Test said. "It's home. The fields, the sledding, cutting our own Christmas tree. The kids have friends. Teach some classes locally. At Lyndon or Johnson, or—"

"Let's scrap it, for now. The position wouldn't start for nearly a year anyway. Nothing would be 'just' move. And if Barrons passes you up for—"

"Don't even say that, it—"

Test's cell phone rang on the counter.

Barrons. This late in the day, it had to be about Dana Clark. "Chief," Test said as Elizabeth screamed. Claude wandered out of the kitchen, shouting, "Stop torturing your sister!"

"I need you at the end of Pisgah Wilderness Road," Barrons said.

"What's this about?"

Barrons filled her in.

"Shit," Test said as she hurried for her coat and keys.

23

Rath awoke with a start, crying out.

Bone cold.

Where was he?

He blinked, could not focus his vision.

Outside. He was outside. In his damned tree stand.

He'd fallen asleep.

Jesus.

Though his body, slumped against the makeshift harness that had kept him from falling, was clammy and cold, the air had warmed. Tendrils of fog twined around tree trunks like vaporous serpents and clung to their branches like spiderwebs.

Preacher's pickup truck still sat in the yard. Had Preacher been out? Rath would have heard the truck start up, the door close. Wouldn't he have? There was no way to know. Rath's sleep had been deep and sound.

Rath stood, stretching, peered through the trees at the house. The fog would soon obscure his view of Preacher's house entirely and he'd have to climb down to observe the place from the hemlocks at the yard edge.

There was no cell service here, but Rath turned on his phone to check the time.

He'd been asleep for nearly three hours.

Fuck it all.

The woman's Subaru had not returned. Or if it had, the woman had driven off again.

Rath heard an engine as a mail Jeep drove into the yard. A mailman hopped out and stuffed mail into each of the metal mailboxes outside the doors. He picked up the shovel that had fallen earlier and leaned it against the house.

Then, he drove back toward civilization.

Preacher's door opened and Preacher stepped out onto the porch.

Just like that.

There he was.

The man who'd raped and murdered Rath's sister, in the flesh. Free.

At Preacher's last parole hearing, Rath had been forced to endure Preacher's lawyer heaping praise on the murderer for all the *good* he had done in prison. To deepen Rath's rage and humiliation, Rath had needed to testify against Preacher's release, as if Preacher's record didn't speak loudly enough. Which, apparently, it did not.

It had taken all of Rath's resolve not to charge at Preacher and beat him as he sat smirking. Preacher had been lucky there were armed officers at the hearing.

There was no one out here now except Rath and Preacher. Just the two of them. Alone.

Rath dialed Preacher in on his binoculars.

Black jeans hugged Preacher's long legs, and his white shirt was buttoned to his throat as he stepped out in brown slippers. He was impeccably shaved, his hair trim and wet.

As at the parole hearing, Rath noted that Preacher, now in his fifties, looked younger than he had when he'd gone to prison sixteen years ago. He appeared in better shape than Rath, like a man who had lived well, without regrets.

From his mailbox, Preacher dug a cache of mail bound with a red rubber band. It seemed like a lot of mail for a man just freed after sixteen years and barely settled. A man with no friends or family who bothered to attend his hearing.

With a folding knife he fished from his pocket he sliced open a large envelope and took from it a pink piece of paper.

He read the letter. Smiled. His two overlapping front teeth exposed as his upper lip curled upward.

He looked in the envelope and sniffed. Smiled wider.

He turned, his back to Rath, face to the sky and arms slung back as if offering himself to abduction by aliens.

Rath made a pistol of his finger and thumb and aimed it at the back of Preacher's head.

Preacher spun on his heel and looked toward the woods, directly at Rath.

His eyes seemed to lock on Rath's, look into them.

Impossible. Preacher could not see Rath, not with the naked eye, not with this fog and drizzle, and with Rath in full camouflage.

Rath kept perfectly still, as if he were watching a deer approach his stand, a deer so keyed to each scent and sound and movement in the woods that Rath dared not blink or swallow for fear of being given away.

Preacher stared.

Water dripped from the snow melting in the branches.

Preacher squinted. Licked his lips.

Finally, he turned away and disappeared inside the house, the door shutting behind him and shutting Rath out.

Rath exhaled and scanned the trees near the house, spotted a grove of birch trees at the edge of the hemlocks, an old wooden birdhouse nailed to one of the birches.

Unhurried, methodically, Rath worked the stand to the ground and, shrouded in mist, sneaked toward Preacher's dwelling.

24

The boy trembled.

In the fog, he sat on the rear bumper of an ambulance parked on the dirt road a mile from where the road ended at the gateway to the Pisgah Wilderness.

The boy could not have been more than ten years old, thin as a sapling, bangs flopped in his eyes from beneath his camouflage Red Sox cap. Other than the Red Sox logo on the cap, and a blaze orange vest, the boy was dressed head to toe in camouflage. Even his rubber boots sported a camouflage pattern.

A man stood beside the boy, his hand resting on the boy's shoulder in a comforting, protective manner that moved Test. It was as if the man were trying to draw the boy's terror from him and take it on as his own. The man dressed identically to the boy, down to the camouflage Red Sox cap and orange vest. No doubt, the boy's father.

Test glanced at a rifle leaning against a nearby tree, an old lever action .30-.30. Iron sights. The barrel pitted from bouts of rust.

"That loaded, sir?" Test said.

"No," the father said, emphatic. "As soon as we— As soon as we finished hunting, I unloaded it. What's the rule?" The man looked at his boy.

"As soon as you're done, unload your gun," the boy said.

"And?" the father said.

"The only place a loaded gun is good is when you're hunting in the woods."

An EMT shined a light in the boy's eyes as the boy shed his cap and squeezed its brim so it curled into a tube.

"Where are the state police?" Test said to the EMT, a woman in her twenties with a pierced nose and eyebrow. Test knew her from a few car crash scenes, but could not place her name. Sally. Or Sarah. Or Sue. "We often beat them to a call. We're local. Like you," the EMT said. "Nearest state cruiser could be an hour away. More in this fog."

It was to Test's advantage to be the first law enforcement on the scene. If she examined the scene first, the state police would need to defer to her for initial information, instead of her having to peck for scraps in a supportive, ancillary role should they have arrived first. If it were a homicide, or even a suspicious death or a deer hunting accident, Barrons would have the state police take lead on the case, but they'd need Test for input. Right now, it was unclear what she was dealing with out in the woods.

If the weather weren't so terrible, she might have been forced to stand down until the state police arrived. But with the cold rain and temps hovering at thirty-eight degrees, Test was losing evidence in the way of boot tracks and other indicators that might be left in what little slushy snow remained of the nearly two feet they'd received in the recent blizzard. She needed to act.

She hit her radio to get dispatch. "I'm ten-twenty-three at the

possible ten-sixty-three. I need an ETA on the state police for Pisgah Wilderness."

"Roger ten-twelve."

Test glanced at the boy.

The dispatcher came back. "Forty to fifty minutes on the state
police's ETA."

"Ten-four. Can you ten-five my husband, my ten-twenty-one A
is unknown. Late. He'll have to manage."

"Ten-four."

The EMT looked the boy in the eye as the boy leaned into his
father's shoulder.

The fog here seemed to be lit eerily by a silvery, translucent
light, like a spider's web damp with dew in the early dawn.

"I'm sorry for your shock," Test said to the boy who looked at
her with eyes clear and bright and attentive. A respect there, not
just for authority, not the kind drummed into a kid, not a forced
respect sticky with resentment and trepidation, but a genuine,
easy respect. A goodness.

This was a good kid.

Who'd stumbled onto something very, very bad.

"I'll need you to show me," Test said. "And to try to tell me every detail you remember as best you can. Can you do that for me?"

The boy nodded. Wrung his hat brim more tightly.

"If it's necessary," the father said.

"It is," Test said. Despite what the boy and father presented to
Test, she could not dismiss the possibility that they were involved
in what took place in the woods, however unlikely. The quicker
she could reach the site, the quicker she could dismiss the father
and the boy. She needed to do it officially. Otherwise the state police would be in her face and up her backside for being slack.

"You might wanna see this." The father showed her an image on his cell phone.

The image was blurred, in part from the fog and rain, in part due to the photographer shaking and standing at a good distance from the subject.

One thing *was* clear: the photo was of a female's body. She lay on the ground, on her back in the wet leaves and sloppy snow, face turned from the camera. Near where she lay on the ground lay a boot, laces undone as if the boot had been yanked on quickly as one does when going out quickly to snatch an armload of firewood off the porch or take the dog out for a morning pee. The foot without the boot was bare.

Was the body that of Dana Clark? It was impossible to tell, but other details, blurred as they were, startled Test. The hair peeking out from under the knit toque was so blond it looked white. Platinum. The coat dark. A peacoat? Perhaps. Test had met Rachel Rath a few times in the past months. Her hair was dyed platinum. Her coat a peacoat.

Jesus.

Test swiped the screen to zoom in, but the pic smeared.

Test handed the phone back to the father.

"I have the coordinates marked exactly on my GPS," the father said. "Perhaps you can go in on your own and—"

"I need you to show me."

A Ford 150 pulled up, and the regional ME, Lloyd Jorgensen, unloaded himself.

Jorgensen grabbed his belt with two hands and tugged, adjusted his red, white, and blue suspenders to keep his pants over his girth. He threw on a rain slicker, zipped it to his chin, pulled up the hood, grabbed a backpack from the truck. "What the devil were they even doing hunting in this crap?" he said to Test, the father and the boy apparently invisible to him.

"It's a tradition," the father said to Test. "I didn't expect we'd see deer. But we've hunted youth weekend every year since he was eight. It's good for a boy to be in the woods with his father."

"I understand," Test said and gestured for the boy and his father to lead the way.

25

The rugged terrain proved arduous hiking.

The rain fell, a din that started in the leaves yet seemed to take residence inside Test's head as she swam through a fog as thick as forest fire smoke, barely able to tell that the ethereal figure just ahead of her was the father, his ghost arm slung around his son's shoulder as if he were afraid that if he let the boy out of his grasp the fog would claim him. The only evidence to suggest Test was in the deep woods were the trees that slowly crept out of the fog like fuzzy black-and-white photographs failing to fully develop before they faded again as she moved past them toward more trees.

Anyone could be hiding a few feet away in this soup.

The father tried to follow his earlier, quickly vanishing tracks back in toward the body. Every once in a while the old tracks stopped their linear march out of the woods and bunched up, revealing how the boy and father had stood around, likely for the boy to catch his breath. Or perhaps they'd both needed to gather their thoughts and rest their minds before they set off again.

Jorgensen snorted and wheezed behind Test. She glanced back to see him in the mist, his hands planted on his hips as he gazed up into the white void, his face flushed pomegranate. This was no trek for a man his age whose exercise, as far as Test knew, consisted of lifting the anchor from his boat on summer weekends on Winnipesaukee or Willoughby.

"You OK?" Test asked Jorgensen.

"Do I look it?"

"No."

"OK then, onward."

They reached a bench on the ridge, a stand of oaks.

The wind raked here, thinned the fog a bit.

Being able to see her surroundings for more than twenty feet made Test breathe easier. Here, the father and son's deteriorating earlier tracks told the tale. Twice, the boy had fallen as he and the father ran from the macabre scene.

In the past year, Test had seen the bodies of two teenage girls. One being that of Mandy Wilks, curled up and frozen in a car trunk, head caved with a tire iron. The other being Jessica Cumber, the front of her skull destroyed with the blow of a hammer just an hour before Test had seen her. Still, Test needed to prepare herself for what the photo on the father's phone showed, whether it was a hunting accident, exposure, or, with Dana missing and the peacoat and platinum hair, an act more sinister. God, if the body were Rachel Rath, how would she tell Frank?

Test continued in the fog. As in shape as she was from years of running, she was getting it handed to her by the upheaved rocks and roots and downed trees.

A sharp piercing cry escaped the boy.

Test staggered backward as the boy cried again and the father shouted, "Go back!"

The boy tripped past Test, the father at his side. Test stood stricken by the scene before her.

It made no sense.

What the hell was going on here?

26

As Rath picked his way down the ridge, he slipped on the greasy leaves and smacked his tailbone on a rock.

He bit back the pain and crept to the edge of the woods at Preacher's yard and stared at Preacher's lit window. He unzipped his waist pack and from it took his motion sensor game trail camera. He set the camera to photo mode and moved quickly to the birch tree to which the old, crooked birdhouse was nailed. He opened the birdhouse lid and situated the camera inside so the lens and infrared eye faced out of the hole. He wove his hand in front of the hole to test the camera. It worked.

A roar erupted behind him. He dove to the ground as ice and snow on the duplex roof avalanched onto the porch, shattering the wooden rail.

Rath stayed pinned to the ground, just able to make out the vague shape of Preacher at the window, peering out. Then, Preacher was gone.

Rath remained motionless, his tailbone splintering with pain where it had struck the rock.

The front door opened. Preacher stepped out onto the porch, looked into the trees where Rath hid just twenty feet away. He held an object in his hand, which Rath could not make out, and looked down at the snow and ice and the broken rail.

He looked out at the woods, toward where Rath's tree stand had been, though there was no way to see that far with the closing fog. Then he went back inside, shut the door, and was gone again.

Rath lay still for a good half hour before he stood and shut the birdhouse's lid.

The camera lens and eye, trained on the porch, were all but invisible unless someone looked directly at the hole from a couple feet away. It was a risk Rath had to take.

He triple-checked the camera and retreated up to the ridge. He climbed back up into the tree stand and sat where he dedicated himself to wait until night fell.

27

Test hadn't seen the girl's body at first.

Because the body wasn't on the ground.

The body was in the trees.

More precisely, hanging from a tree, its back to Test.

"Calm them down," Test barked at Jorgensen, though it was not an ME's place to tend to witnesses, and Test had not meant to bark. Professional command should be calming.

The body hung by its neck from a rope slung over a stout oak tree branch.

The rope stretched taut over the branch, its other end tied around a tree trunk. Except, it wasn't a rope tied around the body's neck. The last few feet of the rope was some sort of metal cord encased in plastic, in the fashion of a coiled bike lock cable.

Had the woman or girl been alive when the boy and father discovered her? Had she awakened and followed through with a suicide?

Test could see only the back of the body from where it hanged suspended perhaps three feet off the ground, above a stump on which the girl must have stood. Her dark coat lay unzipped, and the boot that had been on the ground in the photo was back on the girl's foot.

Test dug her camera from her backpack and shot photos of the scene, the body, the disappearing tracks. The boy and the father had stepped closer to the body than the photo had suggested. Their tracks were all around the body.

The wind kicked up. The body twisted to face Test, as if to say: *Let's get beyond this humiliation so we can find who did this to me.*

"Fuck," Test whispered.

The girl's hands were tied in front of her.

She'd not hanged herself. Someone had hanged her.

Test scrutinized the soggy ground.

The tracks beneath the body were likely not the father's or son's. And, Test saw now, faint drag marks in the wet leaves and remaining snow. No blood.

Someone had slipped the cord around the victim's neck and hauled on the rope to lift the body off the ground.

Someone powerful. Dragging and lifting dead weight by a rope demanded strength.

The victim's face was still not visible to Test, its head hanging limp, chin to chest, as if the corpse were staring down at its feet musing on how silly it was to find itself levitating.

Is she Dana Clark or Rachel Rath? Test wondered.

She peered more closely.

The coat was a black barn jacket. Not a pea coat. What had looked like platinum hair was the lining of the hat, torn. It was not Rachel Rath. Thank God.

Not that Test wanted it to be Dana Clark, either. She did not want it to be anyone. Did not want to be out here on this grizzly afternoon looking at a dead body found by a father and son whose tradition was ruined. Yet part of her wanted it to be Dana Clark. Because if it were not Dana, then Dana remained missing, presumably dead. Which meant there were now, very likely, two dead female victims.

Test took out her radio and tried dispatch. "I've got a one-eighty-seven in the woods off Pisgah Wilderness Road. A two-forty-four." She gave the coordinates. "Are those state police any closer?"

"Ten-twenty-three while I ten-five."

Behind Test, Jorgensen spoke to the father and son. "OK, OK," Jorgensen said and huffed over to Test.

The dispatcher returned, voice staticky. "ETA now a good hour. Officer encountered a flooded road and closed bridge, needed to detour."

"Ten-four."

Jorgensen stared at the scene. His breathing clattered like an old diesel engine.

Test paid him no mind. Nor he her. Both absorbed the site. First impressions were vital.

"He came back," Test said, finally. "While the boy and father fled, he finished what he'd started. In what? The last hour? He's probably still out here." She looked around, at the fog, and knelt at the clearest of the killer's tracks, made in the mud more than in snow. She brought a Shake-N-Cast bag from her backpack and squeezed its internal water bladder, shook it to mix the water with the dental stone powder, poured the slurry into the lousy track. She ignored the cold, stiff ache in her fingers, a mild discomfort to what this victim had suffered.

She knelt and looked up into the face of the victim.

Not Dana Clark's face.

A girl's face.

A girl like so many others.

Like no other.

"Why put her boot back on?" Test said.

28

Test took photos. *Break this case,* she thought, *and the promotion to senior detective is yours.* She stifled the thought. Chastised her disrespect toward the victim for entertaining the notion, natural as it might be. Murder was not a career move.

Test took photos of the knot where the rope was tied to the tree. Forensics would determine how common, or rare, the rope was. And its knot. It appeared to be a rope like any found in a million hardware stores across America. What was not common was the sheathed metal cord squeezed around the girl's neck. It had a latch of some sort, a swivel. It fed through its own loop.

With each raindrop, evidence eroded, the tracks now mere ghostly impressions in the leaves.

Test walked over to address the boy and his father, the son's back pressed against his father's hip as the father wrapped his arms around him.

"How you doing?" Test looked the boy in the eye.

"I want to go home," the boy said.

"I understand. What did you see here the first time?" Test asked the father.

"What you saw in the photo. The body, on the ground."

"You didn't touch it?"

"No. I thought she was dead."

"Why?"

"The way she was. And she didn't answer when we spoke to her."

"Why'd you take a picture of her?"

"So you'd believe us, not think we were crackpots."

"And you saw no one else?"

"No."

"How much snow has melted since you were here?"

"A lot."

"Did you notice anything about the tracks around her, that there were another person's tracks besides her own?"

"Not really."

"Not really?"

"We were in shock. And I tried to keep him"—he nodded at his son—"from getting closer than we were when we spotted her." He gazed at the hanged girl.

"You saw nothing? Heard nothing?" Test said.

"No."

Test squatted before the boy. "Did you see anyone or anything weird, besides the girl, I mean?"

"No, ma'am."

"Try to keep warm. I'll get hold of dispatch and see if I can get the state police to bring food and something warm to drink. But you need to stay put to speak to them."

Test walked to Jorgensen.

"Why hang a dead girl?" Test said.

"Maybe she wasn't dead."

"If she'd been alive, there'd be evidence of a struggle where he dragged her."

"She might have been unconscious, or otherwise incapacitated," Jorgensen said. "I'll find out either way during the autopsy."

"His plan was to hang her. Dead or alive. He was interrupted but came back to hang her. Why?"

"As a message. To study his work? Ritual. I don't know. I'm not insane."

"If he'd wanted her to be a message, he'd have left her someplace visible, not dragged her into the woods. That's hard work done to seek privacy. And he didn't just happen to have a rope on him, or whatever the hell that thing is around her neck. He didn't get the idea on the fly to"—she was going to say "string her up" but the words were callous—"to do that. His tracks have all but melted, but by the impression, he stood here a long time pondering her. He saw the boy and the father, ran up there." Test pointed up at the knoll. "Watched them." A thought struck her.

"What?" Jorgensen said.

"If the perp thinks they saw him"—she glanced at the boy and the father—"they could be in danger."

"If he thought that, he'd have done something then."

"Not if he saw the father's rifle and he wasn't armed."

"Why risk getting caught to come back to hang her?"

"Arrogance," she said. "Foolishness. Ritual. Not to mention simple meanness."

29

Rachel felt the eyes of a dozen locals on her as she entered the gun shop. When she matched each man's stare, they returned to trading quips as they handled pistols and aimed deer rifles at the ceiling, tested the rifles' actions. Shelves between narrow aisles were crammed with gun and hunting supplies. From hundreds of crowded pegs hung game calls, gloves, hats, and gadgetry of every sort. One wall of shelves stood jammed with boxes of ammunition stacked like bricks.

Rachel used to love going into shops like this with her father in August and September when he started to prepare for deer season. This year, he wouldn't have time to rifle hunt.

A man at the end of the counter examined a handgun that lay in pieces on a white cloth. He peered up at Rachel over the glasses perched on the end his nose and said: "One moment, miss."

Rachel glanced out the shop window. She hoped to God Felix did not happen by and see her in the shop, or on the street. She was supposed to be studying with a girlfriend at the Lovin' Cup.

The shop owner came down to Rachel's end of the counter.

"What can I help you with?" His left eye was smaller than his right. Rachel wondered if it were made of glass.

"I'd like to buy a handgun."

"What kind were you thinking?"

"I'm not certain."

"A lot depends on the purpose. Is it for recreational use, plinking cans and the like, serious target shooting, hunting, bodily or home protection, or—"

"Defense," she said. *Perhaps offense,* she thought.

The shop grew quieter.

"I hope it never comes to that," Rachel said. "But—"

"I understand. Do you have experience with a handgun?"

"It's been a while."

"Training?"

"Just from my father. He was a state cop a long time ago, so—"

"Excellent. We offer classes, in the back firing range. If you feel rusty. You really got to be trained to use a handgun under threat. If a weapon is used for defense, then you will be using it under stress, which is not the same type of training for just shooting cans off a fence post. You need training for the circumstances, how to maintain calm, control your weapon under duress, use it for its intended purpose. Not have it taken from and used against you, God forbid."

Rachel felt her nerves jangling, her confidence ebbing.

"I'm not trying to scare you," the shopkeeper said. "But if you're not trained good and get yourself in a bad spot and pull a gun or even *try* to pull a gun, you can end up hurt."

"I plan on getting training."

"What caliber do you have experience with?"

"A twenty-two."

A man behind her by the wall of ammunition scoffed, then cleared his throat.

"A twenty-two isn't enough," the shopkeeper said. "You don't want to go too big, either. You want to shoot level and not have too much recoil. A thirty-eight."

"OK."

"And were you thinking revolver or semiautomatic? How much do you have to spend?

"My father's gun is a revolver. How much are they?"

"They aren't any one price. Revolvers are generally cheaper than semis. We have about a dozen revolvers in thirty-eight that range from just over two hundred, up to about six fifty. Ammo runs twenty to thirty bucks a box. You'll want to get a couple boxes, at least; and the training is two hundred or so for three one-hour courses."

"Oh." Rachel did not know what she'd been thinking as far as price and had not factored in the ammunition or the courses. She had three hundred dollars *maximum*.

"I can throw in a free box or two of ammo, and maybe we can work out something for the course. Payments," the shopkeeper said. "There are other options too. Stun guns. Tasers."

"Do they really work?"

"Oh boy," said a man who gazed through the scope of a rifle.

"They incapacitate," the shopkeeper said. "And you don't have to be nearly as accurate. Of course, while they incapacitate, they aren't lethal. Normally."

"Normally?"

"If the person on the wrong end has a heart condition, for example, it might prove lethal. But should something go wrong while you're defending yourself, the assailant getting possession of your handgun or the Taser, you wouldn't be killed if a Taser was turned on you. And you don't likely want to kill an assailant. The point of defending yourself isn't to kill but to dissuade. Perhaps incapacitate long enough to find safety. You don't intend to kill anyone while defending yourself, do you?"

"Let me look at the revolvers," Rachel said.

30

In the dark night, through his binoculars, Rath kept his eyes locked on the grim light from Preacher's window. The light rain had become a downpour.

At 9:47, Preacher's window fell dark.

Rath remained in the dark for another hour. Then, convinced Preacher was asleep, he trekked back to the Scout. He'd need a few hours' sleep before he returned at 5:00 A.M. to take up watch again, but knew he would not get it. He'd lie awake until he had to get up and sit beside Ice Pond again.

BACK IN CELL service on the slow drive home in the fog, Rath's phone buzzed with three voice-mail messages.

The first from Rachel. "Hey. It's me. Thought I'd call, old school for once. Instead of text. I'm going to sleep soon, but just wanted to let you know I'm OK. No"—she paused—"no incidents to-day. Felix and I had a good day. And—" Rath heard her click her tongue, as she did when she was mulling what to say next. "I'm sorry. That you had to find my mom like that. I mean. She was

your big sister. You grew up with her. I don't even remember her."
She paused again. "Anyway," she said, brightening her voice, forc-
ing faux cheer into it, "everything's A-OK here, I hope it is for you.
Good to hear your voice even if it's recorded. Love ya."

Rath looked up. The Scout had come to a stop in the middle
of Forgotten Gorge Road, the white fog like a wall of snow in the
headlights. He'd let his foot off the gas pedal and not paid any attention to his driving during the message. He was lucky he'd not
driven into the abyss. How was it one could travel so far without
paying attention and not get hurt? He imagined the subconscious
took over, an ancient survival technique.

He listened to Rachel's message three more times.

Checked the other messages.

Chief Barrons had called at 5 P.M.

"We have a situation. You do, anyway," he said. "If you can't
make it to the station tonight, come by first thing in the morning.
I'm in at eight. Or if you're up all night as usual, stop by my place
before I leave for work. But see me in person. Unless you want me
to send an officer out to arrest you."

Rath hung up. Situation? *Arrest?*

Rath would have dismissed the last bit as a joke, except Barrons's voice lacked any levity.

"I don't have time for this," Rath muttered, but knew he'd have
to make time. Knew he'd have to leave Preacher unwatched, if for
a few hours. The next message was Test. She'd left it just an hour
earlier at 10:22 P.M.

"We need to talk. We've found a body. I'm interviewing the
parents in the morning. I hear you're coming in tomorrow to see
Barrons for some reason. I'll find you."

PART III

31

The dead girl's name was Jamie Ann Drake.

A pair of matching silver VW Passats sat in the driveway of her parents' home, the driveway paved, a rarity in these parts, most driveways up here in the Kingdom were dirt or crushed stone.

Test stared at the house, dreading what came next. Interviewing the parents of a murdered child exhausted and depressed her like nothing else. There was no delicate approach. She had to sit with a mother and father still so shocked they had yet to begin to grieve, ask them to lay bare intimate secrets, troubled behavior, drug use, or promiscuity. Most families had never had their secrets exposed to an outsider's scrutiny. Now, all the secrets would be dissected. The questions were cruel by the very act of their being asked.

The home was much like Test's, alarmingly so, what she thought of as adorable, a mid-1800s eyebrow Cape that, she could tell even in the fog and rain, was lovingly tended while maintaining the rustic integrity of the farmhouse. Dried cornstalks framed the black main door on the front porch. A wreath of bittersweet adorned the center of the door itself, and a wicker cornucopia of pumpkins, squash, and gourds rested at the sill.

Test walked up the driveway to the side door; no one in Vermont used the front door. The side kitchen or a mudroom was the everyday entrance. The front door was used by distant relatives converging for the holidays, peddlers of obscure religions, kids pushing candy to fund D.C. trips. Test's kids had been drilled to never, ever, answer a knock at the front door.

Test knocked, her chest tight.

A dog barked once; the door opened.

A couple, midforties, stood before Test, the man tall and lean, his posture erect, proper, though his maroon cardigan sagged on his frame to give a false impression that he was slouching. A black Labrador retriever sat at the man's bare feet, leaning slightly against his owner's legs, wetting the man's trousers with drool.

The woman, petite with alert blue eyes, offered a smile of teeth as white as cream as she squeezed her husband's hand in hers. The couple were not exactly the picture of grief a layperson might expect, but as a police officer Test knew grief had as many outward appearances as there were people grieving.

"Detective," the man said and held out his hand for Test to shake. "Stephen Drake. My wife, Shirley."

Shirley Drake kept smiling, as if afraid to stop.

"Come in," she said.

Shirley asked Test if she would care for anything to drink. Test declined, then wished she'd accepted. Ritual tended to calm the bereaved. The Drakes sat on a love seat across from her, the Labrador retriever collapsing in a heap at their feet with a dramatic sigh.

Test expressed her condolences. The parents of the murdered Jamie Drake nodded. Shirley Drake went on smiling as if she were stoned.

"I have to ask insensitive questions," Test said, wishing again she'd accepted the offer of a drink. Her throat was dry. The air dry in a way only a house heated by a wood stove could be dry.

"We understand," Stephen Drake said. "But we were asked many questions already by the state police, late into the night."

"I apologize to have to ask again," Test said, taken aback, not realizing the state police had already been so thorough. Whatever the case, Test was here now, forward her sole option.

"When were you last in contact with your daughter, in person or otherwise, by phone or texting?" Test said.

"We saw her just yesterday morning, just two hours before—" the mother said. "We both went to work. I work at the Connecticut River Bank, as a teller." She said this as if she were apologizing for her chosen work. "My husband has his own accounting practice. We said good-bye, left Jamie at the breakfast table."

The dog whimpered at the mention of the Jamie's name.

"And did you notice anyone strange, men in particular, near the house or near your daughter, or did she mention anyone or anything that had bothered her lately?"

"Nothing," the mother said.

"Was she upset, angry, or blue?" Test asked.

"She was normal," the father said. "Upbeat, for the most part, into her music and acting, frustrated she didn't get the lead in the school play, typical stuff."

"I hate to ask," Test said. "But I need to. Was your daughter involved in anything you disapproved of?"

The mother blinked, in a way that made Test think she wanted to glance at her husband but did not dare. The father blinked in the same manner and his head had started to turn toward his wife, but stopped.

"We all do things as kids," the father said. "I think of the way I behaved as a teen and I pity my poor parents."

"Did she do *things*?" Test said.

"Like what?" the father said.

He and the mother shifted uncomfortably. Perhaps the state police had asked only rudimentary questions.

"Drinking? Drugs?" Test said.

"Our daughter's murder is not her fault," the mother said.

"Of course not," Test said.

"Even if she'd been a junkie," the father said, "or promiscuous or— Which she wasn't. She—"

"We don't know if she did drugs or drank," the mother said. "We assume she did to some extent. Drank anyway. She's a teenager. We kept a close eye on her. She gave us access to her Facebook account; we let her stay out to eleven on Saturday night. We're firm but open. And never saw any crazy posts. We didn't see any signs of her being in trouble despite who she'd started to hang around with."

Test's antennae raised. "Who had she started to hang out with?"

The mother and father looked at each other with what appeared to be confusion.

"We'd have thought the state police would have told you. Aren't you in communication?"

"We haven't been on this precise point yet. I'm sorry, but you'll have to fill me in."

"We had no signs of, as you put it, things to disapprove of. But the girl she took up with. We knew she—"

"No," the father interrupted. "We didn't *know.*"

"I *did.* I knew," the wife said. Her hand slackened its hold of her husband's.

"To be honest," the father began, "my wife did *suspect.* We talked about it, though not to Jamie. Because there were no outside signs, not even subtle ones, that this girl Jamie had become friends with was influencing her in a bad way. We were apprehensive, naturally. You want your kids to hang out with so-called good kids from so-called good families. But you also want to give the benefit of the doubt to a kid who comes from a tougher, more challenging situation. Those kids get ostracized enough. I know. I *was* one. Had a single mom. Poor. Anyway. We gave Jamie's friend the benefit of the doubt."

"*You* gave her the benefit the doubt," Shirley said.

What are these two going on about? Test wondered.

"But neither of us," the father said, "*knew* our daughter's friend was *that* kind of trouble."

"Of course not," the mother said. "Who would *ever* think *that*? But now—" She wiped at tears.

"Who is this friend?" Test said. "Who are you talking about?"

"She and our daughter both loved acting and bonded because of it, despite having absolutely nothing else in common." Shirley Drake glanced at her husband. "Despite my knowing nothing good could come of that girl."

"*What girl?*" Test said.

32

8:07 A.M. Unslept and famished but without appetite, Rath sat in his Scout outside the Canaan Police Department, wondering about Barrons's mysterious need to see him first thing this morning, and his mention of Rath's *arrest*. Before he went into the station, Rath phoned Rachel. Incredibly, she picked up. "Hey," she said. "Sorry my message last night was so sappy."

"Sap makes sweet syrup."

"Now *that's* sappy," she said. It was an old exchange, comforting. Normal. "Where were you when I called?" she said. "You always pick up."

Her question surprised and pleased Rath. It was the question he was supposed to ask her, most often receiving a sigh that implied she didn't have to keep her father abreast of her every move.

He pondered confessing to her that he had been watching Preacher. It might put her at ease; it might upset her, too, to know he felt Preacher needed constant observation.

"I fell asleep. You OK?"

"I had pretty much a normal day yesterday, other than living among doilies at the inn." She laughed, her signature snort that reminded Rath of the times as a kid she'd laugh so hard she'd snort strawberry milk at breakfast. Except the laugh felt false now, a cover for worry. She was worried.

"Those dastardly doilies," Rath said.

"They're awful," Rachel said, pausing, tentative. "When you go grab me new clothes, could you maybe see about a jacket? My peacoat is drenched and weighs a million tons. I can't put it in a dryer, and I can't wear Felix's jackets, I swim in his clothes and— If you can't, I'll figure it out. There's a secondhand shop in Johnson that's—"

"I'm on it. Promise." He'd forgotten about the Dress Shoppe, but he was happy to perform a common act of devotion, especially now when every exchange with Rachel, every deed carried out on her behalf, felt tainted with the radioactive presence of Preacher. He knew his daughter well enough to realize her mention of the clothes and jacket was not out of a real pressing need for new clothes, but an attempt to establish normalcy amid lunacy.

"OK?" Rachel said. But Rath had missed what she said.

"What? You broke up for a second," Rath lied.

"I said sorry. I swear I didn't call to pester you about clothes or a jacket, really."

"I'm on it. Promise."

"I just wanted to check in."

Check in.

She was beyond worried.

She was scared.

33

"What's this about?" Rath stood in Barrons's office, declining the chief's offer to sit. He wanted to get the mystery over with and see Test about the body she'd mentioned. He was anxious to get back to watching Preacher, too. And somewhere in his day, somehow, he needed to hit the Dress Shoppe. "And what's this about a body?"

"Test will fill you in." Barrons finished the cookie he was eating and stood brushing crumbs from his sadly wrinkled chinos. He'd not shaved his normally bald head this morning, and a stubbly horseshoe of hair, silver as a dime, was making a rare cameo on his skull.

"As I said. We have a problem. Or you do. Your old friend, Dr. Langevine, wants to press charges against you for your past *misdeeds*: criminal trespass, B&E, and your attempted murder of him in his manor."

The investigation of Mandy Wilks a few weeks ago had led Rath to interview Langevine in his secluded mountain manor, where Langevine had laced a scotch he served to Rath. The *doc-*

tor had meant to disable Rath and dispose of him, perhaps in the incinerator in which the ashes and bones of three girls he'd murdered had been discovered.

"He's no doctor." Rath started to leave. He didn't need this shit, not with Preacher unwatched.

"This is serious," Barrons said.

Rath turned on Barrons. "He *poisoned* me."

"Your blood work was inconclusive."

"Because I heaved his poison up."

"Nevertheless."

"Not nevertheless."

"You *did* break into his house."

"Legally, I didn't. I slipped through his Rottweiler's back pet door, which is the same as an open door."

"You beat Langevine badly."

"In self-defense." Rath tapped his fingers against his skull where Langevine had bashed a cue ball. It was still knotted and tender. The wound in his side where Langevine had stuck him with a knife burned like fire ants chewing his flesh.

"That's not his story," Barrons said.

"Of *course* not. He's *innocent. Misunderstood.* I guess the girl he was about to give an involuntary C-section to, and the remains of the three girls in his backyard *incinerator* got there by magic."

"Magic or not. Langevine's a citizen. With rights."

"What is it with these psychopaths, believing they're the victims?"

"They're psychopaths. The center of their universe, empty of empathy, with the emotions of toddlers. I'm speaking for the law here only. The D.A. sent word to arrest you. Peaceably. Respectfully."

"*Respectfully?* That's a good one."

"I haven't gotten back to her, but she doesn't want this shit show either. You plead to misdemeanor charges of trespass and simple assault, we're done. You get fined."

"No," Rath said.

"You did trespass."

"I *thought* Rachel was in there."

"She wasn't."

"And the girl who *was*? If I hadn't—"

"I *get* it. But your motive is as legally moot as Langevine's motive for murdering those girls. You broke in. Accept it, move on. There's not a person who wouldn't do what you did, *if* they had the balls."

"If the D.A. wants to make a mockery of the system, she can charge me—the guy who *got* Langevine—with the full charges, and deal with the media backlash. It'll ruin her."

"I knew you'd do this."

"Good."

"Not good. When it makes the papers, it will give Langevine what he *wants. Exposure.* He *wants* his idea out there, that his crimes can be defended through Vermont's Defense of the Defenseless law; that he acted in defense of the young girls' defenseless fetuses when he abducted them to change their minds about aborting. If you don't plead, *he* gets exposure. Credibility. Interviewed by a dozen outlets. That's how it works."

Rath knew how it worked.

"There is another way." Barrons sounded like a car dealer saying "one more thing" just before he pitched a cockamamie warranty. "You weren't deputized when you went into Langevine's home."

"So?"

"If you had been, you'd have had legal authority to reenter Langevine's house, through the dog's flap door or down the fucking chimney. Making everything else that ensued legal action as a law officer."

"So we tell the DA I *was* deputized, my entry legal."

"One condition."

Rath waited.

"You take the senior detective role I offered you when Grout first left," Barrons said.

"Forget it. I don't want structure. I don't want to have to wear chinos. I like working in my pajamas and Carhartts when inclined, which is daily. And I don't want to have to deal with politics or paperwork or—" Each of these reasons was valid, but none would have normally kept him from helping his friend get this nonsense off his back. The real reason was he could not let anything keep him from watching Preacher. He should have been at Preacher's place right now, since dawn.

"Your only responsibility would be the Dana Clark case," Barrons said. "If she shows up today, I'll still tell the D.A. you were deputized. Problem solved."

"Dana Clark isn't showing up today, or any day, on her own power. We know that."

"All the more reason for you to be involved. You have a deep personal connection with her. We both do."

I have a deep personal connection to my daughter, Rath thought. *And to Preacher. Those are the only two. One for the better. The other for the worse.* Outside those two, and a few guys with whom he played darts on Thursday—guys busy with jobs and wives and kids still at home—Rath had no relationships. He felt for Dana

Clark. He owed her, especially if Preacher were involved in her disappearance. Her death. Let's not kid ourselves. But Rachel needed to be his focus.

"Why the fuck didn't you tell me it was Dana who was missing when you sent me over to her daughter's house?" Rath said.

Barrons scratched at the sprouting ring of hair at the back of his head. "I thought Dana was just trapped in the fog on the roadside. I believed that. I wanted you to go in fresh, not see it through the lens of the past crime against her, and see if you would read it the same. And however it turned out, I wanted you there. Now that we know she's not just lost in the fog, I know you want to find out what's happened to her. If it's linked to the CRVK, or to Preacher. Both. You want Preacher back inside as fast as you can make it happen. Take this post, you'll get him there quicker."

"I can't believe you're playing this card."

"Of *course* you can. I'm doing you a favor."

"I'd be doing the favor."

"We're both doing a favor. Your other two options are untenable. I appoint you, we move on. You get Dana Clark's case. That's it. Unless you want more."

"What more would I want?"

"The case Test fell into yesterday, the body in the woods. It might be linked to Preacher. Like Clark might."

"What was the time of death?"

"Yesterday, midafternoon, I gather."

Damn it. If Rath had stayed awake, he'd know if Preacher had left and committed a murder, or stayed and made Rath his alibi.

"So," Barrons said. "You play senior detective for a spell, and maybe get Preacher— However this nut cracks, and it will crack, *when you* crack it, when you're done, we both get on a plane to the Bahamas and do some serious fishing for bones and permit, relax with cold Kaliks and warm Bahama mamas. Meantime, all the official connections and power you need are at your disposal, for Dana and this new body, if you want. Records. Files. If it's Preacher, you'll get him faster than you will alone."

"What makes you think I'm trying on my own?"

"Please."

"I can access records as a citizen," Rath said.

"Not information not made public. And you'll have Test and Larkin at your disposal to investigate leads you might not get as quickly, or at all on your own."

"I haven't been a real cop in sixteen years. I can't just be appointed. I haven't carried a sidearm bigger than my rat shooter twenty-two in ages."

"I'll iron it out. I *have* ironed it out."

The idea of hauling Preacher in, caging him in a holding cell, it was worth something. Everything. Even with Preacher detained for twenty-four hours, it would be twenty-four hours Rath would not have to worry about Rachel.

"Appoint me junior detective and Test senior detective," Rath said.

"Not negotiable."

"When I step down, Test gets the position."

"I can't just appoint—"

"You're *appointing* me."

"It's temporary, interim, that's how I can get away with it, that and cashing in ancient favors on the select board, for approval. I can promise to give Test the fair consideration she deserves."

Barrons took a Smith & Wesson M&P45 out from his desk drawer and set it on the desk. He set a police ID filled out with

Rath's name and information, the place for his picture blank. "Just get a photo taken," he said. "And"—he took out a cache of papers—"sign your John Hancock."

"Your best detective is going to be rip shit."

"You're my best detective now."

"We'll see about that."

34

W hat bullshit."

Detective Test contained her fury better than Rath would have if passed over for a deserved position, especially by a buddy of the chief. A man.

She sat in the chair beside Rath's, facing Barrons as she absorbed the news, her hands flat on the arms of her chair, but their tendons raised.

"It's temporary; I don't even want the position," Rath said to relieve the tension, realizing too late his apathy was salt in the wound.

"Then don't take it." Test trained her glare on Barrons. "And why offer it? You gave me a line about a process that needed to be followed, a national search."

"This possible reopening of the CRVK case takes precedent," Barrons said. "Rath is interim. Don't think I want to see his mug around here more than necessary. And you can be the lead. Or colead. Despite titles."

"Then why bother with titles?" Test said.

"This is it. For now." Barrons nodded at Rath. "He fought for you. I need to put the person with the most knowledge of the old case at the lead. Officially. Publicly."

"Someone who couldn't solve it the first go-round," Test said. "You still dig into the old CRVK files. And when I proposed that the recent missing girls who led to Langevine might be the CRVK's work, it chafed you."

Rath had expected Test to take umbrage, but not a pointed shot at her chief's failure. It was a mistake.

"A necktie chafes me," Barrons said. "The idea that you proposed the CRVK might not be dead hit a nerve because, frankly, that's a worry Rath and I have shared for sixteen years. That the CRVK had moved to new turf or stopped because something happened. Jail. Illness. Death. Most cops thought the CRVK was Vern Johnson. Rath and I thought Preacher was good for it. He damn well could be. Look. Rath is senior by title alone. On the ground, you two work it out however you want; the sandbox is yours. But if a tough call comes, it is Rath's to make, in the end."

"The Dana Clark case only?" Test said.

"Fill him in on the body found yesterday. If they're not connected, it's your job to find out. It might be wise to suspect they are. And suspect Preacher."

"It might," Test said.

35

Test's office had been Harland Grout's originally, but Grout's scuffed desk with mismatched drawer handles had been swapped for a streamlined table with stainless steel legs and a brushed metal top. Behind the desk, an ancient steam radiator hissed though it had never seemed to heat the embarrassingly cramped quarters whenever Rath had paid Grout a visit.

Grout's books on home brewing, and his son's and daughter's grade-school sports trophies were swapped out for tomes on criminal investigatory procedure, interrogation techniques, forensic science, police codes and conduct, and abnormal psychology. One shelf dedicated itself to photos of Test's young daughter and son and her husband.

"I obviously take exception with this move," Test said, "but not with you, *if* we work *together*. You don't want this job permanently any more than I wanted to keep Grout's ugly furniture."

"I don't even want it temporarily."

"Yet you took it."

Rath did not want to get into the details about Langevine, so he told a simpler truth. "It gives me access to investigate Preacher."

"*Personal* reasons. Dangerous in this work."

"I want him back inside. If this position gets him there faster, so be it. I can't have him near my daughter, I can't have him—" He collected himself. "Tell me about the body you found."

"Jamie Drake. I visited her parents before I got here," Test said. "She had a friend."

"Who?"

"Abby Land."

"Mandy Wilks's killer? That's a fuck of a coincidence."

"If that's all it is."

Here it is again, Rath thought, *coincidence versus connection.*

"Wilks's case is open and shut," Rath said. "We found her body and the tire iron used to kill her in the trunk of Abby Land's Neon. Land's prints are all over the tire iron, in Wilks's blood. Land confessed. Whatever troubles you about this girl and Abby being friends, it can't change your thinking that Land killed Wilks."

"It hasn't. But Mandy Wilks's murder and Jamie Drake's murder *are* linked *by* Abby Land. Land is the common denominator. Maybe it's the bizarre circumstances that have my gears grinding," Test said. "The boy and the father who found Jamie Drake found her on the ground. But when we got to her corpse, it was hanging from a tree."

"They sure?"

"I saw a photo on the father's phone. She was on the ground."

"I mean are they sure she was *dead* when she was on the ground."

"It's to be determined by autopsy. All I know is Abby Land murdered Mandy Wilks, and now Abby's closest friend has been murdered. I don't know *how* Land ties them together. But she does. What's oddest is that Abby and Jamie know each other at all, let alone are friends. The two could not be more different. They had no overlap of social circles. But were best buds."

"I'd have thought our hanged girl was of a similar rough background as Land. Abuse, alcoholism. Neglect."

"Nope. Drake's parents have it together. Professionals, a comfortable income, lovely home."

"Or appears that way," Rath said.

"I bought it. Not a perfect household. Whose is? But compared to Abby Land's situation it's the UFC versus ballet. If not for being in theater together, they wouldn't be friends," Test said.

"A lot of kids with dissimilar homes become friends through music, sports, or arts. Doesn't mean there's a connection to the murder of our hanged girl."

"Something's there. Maybe a love triangle."

"Among our three girls?"

"They have names, you know. Dead girls."

"I don't use names," Rath said. "That's how I was trained. You too. To remain emotionally detached so we can focus on the case."

"I focus better when I remember the girls had names. Lives."

Rath understood the logic, but disagreed professionally.

"So. This love triangle?" he said.

"Not among the three girls. But among Abby, Jamie, and Luke Montgomery."

"Montgomery. Abby Land killed Wilks in a jealous rage over him. But *he* didn't know either girl."

"So Abby *says*. But Abby killed Mandy. And now Abby's friend is hanged while Abby's in prison awaiting trial. Maybe Montgomery knows Abby better than he's claimed. Maybe he and Abby had a thing and he was part of Mandy Wilks's killing, and now this hanging."

"He doesn't *know* the girls. I interviewed him myself afterward. He's a dead end."

"I want to speak with him and look him in the eye to determine that myself. Exclude him myself."

"Fine. But I interview Land first. Before you go to Montgomery. She's facing twenty-five years, so she's more likely to break than him if she's covering for him or there's something there between them. And if anyone knows whether or not Jamie was involved in drugs, or sex, or any behavior that might put her in jeopardy, it's Land. Tell me more about your hanged girl."

Test told him.

Rath leaned back in the chair. "So he hanged her corpse, if she was dead, out of what? Ritual?"

"There's only one person alive who knows."

"It takes a lot of strength to lift and hang a person, dead or alive. Preacher's in shape," Rath said. He needed to tell Test he'd watched Preacher's house. He'd fallen asleep and couldn't account for a few hours; but other than that Rath was Preacher's alibi. Instead, he said: "Pay Preacher a visit. See if he has an alibi."

"I know you want him locked up. But we have no evidence." Test sounded like Barrons as she played with the zipper of her Canaan Police parka, its zipper adorned with a ski tag from Catamount X Country Trails.

"We have *no* evidence pointing to anyone. With Preacher just out for similar crimes, he needs a visit," Rath said.

"Preacher never committed a crime similar to this. Hanging?"

"He'd never used a knife until he killed my sister, either. Pay him a visit." Rath disliked telling someone to do what he could do himself, but he did not trust himself to be face-to-face with Preacher, not yet.

The phone on Test's desk rang.

She answered it, turned her chair to face the window, though there was nothing to see outside the window except fog. "Repeat that. I don't, either. Right. I'll look for it."

Test hung up the phone. She looked as if she'd just been told a loved one was dead. "You were right. Jamie Drake wasn't dead when the father and son found her. Her death was due to asphyxiation by hanging. A very slow, very meticulous, very excruciating and incremental hanging. He held her up and then would let her down again, let her be choked, then lifted her up again."

"He tortured her."

"There *was* a stump under her. He may have used it to perch her on, so she was just on the tips of her toes. Struggling. For air. It's unclear. But it went on for a spell. A good ten minutes. Which"— she exhaled deeply—"is a lifetime. And the end of the rope, it's not a rope. It's like wire cord encased in clear rubber, like a thinner version of those coiled bike locks."

"Sounds like an animal snare."

"It is. A snare used by trappers. It would be easier to slacken it, ease off, than it is to slacken a rope tied in a noose."

"Premeditated torture."

"It's like holding someone under water, then letting them up for a sip of air. Then . . . I don't understand such cruelty, wanting to cause such *pain*."

"I don't either," Rath said, though that was only partly true. When it came to Preacher, Rath wasn't so sure he had a ceiling, or a basement, on the type of pain he'd inflict upon him, if he had the chance to get away with it.

36

Test eased off the main road and onto Forgotten Gorge Road in the fog, inching past a massive rock outcrop that crowded the road, and on which a single wilted red rose had been left to mark a car crash.

The road was a quagmire of muck. Barrons had insisted Test and Larkin take Barrons's Explorer instead of Test's Peugeot or a cruiser. "You'll get stuck in that death trap of yours," he'd said. "You need a reliable vehicle in the winter, as a detective, and as a mother, I'd think."

Barrons's remark annoyed Test, partly because Barrons was right. Her attachment to her Peugeot was irrational and borderline irresponsible when it came to transporting her kids. She'd owned it since her third year at Dartmouth when a professor sold it to her for a song. She still used the archaic cassette deck to play R.E.M. and Violent Femmes tapes; she even appreciated the ripe leathery funk, which remained a mystery since the upholstery was fabric. Perhaps it was her spare running shoes she kept in the way back that smelled so pungent.

Larkin sat in the passenger seat, his posture so erect his buzz cut touched the vehicle's roof. "You think Preacher did it?" He gripped the handle over his window, as if it might save him should the Explorer plunge into the abyss.

"No evidence points to him or anyone."

Test wanted to look Preacher in the eye, read him. She had trepidation, too. She'd faced a brutish bull named Jed King a year earlier, during her first solo murder investigation. He'd goaded Test into drawing her weapon, and she'd nearly shot him. He'd also poisoned Test's dog.

Test steered the Explorer carefully around a hairpin corner, feeling the vehicle, even with 4WD, wanting to slide toward the cliff. Ahead, a house lurked in a scrubby clearing in the woods, a muddy parking space serving as most of the yard. This was where men like Preacher ended up: five miles outside the remote town of Canaan, at the end of a ruined dirt road, in a 1970s raised ranch that—judging by the two front doors side by side at the top of the wooden steps—had been cobbled into a makeshift duplex decades ago.

On the wooden porch steps sat a sunken jack-o'-lantern, originally carved in a way likely meant to be macabre but now rotting and resembling a toothless old man. The porch rails had been shattered by snow falling from the roof, railing pieces strewn like bones.

Test parked beside an old Ford pickup. "Follow my lead," she said to Larkin. "Assess our surroundings and situation, monitor the interviewee's mood and reactions, and stop any threat he might pose. This is a smart man, in his animalistic way. A dangerous, violent man. He's free because he played the system to earn early release. That's patience and guile." Test coughed, her throat scratchy and raw. A sore throat making the rounds in the kids' school was coming her way. She plucked a pack of Esberitox from her coat pocket and chewed four tablets. "There is no telling what he might do."

"I understand, ma'am."

"Drop the ma'am."

Test stepped out of the Explorer into the fog. All around her, water dripped from the trees, so at first she thought the rain had started again. She shivered, realizing how toasty the Explorer's heated seat had kept her.

She walked through the dead muddy lawn, puddled with rain-water, to the porch, to Preacher's door. Number 1.

Despite shivering, Test felt too warm. She unzipped her jacket, her sidearm visible. She'd worn a hip holster instead of a chest holster. It permitted her easier access and confidence in drawing it swiftly.

Unlike the entrance for number 2, there was no storm door on Preacher's entry. The solid, main door gave a dull thunk when Test pounded the side of her fist on it three times.

The door opened so quickly Test flinched, startled. *He's been watching,* she thought.

The man before her startled her, too. For an instant, Test thought she had the wrong entrance or the wrong man.

Even with the photos fresh in her mind, she barely recognized him.

Except for the eyes.

Black. Deep, glassy, black, reflective and impenetrable as polished obsidian.

Preacher smiled. The mirrored quality of his eyes dulled. His smile was that of a schoolteacher or mail carrier. It did not over-reach, it was not used in a manner to disarm or deflect or ingrati-ate. It was subtle, curious, yet not put out to find someone on his porch midweek. Neighborly.

It was a mask. A damned good mask.

He looked strangely younger than any of the photos Test had seen of him. And healthier. Fit and trim, with a physique more akin to that of a triathlete than the massive bulk many convicts achieved while serving hard time. He looked powerful. Yet agile. Powerful enough to hang and torture Jamie Drake with ease.

His face was pink and moist, freshly shaved; a pine scent of aftershave rippled off him, as if he were trying to mask an appall-ing odor. He did not look like a man who had raped and killed five young women. What did such a man look like? Like any other man on the street.

From his shirt pocket he took a pack of gum, tapped a stick free, peeled off the foil. He looked Test in the eye as he laid the gum on the flat of his pale tongue and folded it into his mouth, chewed it with his front teeth.

Test introduced herself and Larkin, whose eyes remained fixed on the interior of the home behind Preacher. "We'd like to ask you a few questions."

"Of course you would. I've been expecting you. I knew this was how it was going to be."

"How what was going to be, Mr. Preacher?" Test said.

Water trickled from the eave above onto Test's boot. Test wanted to look up to assess if there were more snow clinging to the roofline above her, about to fall, but she needed to keep eye contact.

Preacher chewed his gum. "I think we know. The harassment. I suppose you'd like to come in. I suppose you'd like to ask me questions about something that's happened?"

Did he know what had happened? Test wondered. Did he know what had been discovered in the woods from hearing the brief, vague news item that had gone out this morning about a body found in the woods, or was he speaking in general, insinuating that with any crime remotely like those of his past he would be a suspect by default? As he ought to have been. Or did he know because he was the one responsible for Jamie Drake hanged in the trees?

Test nodded, indicated she'd like to come inside.

Preacher backed up against the door to open it wider, gesturing with his long slender fingers for Test to step past him inside.

"After you." Test would not risk squeezing past Preacher, give him an opportunity to try to shove her inside and lock Larkin outside.

"Your wish—" Preacher snapped his gum and backed inside to permit Test room to enter.

Test stepped inside. Larkin followed.

The entry smacked of the 1970s with a floor of multicolored slate tiles set in a haphazard jigsaw puzzle design. Above her, a chintzy brass-and-etched-glass fixture scattered diamonds of light onto the scuffed, gray walls.

The house was divided vertically, so each tenant had access to both the upstairs and downstairs. A set of steps ascended to the main floor, four steps to the right descended to a closed door that surely opened to Preacher's half of the basement.

Again, Preacher swept a hand to demonstrate he wished for Test and Larkin to go up the stairs first. If Preacher were a private citizen with no criminal background, his gesture would have been one of courtesy. Preacher could not be so naive as to think Test would put her back to him; yet he behaved as if he were any other citizen, offering his home to police officers who'd stopped by to inquire about Halloween vandalism. Is this how he saw himself? Free? Just another citizen? He'd paid his debt, and now he was just like the rest of us who had never raped girls, never broken the neck and mutilated the body of Frank Rath's sister? Was he that delusional? No. He was playing a game, as if he wanted Test to call him out, make it clear they knew what he was. He wanted to hear all about himself and the damage he'd wrought, so he could bask in it.

"As you wish." Preacher led them up the stairs.

Larkin flicked his gaze at Test to indicate that he'd be first to go up behind Preacher.

In the living area a forsaken couch slouched facing a brick fireplace, the couch's plaid pattern so faded it was barely perceptible. Dust clung to its skirt. Test saw no TV. The walls were blank, except for a small wooden crucifix above the fireplace mantel. It was not possible to determine if the crucifix was a recent adornment or not.

On the kitchen entrance hung louvered, saloon-type swinging doors stained a dark brown, the bottom edges scribbled with black magic marker. The dark baseboards were gouged and scratched with the claw marks of a cat.

"The kitchen." Preacher pushed through the swinging doors.

Larkin followed.

The saloon doors flapped behind Test as she entered.

The kitchen was just spacious enough to fit a card table and a mishmash of three folding chairs set around it.

A bible sat on the center of the table, opened to a page some-where toward the last third. *A prop,* Test thought.

Preacher nodded for Larkin and Test to sit. They declined.

Preacher shrugged and folded himself into a chair at the op-posite side of the table, stretched his long legs and crossed them at the ankles. With his long fingers he closed the Bible. "So?" he said.

A fly buzzed at the sink window, tapped against the glass pane.

Preacher fixed his black eyes on Test, composed and patient. "You're here to ask me where I was at a particular time yesterday," he said.

Test had expected a coarse man who refused access, defied in-quiry, stuck out his chest, and spat vile words; someone like Jed King. This man was not Jed King. This man was far more devious. Yet, as hard as he tried to project a respectful and accommodating manner, he could not entirely conceal a certain cold menace.

"In fact—" Test began.

"I'll save you the time, since your time is almost as valuable to you as mine is to me. I was here. For a spell. Enjoying the fog."

"Enjoying?" Test said.

"It's beautiful and mysterious. The fog. It never rests, it's always shifting and taking new shapes, quiet and peaceful one moment, ominous and . . . suffocating . . . the next. It's miraculous it's just water droplets. There's so much to see just out your window. You'd be surprised what's out your window. Though after a while the fog kept me from seeing most of what's out there, from seeing much farther than the end of my fingertips." He flexed his long fingers. The fingers of a strangler. Fingers that had squeezed and crushed the windpipes of young girls after and sometimes during, their rapes. Rath was right: it was not a reach, even without a shred of evidence, to put Preacher at the front of the line as a suspect for Jamie Drake's murder.

"You were here for a '*good spell*'?" Test said. "You went out then?"

"I took a stroll."

"To?"

"Town. I had planned to just go to the main road and back. But when I reached that goal, I just kept going."

He smoothed his hand over the cover of the Bible.

"What time?" Test said.

"I assume we're talking about the times roughly around that girl being hanged."

Hanged. This detail had not been released to the media. Preacher could not know it. Unless he had done it. Or knew who did. Jesus.

Test tensed, a hand going to her sidearm, and glanced at Larkin to be ready. She didn't care if Preacher saw her gestures. Hoped he did. Perhaps Preacher believed the detail of the hanging had made the news as it would have by now if it were not intentionally held back.

Test had to tread with caution now, could not let Preacher know he'd slipped up. He'd done it. He'd hanged Jamie Drake. Tortured her. Stepped up his desire for sadism.

"You *walked* to town? Five miles one way?" Test said.

Preacher nodded.

Bullshit, Test thought. *You didn't walk to town. You drove your fucking truck, parked near the Drakes' home, and waited in the woods for Jamie.*

"You didn't take your truck?" Test said.

"That's not my truck," Preacher said. "And I like to keep in shape. It isn't far. Town. An hour and half or so each way. I've got all the time in the world now."

No, Test thought. *You are just like me, just like the rest of us, in that regard. Your time is brief, finite. And you've used it to rob other people of their time here, to make it painful for others.*

Test felt herself coiling tight but needed to relax. She did not need more than Preacher's admission of the girl being hanged to take him in for questioning. It was best to get whatever else he might say videotaped at the department. But she did not want to incite him, not yet, not if it could be helped.

The fly buzzed past Test's ear into the ceiling light fixture, where it ricocheted inside with an annoying tick.

"Why do you think I'm here to ask about where you were?" Test said.

"Why else would a moderately attractive female detective waste her precious time? You're not one of my admirers. Not so mis-guided, so *insane* as any of those poor birds that send fan mail." Preacher's mouth stretched into a slow smile, leaking a malicious confidence. His dark eyes had a brightness in them, a savagery. His teeth shone too white, as if he bleached them in Clorox. "Of course, you pay a visit to the convict recently paroled for past sins, the outside world never able to forget or forgive."

Test wondered what had happened to Preacher's gum. He was no longer chewing it or snapping it. She'd not seen him take it out of his mouth. Had he swallowed it?

Preacher smacked a palm on the table. Test's hand flexed on her weapon's grip. Preacher lifted his hand to show a red splat of blood in the center of his palm. It looked like a stigmata. "What kind of creature feeds on the dead and shit?" he said.

"To be clear," Test said, "between eleven A.M. and one P.M. you were walking to town?"

Preacher blinked, a blink that lasted a half beat longer than his previous blinks. He knew. He knew Test had purposely misstated the time frame. The girl had been murdered between the hours of 2 P.M. and 3 P.M., that much was clear. Preacher could not know Test had given him a misleading time unless he *knew* the time.

Preacher tried to give the same smile as before, but missed by a shade; this smile was oily and knowing as the glassy impermeable blackness returned to his eyes. "If *that's* the time frame, I was here napping, reading my fan mail. Alone. The time I was speaking of was the afternoon. Say two o'clock or so?"

Preacher started to reach into his pants pocket.

Test gripped the butt of her M&P45 more tightly.

Preacher raised an eyebrow. "Just getting my phone," he said.

"Put your hands on the table. Palms down. You can come with us for questioning at the station without resistance, or you can resist and be arrested. And *that* will be a violation of your parole. You will be jailed."

Test glanced at Larkin, who had his M&P45 out, leveled at Preacher.

"Right," Preacher said, smiling like a child who delights in misbehavior. He placed his palms flat on the table. "You people."

Test went to his side, prepared for him to resist. He did not. He laughed, as if at a sick joke to which only he knew the punch line.

"Up," Test said. "You know how this works."

"You'll live to regret this."

"I hope that's not a threat," Test said.

"You will wish it were."

OUTSIDE IN THE Explorer, the sole of Test's left boot stuck to the floor mat. She lifted the boot off the floor to look at what was causing it to be so tacky.

Chewing gum.

She got out of the vehicle and scraped the gum off her boot onto a rock. She didn't want anything that had been in Preacher's mouth touching her.

37

It's him," Test said.

Rath looked up from a topographic map he used for deer hunting, a map now spread out on the card table he'd set up in his makeshift office at the station. He'd been determining distances from Preacher's new place to three other points on the map: Johnson State College, the Wayside Country Store, and the Pisgah Wilderness Area. Each point, by car, could be reached in thirty minutes, give or take, from Forgotten Gorge Road. A perfect triangle, with Preacher at the center.

"Who?" Rath said, working out the time frame. Preacher could have been watching Rachel and had time to intercept Dana Clark at the Wayside. If Preacher knew Dana's pattern. And he'd had plenty of time to murder Jamie Drake in the time Rath had slept.

"*Who?*" Test said. "Preacher. I've got him next door."

Rath stared at the thin wall that now separated Preacher from him. In a minute, nothing would separate them, save a few feet of air across a narrow table.

"Did you arrest him for Clark or Drake? Or both?" He felt almost dizzy with relief.

"I didn't arrest him," Test said.

"You just said it's him," Rath said. "Is it or not?"

"He slipped up. He mentioned Jamie Drake being hanged. That's not in the news. And he knows the time frame. We kept both of those facts out. There's hardly any news reported except a young female body being found. There is no way he could know unless he did it. Or knows who did."

"Then arrest him."

"It's not enough. We arrest him, he'll backtrack, say he guessed, was playing with us, and the D.A. will tell us to cut him loose. We need physical evidence, too. Hard evidence. I requested a warrant for his premises."

"Be sure to include his—" Rath was about to say truck, but caught himself. "His vehicle. If he has one, in the warrant."

"He claims a truck in the yard isn't his. I don't believe him. I'll run it," Test said.

Rath thought about Preacher looking up from his front steps at Rath in the trees. Had Preacher seen him?

"What is it?" Test said.

"Nothing."

"Video is running in the room. Maybe you can press him, get under his skin, and get more out of him, enough for an arrest. Ready?"

Rath wasn't ready. He did not know if he could deny the violence in him. *Be careful,* he warned himself.

He let out a breath. "Ready."

38

Pine-Sol, Rath thought as he entered the Spartan interrogation room of one table and two chairs, one chair empty across from the one in which Preacher sat, his hands folded on the table, posture proper, chin up with a slight, yet unmistakable air of superiority; or at least an attempt at it. *The guy stinks like he bathed in Pine-Sol.*

Preacher's eyes followed Rath as Rath shut the door, the bolt finding its recess with a metallic clack.

"Senior Detective Rath entering the IR," Rath said for sake of the recording.

Rath sat. His eyes met Preacher's black eyes. Rath supposed one might see Preacher's dark eyes as menacing or mysterious. To Rath they were as dumb and dead as that of a doll.

Preacher was not cuffed. Nor shackled. Since he was not under arrest, use of restraints was not permitted. One could not just drag in any old rapist and murderer in cuffs on a whim, after all; that would be a humanitarian outrage.

Rath's blood swam inside him, hot and tidal. He thought of his sister, Laura.

Laura who, when Rath had been a boy, had protected him from bullies who claimed his father had left because Rath was a "stupid little fag." Once, a bully had pinned Rath in the dirt of the playground and had pulled his shirt up and was giving Rath an Indian burn as Rath swatted futilely at him, swatted and cried. Until the torture had stopped instantly, and Rath looked up to see Laura towering over the bully, a rock in her hand as blood streamed out of the bully's cheek. "Do it again, I'll crack your retard head open," Laura had said. Laura who'd had no one there to help when Preacher had attacked her. Laura who'd been expecting Rath for his own birthday dinner, but who'd shown up too late.

Rath thought of Rachel, too. Of Preacher's phone call.

"Frank Rath," Preacher said. "In the flesh."

Rath stared at Preacher. Three feet away. An arm's length.

Rath's presence must have surprised Preacher, yet neither Preacher's expression nor voice betrayed surprise.

Preacher's Adam's apple jutted just above the primly buttoned collar of his stark white shirt, his skin raw where a razor had tracked it. The shirt was a shade tight and gave the impression of his solid frame beneath. Dry skin flaked at the wings of his nostrils, as if he were shedding.

"You're an officer of the *law* again," Preacher said. "I regret you have to be here."

Steady, Rath told himself. *Careful.* "You don't regret anything, except being caught."

"It must be hard. To see me. I can barely look in the mirror myself. In fact, I don't. I don't have mirrors in my home."

"Why do you believe the girl was hanged?" Rath said. *Sixteen years after Laura's murder,* Rath thought, *and here I sit asking her murderer, days after his parole, about another dead girl.*

Preacher touched the tip of his tongue to an incisor. "*Believe* she was hanged? I *know* she was. News travels fast."

"It's not in the news. There's one way you could be certain. You were there." *Or the person who did it told you.* Rath did not want to speak of this possibility. The odds were too slim that Preacher involved anyone else. And he hated to think of what it meant, two men like Preacher unafraid to realize each other's dark fantasies.

Preacher leaned forward, in an odd bow, as if he wanted to touch foreheads with Rath. "You and I both know I wasn't there," he said and leaned back, head dangling over the back edge of the chair, arms spread wide to his sides, as he'd done out on his porch, just before looking toward Rath in the woods, as if he were in the beam of an alien ship awaiting abduction to another world. Did Preacher know Rath had been watching, had he seen him, after all, had he found the trail camera?

Rath clawed his fingernails into his palms. *Careful.* "Dana Clark," he said.

Still leaning back, Preacher folded his arms across his chest, hands overlapped in the manner of a corpse about to be wrapped in a shroud.

"Dana Clark," Rath said again.

"You've lost me."

"The Wayside."

"What is this Wayside?"

"You know what."

"Rings a . . . foggy bell."

"After you were in Johnson. After you harassed my daughter and called me, you went to the Wayside."

"This fog has seeped into your brain. I am not the only man in the world capable of bad things. I've done nothing. And I can't have police showing up at my door with no cause. You can't just haul me in here for no reason. I have rights. I'm free. Just like you. Just like your—"

"Don't you mention my daughter."

"I was going to say your homely partner. She should invest in a little makeup. And *your daughter*? *Your*?"

"Don't you mention her."

"Your so-called daughter."

"Sit up like a fucking human being."

Preacher obliged. "I think you should have that homely detective drive me home now."

"You're not free. You're paroled. And you have privileged information about a crime that you could not have unless you were there."

"So you keep saying. But. I was home. I just. Hear things."

"You have no alibi."

"Don't I? And what about you? Where were you while this girl was killed? Do you have an alibi?"

"I'm not under suspicion."

"Yet, I am. Why? Personal revenge? I've paid in full."

You could be imprisoned for a thousand years and not pay back what you took, Rath thought. He leaned in close and whispered so the video would not pick up what he was saying: "It stops here. I won't let you hurt anyone else."

"Ah, threats."

"It won't go easy for you."

"Yet, here I am, unharmed. How much more would a man have to do for you to harm him? Hmmm? And. Yet. Here I am.

Free. How does the saying go: 'I wouldn't harm a fly.' I value my freedom. Hurting the flesh, that's unlawful. And, so . . . ordinary. Boring. I see you looking at me, the fear in your eyes, searching my face, trying to see, is there a similarity, a trait your adopted daughter and I share? Is it true? I can tell you I am only interested in the truth. I am the truth. What are you going to do if she is who I say she is? If she is mine?" Preacher plucked a hair from his head and set the hair down on the table between them. "One simple test. And you'll know. You'll have your answer. Proof. But you don't want to *know*. You want to live in a fantasy, need to *believe* I'm a liar. I bet you lie sleepless wondering if you should tell her. It must feel like a lie to hide it from her. If you tell her what I said, and it turns out I'm lying, you'll have fallen for a sucker's con and helped me torment her. If it turns out I'm telling the truth, you'll have helped me ruin her. Of course, *I* could tell her myself. It is probably best if it came from me, since you're too afraid. Are you going to tell her? Or am I?"

Preacher was right: Rath was afraid. Afraid that if he did not force himself to leave the room, now, he would attack Preacher.

"I don't need to cut flesh anymore," Preacher said. "I know how to crawl inside the weak now. I'm inside you. You think about me more than you think about your sister. You dream of me, when I'm not keeping you awake. Obsess. I see it. There are other ways to turn the screw. I don't need to torture you when you torture yourself because you are weak, and the truth is too much for you to bear. You won't do anything to stop me. Only react to me, as cops do."

Rath leaned in close again, whispering. "I'll give you a truth," he said. "You're safer in here than out *free* in the world. If you're released today, you'll be back soon. Because we'll have eyes on you. There will be a cruiser parked at the end of your road, round the clock. You won't be able to walk or drive anywhere, do anything without one of us following you." It was a lie. Rath could put Larkin on a detail and do some himself, but they could not watch Preacher at all times. They did not have the resources or the bodies. But he wanted Preacher to know, needed him to believe, he was being watched at all times.

Preacher shrugged. "I don't plan on going anywhere."

As Rath rose, he sneaked the hair Preacher had placed on the table into his palm, then left, locking the door behind him from the outside.

He looked at Preacher's hair pinched between his thumb and finger, tucked it in his shirt pocket and leaned back against the door to breathe.

After a moment to collect himself, he ducked inside Test's office quickly, rooted around, found some envelopes in a wire rack on a bookshelf, and slipped the hair into one, put the envelope in his jacket pocket.

He hurried back out in the hall as Test came out from the room on the other side of the room next door, where she'd been watching the video feed.

"Arrest him," Rath said.

"We can't."

"He can't be released on the public," Rath said, though he was not concerned about the public. He was concerned about Rachel. Preacher was playing a game, trying to slowly torture Rath, to see if Rath would tell Rachel what Preacher wanted him to tell her. Do Preacher's bidding. Rath refused to believe Preacher's claim, but only because he was afraid to imagine his sister would sleep with Preacher willingly, even if she had not known the monster he was. Laura had struggled with promiscuity in high school and college, cheated on many of her boyfriends. That had ended when she'd met and married Daniel. So Rath had believed. Whether it was true or not did not matter if Preacher told Rachel he was her father. It would wreck her. Rath could not sit back and let Preacher tell her. That would be worse. Preacher would not stop with merely telling her. He'd tell her, then—*Finish* her. So she died with that being the last thing she ever heard.

"Arrest him," Rath said. "I don't care if it's for looking at you the wrong way."

"The D.A. will laugh at us. We need physical evidence."

"He says he knows the time and the means. He has no alibi."

"It's not enough. He'll retract it as soon as we arrest him. Make a mockery of the case against him. What was he talking to you about, you and an alibi? And when you leaned in and whispered. What were you two saying?"

"He was talking shit, trying to get under my skin. He's a sadist. He'll hurt people any way he can. I want him locked up."

"At most, he's a material witness for having information about a crime. If we want to detain him for that, we need to file an affidavit. I'm already on it. Until it's turned around, unless he confesses, we *have* to release him. Otherwise we could blow our case."

"I'm *running* this case," Rath shouted.

"And you're going to sabotage it."

"Don't you dare release him."

Barrons appeared at the end of the hall and walked slowly toward them. "What's this?"

"She refuses to arrest Preacher," Rath said. "He knows Drake was hanged. The time. Neither made public."

"Is that right?" Barrons looked at Test.

"It makes him material at best," Test said.

"What else do you have?" Barrons said.

"*What else?* What the fuck else do we *need*?" Rath said.

"Was it a confession?" Barrons said.

"No, sir," Test said.

"File the affidavit. Let him go until he's an official MW, then haul him in," Barrons said.

"I want him *arrested*," Rath said, "charged with obstruction or—"

"No." Barrons walked back to his office.

Rath's phone chimed in his pocket. He took it out and glanced at it. A text from Rachel: What this in news? Dead girl in woods?!! Is it him? Is it?

Test turned to Rath. "Look," she said. "We hit a snag while you were in with Preacher, makes me think maybe he didn't do it, not alone anyway."

"He'd never share his fun with someone else," Rath said, though he was uncertain. If Preacher had been at home, yet knew about the hanging, did he have a minion? "And what do you mean, snag?"

"On the truck parked in Preacher's yard, we can't get warrants. It belongs to an Andrea Diamond. Not certain who she is. And, the neighbor woman, Larkin reached her at her work and asked about the window of time Jamie was hanged, to see if she saw Preacher leave or not. She was out. She can't help."

"If Preacher did it, he's got a vehicle stashed somewhere. Or an ATV. Has to," Rath said. "He was in Johnson, stalking my daughter. There's no bus service. No one picks up hitchhikers anymore. He's got a car stashed. We need to find it. We need to get him on something. Anything."

"We *will*," Test said. "If he didn't do it himself, he's got an accomplice, or he knows who did it. Maybe a convict in prison bragged about how he was going to torture girls when he got out. Or maybe Preacher hanged her and got a fellow ex-con to drive him."

"Have Larkin go through the Northeast prison files and make a list of prisoners released the past six months from population with Preacher. We'll look for a car within a two-mile radius of Preacher's place. You can put out an APB on a lone car. Or ATV. Parked in an odd spot."

"You're going to look for a hidden car in this fog?"

"Every angle, no stone," Rath said.

Rath looked at the door to the IR where Preacher was held. If Rath could have Preacher kept here even for a day, Rath would not have to set up camp outside Preacher's house. He could at least get to Johnson to see Rachel, get to the shop, see two other people he needed to see, *and* know Preacher was at heel. "Do this. We can't arrest him. So we keep interviewing him. Grill him. Delay his release and keep him here as long as legally possible while I track a few things down and tell my daughter she can at least feel safe for a day."

"What things?"

"I want to meet with Dana Clark's daughter. Let her know in person Preacher is a suspect in her mother's disappearance. She deserves that much. And visit Abby Land. You're right. She and Drake were close. Maybe it's nothing. But if anyone knows what dark past Drake may have kept secret, it's likely Abby Land."

"I'll pay a visit to Luke Montgomery before this day is out then. But I'll interrogate Preacher now, then have Larkin put the screws to him. Have him ask the same questions. It will do Larkin good.

Between us we'll keep Preacher a good spell longer; maybe fatigue
will trip him up."

"Keep him as long as you can."

RATH RAN THROUGH the rain and fog, hopped into his Scout. Rachel was in class now. She couldn't answer a call, but she might see
a text if she had her phone on vibrate.

Rath texted: I'll come out to see you as soon as I can. Sometime
late afternoon today or tomorrow. I'll explain. Be careful. Stick with Felix.
Love you

Before Rath could start the Scout, Rachel texted: Is it him? The
girl in woods. He do it? Do u know?

Rath didn't know. Yet, even if it weren't Preacher, Rath wanted
to make certain Rachel took as much precaution as possible, even
if it meant she was frightened for the time being. He'd rather she
be frightened *and* safe than the alternative.

Rath texted: Just be safe.

Rachel: K

Her coat, Rath thought, *the clothes. Damn it.*

39

Rachel slipped her cell phone into her pocket and peered around the library where she sat at the counter of her work-study station. She lifted her backpack onto her lap, the heft of the handgun in it reassuring. If anyone knew she had the gun, security would be called, she'd likely be arrested, almost certainly expelled. It was worth the risk.

The past three days fear had hijacked her routine, her life. It had killed her appetite and tattered her sleep, left her body exhausted and her mind jagged.

No more.

She was done with darting from class to class like a mouse skittering atop the snow.

No more. Her plan incubated in her mind. The gun shifted her instincts, from flight to fight.

She'd selected the .38 revolver because it packed punch but its recoil was manageable. The gun shop owner had invited her to shoot several boxes of rounds in his range in the rear of his shop, the ammunition *on the house*.

She'd also signed up for the personal defense classes. Her shooting needed to be better. Much better.

40

Rath got out of the Scout down the street from the Dress Shoppe. Running into Madeline was the last thing he wanted.

He stood on the sidewalk and took in the street. The church at the top of it, the fire station just across and up from the Dress Shoppe. Perhaps Test was right. Perhaps there was something to Luke Montgomery. Test's instincts were sharp. Better to be thorough and at least eliminate all doubt.

Rath took a breath and entered the store, the bell above him clacking.

Gone were the racks of splashy late-summer clothes on late clearance that had occupied the front of the store a few weeks earlier, before his lone, failed date with Madeline. In the place of the summer sale clothes stood racks and tables of sweaters and slacks and cords in fall hues of brown and rust and black. Rath wondered why people wore bright colors in the summer, and drab colors in the winter. He'd have thought it would be the opposite. But, what did he know? His Johnson wool jacket was infested with burdocks and, he noticed now, too late, gave off a pissy scent of whitetail doe urine he'd accidentally spilled from its bottle onto the jacket cuff when going through his hunting gear, and his BORN TO RUN T-shirt beneath the jacket had a coffee stain along the contours of the Big Man's sax.

The store's earlier powdery scents had given over to odors of cinnamon and nutmeg that made Rath want a slab of apple pie à la mode. His stomach rumbled. He'd not eaten in two days.

The shop stood quiet. Not even the low background hum of holiday Muzak. His first time here, several clerks had circled him as a prospective patron. Now, a lone teenage girl stood at the back of the store near the cash register, folding turtlenecks and placing them on a display table.

She did not notice Rath, had not heard the door's bell clang apparently.

Rath took a step to ease into her peripheral vision without startling her.

She whirled around, plucked earbuds from her ears, a blush of guilt shadowing her look of alarm, as if she'd breached store policy by wearing the earbuds and thought for a moment she'd been caught by a supervisor.

In seeing Rath, a strange disheveled man, the girl tensed and her look of surprise morphed to guarded suspicion. She smoothed a palm over the turtleneck at the top of a stack, tucked its price tag inside its collar.

"May I help you?" she said, apprehensive, as if Rath had stumbled in to seek directions to the nearest gun show.

Rath welcomed her caution. He hoped Rachel made strange men earn her trust.

"Are you lost?" the clerk said.

She fingered a strand of her lank brown hair behind her ears as she approached, stopping at a distance that did not permit shaking hands.

"I'm looking for clothes and a coat," Rath said. "For my daughter."

The girl nodded, but the veil of suspicion in her eyes did not clear.

"Madeline helped me, a few weeks ago," Rath said.

"Oh," the girl said, her smile awkward. "OK. How old is your daughter?"

Too quick, Rath thought. *She's too quick to let her guard down to a man who looks so out of place, just because I dropped a familiar name.* Trust via association was misplaced trust. Cons used familiar names to disarm marks. Child abductors often mentioned an abductee's parents' names to lull the child.

While relieved Madeline was not on the clock, Rath wished she were here for her professional input; she'd nailed Rachel's tastes.

"How about I let you roam free," the clerk said as if Rath were a wolf granted freedom in Yellowstone, free except for the tracking collar. "And I'll find what I think your daughter would like?"

She retreated behind the counter, and the song "Horse with No Name" began to play softly over the speakers.

Rath browsed. His desire to get things perfect for Rachel crippled his usual decisiveness.

After mulling over clothes with more deliberation than a juror on a capital murder trial, Rath had selected just one sweater and was not sold on it.

He hummed "Horse with No Name." He'd be humming the damn song all day now. He didn't care for faux '70s folk. Give him Springsteen. Dark Springsteen. *Nebraska. Darkness on the Edge of Town. The River*'s despairing tracks. "Stolen Car" and "Drive All Night."

The clerk strode over, arm draped with apparel. The tops, pants, and jackets were perfect. Where had she found them? Rath had not seen half these items, and the half he had seen he'd dismissed, yet they now seemed ideal.

It was a matter of trust. He trusted the clerk's eye.

The clerk held far more garments than Rath imagined he'd need. The prices terrified him. He selected several pieces, and a black coat.

The clerk rang him up, folded and bagged the clothes.

Three bags total, so heavy their rope handles dug into Rath's palms. The clerk got the door for him. As he squeezed past her, he said, "Tell Madeline I said hello."

"She doesn't work here anymore," the girl said.

"Oh," Rath said. "Do you know where she works now?"

Suspicion returned to the girl's eyes. "No."

"Right." Rath walked out into the fog and got into the Scout to drive toward the Northeast Correctional Complex in St. Johnsbury, realizing facing Madeline had not been the last thing he wanted after all.

41

In the parking garage of the NECC, Rath ejected the clip from his newly issued S&W M&P45, locked the weapon in his glove box, placed the clip in a steel ammo lockbox, and tucked the box under his seat.

Rath detested the M&P45. While the .45 APC cartridge possessed a velocity of roughly one thousand FPS, the weapon's frame was Zytel polymer, with a four-and-a-half-inch barrel. Too light. Insubstantial. Plastic. Rath preferred the .357 with the seven-inch vent rib barrel, if only because it was the sidearm issued in his day; those days as long gone as pull tab beer cans.

He got out of the Scout and locked its door, headed to Building C, the all-female wing of the correctional facility where Abby Land awaited trial for the murder of Mandy Wilks.

FROM HIS DESK at the front of the building, the balding middle-aged administrative assistant peered over his glasses, giving Rath a wary eye. "May I help you?"

Rath handed his new ID to the man. "I phoned earlier for an interview with inmate Abby Land."

"Detective," the man said, glancing at Rath, sizing up his rumpled appearance. "Are you in possession of your sidearm?"

"It's locked in my vehicle. Unloaded."

Rath signed in and headed to the next room beyond the lobby.

"Metal objects in this basket, please," the C.O. said as she adjusted her blue clip-on tie at the neck of her white uniform shirt. She was tall, at least six foot four. Rath emptied his pockets of coins and keys and cell phone. "Belt and shoes, too," the C.O. said.

Rath unslung his belt and shoes and placed them in the basket. Rath handed her his ID.

"I don't need to see that," the woman said.

"Out of practice," Rath said.

"No harm."

The woman requested he proceed through the metal detector to the male C.O. awaiting him on the other side.

The metal detector went off. Rath stepped back out from it. Checked all his pockets again to find a live .30-.30 deer cartridge in the chest pocket of his Johnson coat he wore everywhere except funerals and his lone date with Madeline.

"What is that, sir?" the C.O. awaiting him said.

"Nothing, a—"

"Hand it here."

Rath obliged.

The guard inspected the cartridge in his gloved fingers.

"I'm a deer hunter," Rath said. "I wear this jacket—"

The guard nodded, tossed the cartridge in the wastebasket beside him.

The metal detector remained silent as Rath passed through it again.

"Anything, sir?" the guard said.

"No, no more cartridges."

"Any luck deer hunting, I mean." The guard's face remained professionally neutral, but Rath saw in his eyes he was a deer hunter.

"I wish," Rath said. Boy, did he. "No time to hunt. A small buck back during bow season. You?"

"My daughter got her first deer on youth day. Six pointer. Have a good day, sir."

Rath collected his belongings and put on his shoes, headed down the hall.

42

Because she was a minor as well as female, Abby Land was held in the prison's Administrative Segregation area for her own safety.

Rath nodded at the O.C. outside the assigned activity room in Segregation and entered. At a square metal table in the center of the room Abby Land sat on one of the four metal seats welded to the table and bolted to the floor. She looked like she'd lived thirty stony years in the short time since her arrest. The hot defiance in her eyes had paled to a watery dullness. Her flush pink skin had gone as sallow as that of an aged chain smoker. Her chin, once calcified in an obstinate, *fuck-you* thrust, sunk to her chest as she gnawed at a thumbnail.

On a seat to Land's left sat public defender Joanne Blanc, whom Rath had phoned earlier to set up the meeting. Blanc was already going to be on-site for most of the day, but was resistant to letting Rath speak to Land, until Rath had told the attorney that what he had to say might get Land off the hook. That he believed she had not killed Mandy Wilks, or at least not alone. He didn't believe this, but it had bought him a half hour.

Blanc sat silently in her black suit, its cuffs spattered with dried slush and road salt.

Rath sat across from Land. "Can you look at me?"

Land gnashed away at her thumbnail.

"Luke Montgomery," Rath said.

"What about him?"

"What role did he play in Mandy Wilks's murder?"

"Nothin'."

"You killed Mandy because of him."

"So?"

"So that's not nothing. You and Montgomery, maybe you're closer than you're telling?"

"Fuck you."

"Your friend. Jamie Drake. She's dead. Did you know that?" Rath said.

Abby Land looked up, empty-eyed. A dribble of bloodied saliva trickled down her chin.

She spat a tag of skin from her thumb on the floor. "Are you stupid? Do you think we don't get TV in here? I watch a TV the size of a movie screen, it's ten times better than the piece of shit I had at home. I just saw the *big breaking* news update, the identity of the mystery dead girl."

Blanc crossed one leg over a knee.

"She was murdered," Rath said. "Hanged. That wasn't on your TV."

Blanc cut her eyes at Rath, disapproving his tone.

A quiver worked across Land's lips.

"She was tortured. Deliberately and slowly." Rath would never impart such traumatic information to a teen in a normal state of mind; but in the case of Land, trauma might be just what was needed to reach her.

Land stopped savaging her thumbnail.

"What does this have to do with my client?" Blanc said.

"Jamie Drake died a mean, cruel, slow death," Rath said.

Land swallowed her flesh. She blew on her tattered thumb, wincing, waving it at her side as if it were on fire. "Yeah. What's it got to do with me?"

"That is what I want to know," Rath said.

"If you're implying my client—" Blanc began.

"I'm not," Rath said.

"And. Umm. Hello. I'm in *here*?" Land said. "How can it have anything to do with me? I didn't kill her, obviously. Even you can figure that out, probably." The old shining meanness leapt in her eyes. How did a person, a kid, end up like this? Rath was not looking at evil, not in the way he stared at evil when he met eyes with Preacher. No. What he was looking at he'd seen dozens of times from kids when he was a cop in the nineties; kids he'd give warnings to for partying in a park after dusk or drinking under age, only to be met with a recalcitrant, venomous disrespect for him and everything and everyone else in the world. It was not evil. It was pain. The pain of years of neglect and abuse, of invisibility and disrespect, fossilized into a contempt for and blindness to the very kindness the kids had most needed early on but to which now they were inured. The aftermath of lovelessness.

"Did you come here just to tell me the happy news that my friend was tortured?" Land said. "Is that how you spend your time?"

"I find it odd. That both you and a friend of yours are involved in violent deaths. You bludgeon a girl so hard with a tire iron that you struggled to dislodge it from her brain so you could hit her again. And now, your friend is killed in a ghoulish way."

A look of confusion fluttered in Land's eyes; she didn't understand what *ghoulish* meant.

"Yeah. Well," Land said. "Life sucks."

"Death's worse," Rath said.

"Can't be worse than this hole."

"I doubt there's TV."

Land's eyes gleamed, then dimmed. "That might suck worse. Not that I'll be able stay here forever for the TV anyway. I'm a minor. When I turn eighteen, I'll be released. Free."

Rath wondered who had poisoned Abby's naive head with lies. Abby Land was going to be tried as an adult and thus not see the free world until at least 2036, even if she were Mother Teresa inside of whatever maximum-security prison she got as a present for her eighteenth birthday.

"Did you tell her that?" Rath said to Blanc.

"Certainly not. I've tried to explain—"

"She don't know shit," Land said.

"How did you and Jamie become friends? You two don't exactly strike me as compatible, if you know what I mean." Rath decided to rile her.

"What *do* you mean?"

"You coming from the household you do: unemployed, coke-dealing stepdad; absentee mom, living in that hovel; playing dated cartridge video games; driving jalopies, if they start. Meanwhile Jamie's bedroom is the size of your whole apartment, decorated just so; she wears brand-new, brand-name clothes, the latest fashions; she has the best laptop and the latest iPhone, lives in that big

THE NAMES OF DEAD GIRLS

house on five secluded acres, drives a nicer car than you'll ever own in your life and whines that it's a piece of shit. Not exactly alike. You two."

"What would you know about it?"

"Plenty." Rath did know plenty about growing up in poverty. After his mother had sent his father packing, she'd worked three jobs just to string together enough for rent, thrift shop clothes, and the weekly groceries. He'd been so embarrassed about the state of their cramped, messy home he'd never asked what few fleeting friends he had over after school.

"We had things in common," Land said. "Acting."

"She get all the plum roles, did she? That piss you off?"

"Easy," Blanc said. "You don't have to answer any of these questions, Abby. I advise you not to, in fact."

"I got good roles," Land shot. "I got plenty of good fucking roles, if you think—"

"I don't like this line of questioning, it's upsetting my client," Blanc said.

"I'm trying to help your client help herself," Rath said. "If she knows something about her friend's murder, if Montgomery was involved in either murder, and she can help us with it, we may be able to do quid pro quo."

"Quid what?" Land said.

"Was your friend in trouble? Do you know anything that would suggest your friend's death wasn't random? Was your friend doing anything she shouldn't be doing?" Rath used the word *friend* intentionally.

"Did she do stuff she *shouldn't*?" Land scoffed. "You fuckin' serious? We *all* do stuff we shouldn't. Every day."

"What did your friend do?"

"I wasn't her mother. I just know we all do. I'm sure you got stuff you shouldn't a done. Got all kinds a secrets you don't tell no one. Don't mean you got it coming or deserve to get killed for—" She stopped, as if she were struck for the first time by the fact that maybe Mandy Wilks hadn't deserved to be beaten to death with a tire iron for looking the wrong way at a boy Abby had liked. If that was why she'd done it.

"This is enough. Enough," Blanc said.

"It don't matter," Land said. "I did it. I said I did it. Killed Mandy. I confessed. It don't matter if I say it again."

"We're done," Blanc said.

Land dug at a loose piece of cuticle, peeled back a long strip of flesh, blood rising again.

She stared at Rath. A smile seeped across her face, grim and cold.

Rath thought perhaps his earlier musing was wrong, that perhaps this girl was evil. Not on the order of Preacher—whose evil was malignant and malicious. Hers was a banal and sad evil, but just as deadly.

Abby Land fixed her eyes on Rath. "Just because you don't have something coming," she said, "don't mean it ain't coming anyway."

43

Luke Montgomery was scrubbing down a rear fender of a fire engine with a sudsy brush when Test walked up to the open overhead bay doors of the station. A System of a Down song echoed off the concrete floor of two empty bays, the trucks parked along the curb. The song was a favorite of Test's husband's, not a note of which appealed to a strand of Test's DNA. It amused her that her husband gravitated to music in complete contradiction to his quiet temperament.

Two other young men were lathering the front of the engine with soapy sponges.

Montgomery seemed to sense Test and turned to give her a look as if he'd been lost in a daydream. The look sharpened as he wiped his hands on the front of the yellow, rubber raincoat and overalls that reminded Test of the boat captain on a fish sticks box. His big black rubber boots looked like something an astronaut might wear.

He was tall, sturdy, good looking in that bland, homogenized way of young men who were only a few years beyond bad skin and braces; Test could see why teenage girls might fawn over him, though she had always leaned toward the quirky, awkward, off-beat types her friends deemed homely.

Montgomery looked confused; why was a strange woman here?

The two other young men, also in yellow rain gear, kept at their task, oblivious of Test, their movements in aggressive time to the music.

Montgomery stepped out onto the sidewalk. "Help you?" he said. His eyes shifted to his fellow firemen. Test sensed he hoped his peers wouldn't notice the woman whose attention was all his for the moment. Test hoped they wouldn't notice her, either. She didn't need to deal with false bravado or rivalry for her attention.

Test showed her ID and told him who she was. "I'd like to talk to you about Mandy Wilks and Abby Land."

"Who?"

"Mandy Wilks, she was murdered a couple weeks back. Abby Land murdered her."

"Yeah," he said, "Right. Crazy."

He glanced at his peers again, and this time Test wondered if it were out of wanting to protect his territory, or some other motive. He seemed nervous.

"You knew them," Test said.

"No. Not really."

"I'd like to talk to you anyway."

"Let's get out of this noise."

Montgomery walked down the sidewalk and opened a door to an office of sorts, a concrete floor and white walls, a metal desk and chairs. On a lone shelf above a filing cabinet sat a police scanner, rows of red lights blinking, a half-dozen walkie-talkies perched in chargers.

On the table sat an iPad and a deck of playing cards, on the back of which were images of naked women. Montgomery snatched up the cards and tossed them in a drawer.

"I didn't know them," Montgomery said. "I knew who Mandy Wilks was, of course, but—"

"*Of course?*"

"She was behind me a couple grades. But she was the kind of girl you noticed. Kind of creepy saying that now."

"You were seen at a party with her, there are pictures of you standing near her and her looking at you while you had your arm around Land, laughing."

"Pig roast. Everybody was there. Like four hundred people, probably. Lots of pics taken. Six kegs got tapped in no time. Port-a-Lets. The works. I was pretty wrecked, honestly."

"Were you talking to Mandy?"

"I didn't know her. I told you."

"If you never talk to pretty girls you don't know, how are you ever going to get to know any pretty girls?"

"What? I just didn't talk to her."

"What about Abby Land?"

"I'm twenty. She's like what, twelve?"

"Answer the question. Did you know her?"

"No. I was having a good time. Joking with people. I don't remember having my arm slung around her. I don't understand. Why're you after me? I didn't know them, and I didn't do anything. I told the cops all this shit a couple weeks ago."

"No one is after you."

"Then why are you asking me questions weeks after that skank was busted?"

Test hesitated, then said, "Because Mandy Wilks was killed because of you."

"Are you crazy?"

It was an awful way for Test to put it, but it was the truth, at least *Abby Land's* truth, if you believed what she claimed, that she'd killed Mandy Wilks out of rage spawned of jealousy over Montgomery giving Mandy the eye at the pig roast. Test didn't believe it. Not anymore. No. There was more to it than Land being pissed off over a flirtatious glance. Had to be. Didn't there?

"Land said she killed Mandy because of the way she looked at you."

"So? This Abby Land chick is bat shit. But don't say Mandy was killed *because* of me." He took a step toward her. "If some crazy chick killed a guy for the way he looked at you, would you think you were to blame?" His voice was raised. Test had her parka zipped up, her M&P45 tucked in her chest holster underneath it. She'd not worn a hip holster today.

"Take a breath and—"

"*Take a breath.* I'm at *work.* I volunteer to save lives, risk my life probably more than you do, for free, when other guys my age are whining because someone said boo on Facebook, and you accuse me because a retarded redneck chick killed another girl for looking at me wrong?" The veins in his neck stood out. The music had stopped, and now the other two young men, big meaty guys, stared at Test through the window that looked out to the bay. Their stares were not the ones she had imagined earlier, where she was the object over which the young men would compete for attention, the boys turning to nemeses against each other. No. The looks were those that steeled their camaraderie, fraternity. The young men were on the same side here.

The beefier of the two young men opened the door and they stepped inside the small office.

"She bothering you?" the bigger guy said, his cheeks puffy from too much booze.

What was this? He was asking another young, built guy if a woman half their weight and six inches shorter was "bothering" him.

"She's giving me shit about some crazy chick I don't even have a clue about. I'll tell you what," he said, glaring at Test, "say another word accusing me—"

Test stepped closer. A headache pounded at her forehead, seemed to want to splinter her skull. She'd been clenching her jaw. Could not unclench it.

"Speak to me like that again, and I will arrest you," Test said. "And you two." She pivoted to the other two boys, in part to meet their eyes straight on, and in part to demonstrate that she was unafraid to put her back to Montgomery. "Step out. I'm an on-duty police detective conducting an interview and you two are interfering. Step out or get arrested."

The young men eyed each other.

"We've got no gripe with law enforcement." Puffy Cheeks shrugged as if to say *you're on you own, man* and the two young men left and went back to washing the truck.

Test turned to Montgomery. "Don't speak to me again like that."

Montgomery seemed to release the tension in his body, though his face remained flushed. When he spoke, the anger in his voice was tempered, but the message was the same. "I have work to do.

You want to speak to me again, contact my dad's attorney, Fredrick Bauer."

He left and set to washing the engine.

Test's blood fizzed, not with anger, but with the adrenaline rush that her suspicions might be correct. Somehow, Jamie Drake, Abby Land, and Mandy Wilks were connected, and Luke Montgomery was connected as well. Mandy Wilks had been in the Dress Shoppe and been seen by her mother and two clerks leaving the shop for a moment to stand out on the sidewalk, looking around and acting odd, as if she'd seen someone pass by. Looking toward the firehouse. That night, Abby Land kills Mandy. She admits she killed her in a rage of jealousy spurred by Mandy looking *the wrong way* at Montgomery. Montgomery who claimed he didn't know either girl. Now, Abby was in jail, and her closest friend is found hanged. Test looked out the door window at the bay. Montgomery looked up and gave her a fake smile. She smiled back, not at him, but at the thought that he was going to need his attorney sooner than later, and not for the reasons he believed.

44

Rath sat in the hospital cafeteria sipping coffee from a cardboard cup and staring at a bowl of coagulated oatmeal. He'd gone so long without eating he'd lost his appetite.

At a nearby table, doctors and nurses in scrubs bantered with a tone that bordered on flirtation. At another table, men, women, and children fidgeted in silent glumness perhaps awaiting news of a sick loved one quarantined in the hospital's deeper reaches. Plastic trays clacked on the buffet line's metal rollers as visitors selected yogurts and salads from glass displays. This cafeteria was light-years from the institutional species in which Rath's mother had succumbed. It was as upscale as any restaurant Rath patronized, not a high bar perhaps. Organic Greek yogurt had replaced Jell-O cups, and steel-cut oatmeal had replaced Froot Loops, although if Froot Loops was an option, Rath's cereal bowl would have been empty.

Tammy Clark had chosen to meet here. She was working a double shift and didn't have time otherwise. Rath needed to tell her, somehow, of his belief in the connection between Preacher

and the hanged girl, and Tammy's mother's disappearance. Then
he needed to get to Johnson to see Rachel. He needed more time.

As if to taunt him, a text from Test came through on his phone.
Meet me at the Wilderness Restaurant when you come back through on
your way to Johnson.

He needed *a lot* more time.

He slipped his fingers in his jacket pocket and took out the
envelope with Preacher's hair in it. One simple test.

He glanced up to see Tammy Clark beeline toward him as she
slipped a notepad from the handbag slung over a shoulder, the
bag's rainbow pattern matching that of her scrubs.

She sat and set her cell phone on the table.

"Have you found her?" she said, without greeting.

"Afraid not."

She let out a breath and retrieved a plastic bottle of water from
her bag, chugged half the water so fast the bottle crackled and
burped. "Nothing?" she said with calm reserve. Rath did not know
the type of patients for whom she cared, but he knew her occupa-
tion required calm amid chaos and grave developments.

"Not yet," Rath said.

In some ways, one looked to a detective and to a nurse with a
similar mix of apprehension and hope, in search of answers that
might give one a way back to the life lived before they'd been set
upon by the unexpected. Often it was too late to go back to that
life, because that life no longer existed.

"She's dead," she said.

"We don't know that," Rath said.

"What *aren't* you telling me?" Tammy said.

"I don't know if you heard. A girl's body was found in the woods."

"I heard a brief thing. On my way in, it's a terrib—"

Rath didn't have to tell her. She knew. Yet he told her anyway. "We think . . . *I* think, it's related to a man named Ned Preacher. I can't prove it. Yet."

"Preacher? But he's in prison. For your sister. He's the one who—"

"He's out. On parole."

"How can he be out?"

"I'm the wrong person to ask. We suspected him of attacking your mom back then, the first time. But we couldn't prove it. Had no evidence."

Tammy Clark finished her water and rolled the empty plastic bottle between her palms, her anger clear.

"And you believe the dead girl and my mom—"

"I suspect it."

"*Suspect*. Tell me straight. Have that respect at least. If you only knew half her struggles, even when she believed her attacker was dead. She's never felt safe. Never. She never goes a day without thinking of her attack, and thinking of me having to see her like that. Every time she gets in front of a mirror, which she avoids like the plague, she sees her own scarred body. He *cut her up*. She loved the sun, the beach, the water, but has never enjoyed a sunny day since. She's a ruin of scars. She has to keep covered. Not out of shame. But the sun, the heat, it hurt her scars, physically causes her pain. A lot of pain. Tell me what you *suspect*. I can handle it."

"I think the person who hanged that girl in the woods is Ned Preacher. And I think he's hurt your mom."

45

Rath set off across the hospital lot in the fog.

At the Scout he fished his keys out of his coat pocket.

"Frank?" a voice said behind him.

Rath spun. Fog swirled.

For a moment he wasn't sure it was her. She'd cut her hair, or perhaps tucked it under the crocheted hat askew on her head.

"Hey," Madeline said and fidgeted with her hat.

"You left the Dress Shoppe," Rath said stupidly.

"It lost its charm after that girl you asked me about, the girl I helped in the store, was found dead in the trunk of a car. How'd you know I left?"

"I stopped in for more clothes."

"For Rachel?"

Rath was surprised she remembered Rachel's name. Though it had only been a few weeks since he'd seen Madeline, it felt like months. She'd left a couple messages on his voice mail shortly after the date. He'd never returned the calls.

Madeline wiped rainwater from her eyes, glanced at the hospital as an ambulance siren yelped behind Rath. "What brings you here? I hope nothing—"

"I had to meet someone. Work."

"A case."

Rath nodded.

"It must be hard, working with missing and dead people and violence all the time."

"I hadn't done it for years until the girl who was in your shop went missing. That was extenuating circumstances."

"Extenuating circumstances for this one, too?"

"So it seems."

"I hope it works out better this time."

Rath wanted to say he had listened to her voice-mail messages, in fact saved them, and was sorry he'd not gotten back to her, time had gotten away and other matters had taken priority. He wanted to say he had been sorry not to see her in the shop. Instead, he twirled his key ring around his finger, the keys jangling. As if this were a cue, Madeline said, "I hope Rachel likes her clothes. It was good to see you. Quite a coincidence."

Before Rath could say anything, Madeline had turned and disappeared into the fog.

Yes, Rath thought, *quite the coincidence.*

46

Rath was texting Rachel to tell her the day was getting away from him, he'd have to visit tomorrow, when the door to the Wilderness Restaurant flew open.

He looked up from his booth situated beneath a mounted moose head to see Test hurled into the restaurant on a gust of wind from the squall outside.

Her wet hair hung in her eyes as she raked her fingers through it, peeled a rubber band off a wrist, and cinched it around a soaked ponytail. She scanned the Wilderness, her chin up as if she needed to look over a crowd of people. She didn't. The Wilderness was as desolate as a beach in January. It was normally packed, but this weather . . . this fog. Its persistence was damnable. And the rain. It had doubled down, a brutal cascade, expelled from a sky so black, the midday hour was a marrow-sucking, unending gloom. Even the jukebox in the back stood quiet, and the few old-timers who normally orbited around the pool table as reliably as the earth around the sun were AWOL, the billiard balls racked on the felt, waiting to be cracked.

THE NAMES OF DEAD GIRLS 213

There were only Rath and his Barn Burger Special.

Test sat opposite Rath. She snatched a napkin from the dispenser and blotted her wet cheeks, her face greasy and without makeup, revealing freckles on her nose and cheeks.

Rath bit into his burger; Michigan sauce squeezed out onto his fingers and plate.

Test retrieved a folder from her pack. Rivulets of rainwater ran from her police windbreaker onto the table. Rath had been here a half hour and was still soaked and chilled. He wished he'd ordered soup.

The waitress shuffled over, coughed into her elbow. "Our burgers aren't so good that you gotta put your life at risk with that mess outside," she said to Test. Apparently, since the same waitress had not warned Rath, it was OK for him to put his life at risk.

"It's not the food, it's the atmosphere," Rath said.

The waitress looked at Test.

"Just hot tea for me," Test said.

She spread the contents of the folder out on the table. "Larkin pulled three possibles for fellow convicts released within six months of Preacher."

"First," Rath said, "anything with our fireman?"

"There's something there. I can't grasp it. Yet. But then I think of this Preacher angle. Preacher *knowing* Jamie was hanged. *Knowing* the *time*. He's involved."

"No doubt there."

"Larkin's still working him. You? Anything with Abby Land?"

"Someone's fed her a line about her getting out early, at eighteen, because she's a minor."

"She needs to fire her public defender for filling her head with fantasies."

"It wasn't her attorney. Something's not right there. But then there's Preacher. He's our hot ticket. He excludes our fireman. What do you have on his prison buddies?"

Test tapped a finger on a mug shot of a black male, bald with muttonchops, a gold hoop ring in his left earlobe. "Xanders Geoffries. Thirty-eight. Five ten. Second-degree murder, sexual assault. Served twelve years. He was in the same cell block as Preacher, as were the other two cons I have a line on. I don't think he's our guy. He's housed in Providence, Rhode Island. I checked with his P.O. Geoffries is employed already, a Shell service station and convenience store. I called his employer and his manager. He was on the shift at the time of both Dana Clark's disappearance and Jamie Drake's murder."

"Do background checks on the manager and owner," Rath said. "We don't know these people to trust them out of hand. A lot of times parolees get work with their old ties who cover for them, and they fall right back into it. I want to make sure the owner and manager are clean and straight. If not, we pay a visit to a Shell station in RI."

The waitress brought Test's tea and set it down, asked if there were anything else. Test shook her head, and the waitress strode toward the back, fishing a pack of cigarettes from her apron pocket.

"Number two." Test jabbed a finger at a second mug shot. A Caucasian male, red hair cut short and neat. Chubby face of a guy who looked like he enjoyed his beer a bit too much and a bit too often, though he probably hadn't seen too much beer inside. He sported a crisp line of beard where his jawline used to be before he encased it in fat. He looked like a man you'd see working the floor of a Home Depot or the lot at the local Chevy dealership.

"Timothy Glade. Forty. Five foot six. Served eleven years of a ten-to-fifteen for three counts of sexual assault of a minor, and one of attempted murder. A serial predator. Vicious. Nasty. The things he's done. Unforgivable. These people make me want to pack up my kids and move to a deserted island." Test pushed her mug away, tea lapping over the edge.

"He could be our guy," she continued. "One of his assaults, he had a 'buddy' join him. They took turns, captured the hijinks on video. He was released thirty days ago. Lives a hundred miles from here. Outside Concord, New Hampshire."

"A good poke but in striking distance."

"He's not on parole. Served his time. He's out clean, free as a bird, no obligation to report to anyone, to get a job. Not accountable to anyone but himself."

"Let's interview him. Soon. A weekday night. Catch him out of sorts."

Test nodded and stabbed a finger on the third mug shot. Rath stared at the face.

"Clay Sheldon," Test said. "Fifty-one. Brown and brown. Six feet one. Powerful build."

"Fits the CRVK."

"He's got my attention, believe me. Except he was in prison for murder during the commission of an armed robbery. No predatory history. No sexual assault. No priors. Clean as a NASA space lab until then. He was living in Maine, and his motive for the robbery was purely financial from the court transcript. He pleaded guilty, but not in an attempt at a plea bargain, though his lawyer sought and got that for him. He was distraught by his killing, sobbed in court, and did the opposite of what the Preachers of the world do: he asked the judge to go hard on him, to punish him.

Just put him away for as long as possible and get it over with. He was put on suicide watch."

"Not exactly a match made in heaven for Preacher."

"But get this. He lives in Colebrook."

"Just across the river. Twenty minutes away."

Rath could see that Test wanted to go drop in on Sheldon now. But he didn't want her going alone. "Larkin still keeping Preacher busy?"

"You bet. I told him to try to instigate Preacher into assaulting him, so we can put the cuffs on the bastard. That goes against Larkin's nature too much, though."

"Let's talk to Sheldon. For all we know, his gushing to the judge could have been a ploy."

"Nothing surprises me anymore," Test said.

"We'll see about that."

47

Clay Sheldon answered the door to his efficiency at the North Star Motor Court bare chested, his muscular physique on display, as well as the graffiti of tattoos across his chest. Rath expected a muscular voice to accompany the man's brawny build. It did not. The man's soft-spoken manner was so discordant with his physicality it was as if Sheldon were trying to pull a trick on them.

Rath and Test offered their IDs. Sheldon barely glanced at them. He could smell a cop from down the block and across the street.

"Let me get a shirt." He stepped back into the unit. The place was a throwback to the heyday of mom-and-pop motels and had apparently not seen an update in decor or a new coat of its original, sky-blue paint since cars had fins and *fuel economy* was an alien term.

The nightly rate on the sign out front, which boasted COLOR TV, reflected the establishment's desire to remain locked in the past: $29. $199 weekly.

Rath and Test entered the unit. Sheldon shut the door behind them.

The room was as squalid as expected, damp with a sour pong to the air. The furniture had a dark faux wood veneer, chipped to reveal particle board beneath. The frameless double bed's mattress sagged in the center as if a body had lain in it unmoving for years.

"It's temporary digs," Sheldon said. He turned to grab a wife-beater shirt off the floor. His back was a mural of tattoos, most in old-school greens and blues, symbols that looked Celtic. A few words were scribed in his flesh at the base of his neck below a fold of the only fat on the man's body. He put on the shirt and jabbed an elbow at two chairs at a table in the kitchenette of turquoise appliances. "Grab a seat."

"We're fine," Test said.

Sheldon remained standing, pushed his hands in the pockets of his gray sweatpants.

"Take your hands out of your pockets, Mr. Sheldon," Rath said.

Sheldon pulled the insides of his pockets out to reveal nothing but lint.

"You did time with Ned Preacher," Test said.

"Preacher? I wouldn't say I did time *with* him. I didn't do time *with* anyone. We were in gen pop, crossed paths. I kept to myself. Much as you can. Ain't exactly easy, to mind your own business inside. It's seen as . . . impolite." He laughed. "No one trusts a loner."

"You always been a loner?" Test said.

"I had a family."

"You *crossed paths* with Preacher?" Rath said. "How?"

"Weight room. Library. Rec room for movies."

If Rath didn't know better, he'd have thought Sheldon were describing a stay at a Marriott.

"Sounds like you crossed paths a lot," Test said.

"No more than with anyone else. We all do pretty much the same routine. In shifts. We had the same shifts a lot."

"You talked to him then?" Rath said.

"Like I said, I'm a loner. Just trying to keep cool, get my anger in check."

"Anger at who? The law?" Rath said.

"Anger at me. I wanted to kill myself. Every day I battle the part of me that wants to kill me, that wants this nightmare over. I'd kill myself today if I could manage to do one meaningful thing before I did it. Go out knowing I'd helped someone, done something worth a damn."

"What nightmare?" Test said.

"My life. What I did."

"It's been almost two decades," Test said.

"You think time makes it better? Time makes it worse. The longer I breathe, the longer I know that boy hasn't breathed, because of me. You've never killed a boy, I take it," Sheldon said. "Never shot a kid just working his after-school job as a cashier to make a few bucks for the movies and gas money. You'd have to be a sociopath to get over that. Or want to. I'm no sociopath. Sometimes, I wish I was."

Out on the walkway, a shadow passed by the curtained window. Sheldon's eyes caught the movement.

The scuff and crunch of a plastic scoop digging in the ice machine was followed by the slap of the ice machine's lid. The shadow passed by the window again, Sheldon's eyes watching, alert, body tense as the shadow seemed to linger for a second, then was gone.

"You talked to him, though, Preacher?" Test said. "Over so many years, you must have got a sense of him."

"What is this? What's he done now?" Sheldon asked. "I heard he made parole. Who knows how *that happens*. He right back at it? The sociopath."

"Back at what?" Rath said.

"*What?* What he's always done when free."

"What makes you think he'd be back at it?" Test said.

"I called him the Great Pretender. Not to his face. I don't need to mix it up. I hit the weight room to occupy my mind and to kill the boredom. Not to get ripped so I could pummel other cons. But, it didn't hurt to pack muscle. You can imagine. Now I'm out, I could give a shit about pumping iron."

"The Great Pretender?" Rath said.

"Holier than thou. The Jesus racket. I bought it from some guys. Some guys were the real deal. They struggled. I mean guys who still seemed regretful, ashamed, who realized what they did *mattered*. And what they do, what we all *do, matters*. You can do good or you can do bad. Those guys, you know, they were *working* at being better. Even if they took a step backward. Guys who had to fight against everything they knew how to be in the world in order to even sniff being good. Man, they suffered to be good. I sure the fuck did. There's a lot of mutants behind bars, but one thing that surprised me was at night, the crying. Man, the *crying*. Sounded like a goddamned nursery. Men crying like abandoned babies. Men who'd done terrible things. Things no god would forgive. I guess I shouldn't a been surprised with the crying. I was a crier. But I tried to be quiet about it. Have *some* dignity."

Sheldon was traveling down his own lonely road in his mind. Rath and Test kept quiet to see where the road led.

"Preacher didn't cry," he said. "He didn't regret. Not that many of the guys regretted much. Don't get me wrong. They were too busy blaming everyone else for why they were inside. But Preacher. He seemed to throw a switch when he stumbled upon the 'good book.' A magic wand. 'I'm forgiven.' Presto. 'I'm good now. What I did is in the past. Anyone still dragged down by it, best get over it. Cuz I'm forgiven. I am free of the weight of what I done.'"

"Sounds like you knew him well for crossing paths."

"You cross paths a good shitload in fifteen years. You hear guys. Rumors. See things. You watch them."

"But you weren't close?" Test said.

"What I did. Shooting that kid while robbing that store." He shook his head. "I was desperate. I didn't do it outta meanness, or outta some sickness to hurt others. After the gun went off in the struggle. And I saw him there. On the floor. He was my *daughter's* age. I just sat down and waited for the cops. I tried to shoot myself. They got that on video. I put the gun barrel in my mouth, shoved it in there, and pulled the trigger. And nothing happened. I almost died of a heart attack when I pulled the trigger. My heart almost exploded. But the gun didn't go off. It was old, rusty, and when it went off the first time and killed the kid, its cylinder, it seized or something. Stuck. It wouldn't rotate again to bring in a new, live round. All I wanted in that moment was to die, just to die. And I was being denied it by some cruel twist. I thought, 'This is my punishment, to live. To have to live with myself. To have to see the faces of this kid's parents in hell. A hell I put them into.' But I wasn't Preacher's type. A predator. Who takes joy in pain. Sexual perversion. Violent perversions. Do you know how much it damages people? Violence like Preacher's done?"

"I have an idea," Rath said.

"In your line of work I guess you would," Sheldon said. "We were not close. Sometimes during library duty together, shelving books, he'd try to bend my ear, convince me he was 'saved,' whole. However you put it. He'd— He'd almost convince me he was."

"But?" Rath said.

"But he didn't."

"Why not?" Test said.

"I'm not religious. Spiritual, maybe. Not how I was before. But. I know right from wrong. I knew going into that store to rob it was wrong. Preacher did not seem to know. I'd tell him 'You're empty, man, missing something if you can do what you did and just, just not want to kill yourself,' you know? And he'd say or do something to try to convince me he was changed. Born anew."

"Why didn't he convince you?" Test said.

"I looked into the shit he did. I kind of knew. We all kind of know about each other, but a lot of what we hear is crap. Made to sound even more wicked than the real deal. But I checked it out on our computer, just a few old articles, hard to find, but after he did what he did . . . You know he killed two young parents, right? While their baby was sleeping? That *kid*. How *fucked up* is she now? *No* God can give you peace after that. The man is missing a soul to not just put a gun in his mouth and get it over with. Y'ask me."

He took a toothpick he'd kept hidden behind his ear and picked at his teeth. "I don't know what else to tell you."

"Did you ever see him speaking to other inmates . . . who'd done things like he'd done?" Test said.

"There's a few of his type that like to swap stories, like a sick club, they get each other off on it. *Literally*, they get each other off."

Test grimaced.

Rath felt too warm. Grimy. He couldn't peg Sheldon, figure out yet what was bullshit—because there was always bullshit—and what was genuine, and what the motives would be behind the bullshit.

"I don't think he was in with anyone," Sheldon said. "He seemed like a club of one member."

"No one you think he'd meet on the outside?" Rath said.

"He dug his own company. Loves himself. Worships himself. I think the only reason he talked to anyone was so he could talk about himself." He shrugged.

Rath nodded at Test to indicate they were done, for now.

Test handed Sheldon her card. "Get in touch if anyone comes to mind that Preacher might contact on the outside."

Rath opened the door. The wind and rain tore at his jacket, churned the fog. *When will it end?* he wondered.

48

Sleepless again, Rath stood in his bathroom and stared at the medicine cabinet, the mirror as fogged from his morning shower as the fields and woods were fogged outside, tiny tremors of anxiety buzzing in his hands and fingers. He licked his dry lips. Opened the medicine cabinet door.

Stared at its contents. Shaving cream. Razors. Lotions. Medicines.

Rachel's old hairbrush.

Her long dark hair of her old self tangled in it.

He took hold of a strand of her hair and pulled it free of all the others. Opened the envelope in his hand and placed his daughter's hair in it, next to the other hair.

He shut the cabinet door and left his quiet house to head out on the road again to see his daughter and take her the clothes and jacket he'd bought for her.

49

The ring of his new work cell phone startled Rath as he drove 114 West on his way to Johnson mulling what little he knew of Dana Clark and Jamie Drake. He looked at the phone on the seat beside him, a strange number on the screen.

He pulled over into the Lac Wallace fishing access and answered. "Hello?"

"Senior Detective Franklin Rath?" a voice said in an unmistakable Quebecois accent. It was not anyone who knew Rath: no one called him Franklin.

Rath confirmed that he was Senior Detective Frank Rath, though the title sounded as foreign as the name Franklin.

"This is Inspector Gerard Champine of the Saint-Jean-sur-Richelieu Police. I wonder can I speak to you, *non*?"

"Go ahead."

"I prefer not."

"I don't—"

"In person. I prefer. I am in the Jay Peak Resort, for skiing with family, *les petite enfants. Moi?* I sit and read. But the fog. Rain. Aye. There is no skiing. I could drive to meet at a place you like as the kids enjoy the water park."

"What is this?" Rath said, wondering if this man was even who he said he was.

"You have a murder, *non?*"

Rath nodded, though the inspector could not see the gesture. When the inspector said nothing, Rath realized his faux pas. Jamie Drake's hanging had not been reported as murder. Not yet. "I can't speak to any murder," Rath said.

"I appreciate. Even still, you have a murder."

"What is it I can help you with?" Rath said.

"*Non, non.* It is me who helps you. Or, as I prefer, we helps each other. I am 'omicide. I have dead girls. I am watching your local TV news just now. Your girl. In the woods. I am watching while *les enfants* swim. Your girl. She is hanged, *non?*"

How the hell did he know Jamie Drake was murdered, let alone hanged? Who was this "inspector."

Rath looked out the Scout window toward Lac Wallace. But the lake was not out there. Only fog.

"My three girls are not solved," the supposed inspector said.

Three girls? "Tell me more," Rath said.

"I prefer not on phone, but I see on the news you have the girl in the woods. Hanged? Non?"

Had Test leaked information? "Is that what the news report said?" Rath said.

"It is what is not said."

"Who the hell is this? Tell me about your girls, if you are who you say—"

"As I say. I prefer not on phone. We rendezvous? I can tell you my own cases. And what other links I think we share."

"Tell me what you know, or I'm hanging up," Rath said.

"I prefer not on phone."

Prefer not. Who was this guy, Bartleby?

"How did you know I'm working this case? Or get my number?" Rath said. "I've barely started and—"

"I request from the woman who answers police's line to please speak with the detective of the case. Will you rendezvous?"

"Give me a reason."

"If your girl was hanged, we will meet. If not. We can say *au revoir.*"

Damn it, Rath thought. He could tell the inspector to meet him in Johnson, but if the inspector did indeed have three dead girls, *hanged* dead girls, Rath did not want to chance running into Rachel with him and having her ask questions. "There's a roadside place in Starkville, about halfway between us. Called Borderland."

"We meet in forty-five minutes then, *non?*"

"Twice that, with this fog."

"*Bon,* detective."

Rath ended the call.

Detective.

Rath had not been called detective in sixteen years.

He was not sure how he felt about it.

Desperate, he decided. Barrons had miscalculated. One factor that kept police officers from crossing lines was fear of ruining careers. Rath did not have a career to lose. Did not have to worry about scandal if he acted out of bounds. It wasn't that he did not respect the profession. Or the law. He'd do whatever he needed to do within the bounds of the law. But life was about priorities. Preventing another girl from ending up dead in the woods, that was his priority.

When this was over, and Rachel safe, he would not look back. He would go deer hunting as deep into the woods as he could hike. Away from it all. He'd track and take a big buck, pack away venison to last until spring, and hole up in his home by a fire and read novels and carve decoys and grow a beastly beard. He'd hike up the remote trackless wilderness on the backside of Mount Monadnock and try to find an ancient geologic anomaly rumored to exist up there.

He stared out the windshield. At it. The window was painted white with fog, as if the fog were trying to block out the world in order to get Rath's undivided attention, get him to focus, to tell him something.

Or warn him.

50

Rath had driven nearly an hour without a single pair of headlights passing him in the fog going the other way. Route 114, which scribbled its way west just a few hundred yards south of the Canada border, then southwest toward Burke, was no Autobahn even on a clear summer day, yet Rath had traveled it dozens of times at 3 A.M.—when he was younger heading back from drinking in Quebec and Montreal, where he and friends took advantage of the lax drinking age of eighteen; and when older, heading to deer hunt the backside of Great Averill Lake—and even then passed a dozen tractor-trailers along the way.

Not today. Not a soul.

Rath had the sensation the Scout was drifting through clouds—complete with turbulence from bucking on frost heaves—and that time had slipped a gear.

Ahead, the red of a neon sign stained the fog.

It had taken him an hour to drive the last twenty-five miles.

He pulled the Scout into a mire that was once a dirt lot, relieved to find Borderland was open. The possibility that it might be closed had occurred to him as he drove. Yet places like this never closed. They prided themselves on staying open, no matter what—in spite *of what*—the rest of the world did.

As he stepped out into the fog, his face was wetted with mist. Despite the raw temperature, the fog felt warm, as if it were the damp breath of a dragon.

Several ATVs sat parked near the porch rail, a modern-day substitution for the Old West's hitching post.

Inside Borderland, the clack of billiard balls accompanied boisterous banter from a few men who taunted another man who circled the pool table with his cue, his face fixed with the cold concentration of a sniper assessing the best vantage from which to fire his kill shot.

The men were loggers, their steel-toed boots encased in muck, duck cloth overalls and leather chain-saw chaps darkened with rainwater, the bills of their trucker caps with chain-saw and auto-motive logos blackened with grease. They looked at Rath with his wool jacket, his face unshaven, and frayed Carhartt jeans jammed in rubber boots, as if Rath were wearing a Brooks Brothers suit, then resumed mocking their friend.

The fog made it dangerous to work in the woods, gave the loggers an excuse to break early for lunch and enjoy a beer that would lead to a half-dozen beers and most of the men staying here until closing at 1 A.M. Rath knew. As a teen he'd worked for a logging company marking trees. Worked for a roofer and house painter, too.

Rath took a stool at a bar crafted of a single span of roughhewn old-growth spruce, hundreds of spent brass bullet casings embed-ded in the wood beneath clear resin.

A bent, elderly man shuffled over behind the bar.

Rath did not want a beer this early, but knew to order anything except a beer or booze would be suspect.

"Labatt Blue," he said. The man dug around in a cooler at his hip, popped the cap off a longneck with a piece of deer antler, and slid the bottle along a few feet of bar to Rath. He limped back through the kitchen door.

Rath sipped his beer.

The bar door opened.

Out of the fog, a tall man with wire-rimmed glasses appeared, wiped his black overshoes on a mat visible only to him. He was as likely to be the first patron to wipe his feet upon entrance to the establishment as he was to be the last.

He was older, nudging seventy.

Water dripped from his fedora, the orange feather in the hat band wet and wilting. He did not wear the hat with the forward tip of Sinatra flair or the hipster cock, but squarely, for the purpose for which it was intended: to keep rain off a man's head.

He shed the hat and snapped it against his black wool coat, water spraying as he revealed a head of white hair tidily cropped. A cop's cut. Except this man could not be the inspector. This man was too old for that world.

The man unbuttoned his coat, unslung from around his neck an orange scarf that accented the fedora's feather. Under his coat a checked dress shirt, dry-cleaner pressed.

The men at the pool table halted their bullshitting to observe the stranger as if he were an exotic bird, but quickly gauged him as no threat.

The man walked to Rath, his long legs scissoring.

"Detective?" he said.

"Inspector?" Rath rose as the inspector shook his hand with fingers long but not bony, cool and soft. The inspector settled in the stool beside Rath. He did not take in his surroundings, and while his impeccable dress was as out of place as a tux in a deer camp, he betrayed no awareness or discomfort at the incongruity. He was at ease. He'd been in legions of places like this, and much, much worse, Rath was certain. He'd seen the world's ugliness. While he was lean and dapper, and his age presaged the shadowy beginnings of inevitable fragility, there was no trace of softness about him. He did not need to fit in to his surroundings to be respected or left alone.

Next to this inspector's poise and polish, Rath felt like a roadside chain-saw carving.

"Your girl," the inspector said, pulling down his coat cuff where it rode up over a slim silver watch, "she was hanged or *non*?"

How does he know? Rath thought. If the inspector knew, could Preacher have figured it by watching the news?

"Tell me about your girls first," Rath said.

The inspector smiled.

"I had two earlier girls before this new one. Both November. Both strangled." He paused, reflecting. His eyes narrowed and he smoothed the feather of his fedora resting on his knee. "Rochelle Beauchamp." He paused between the two names, as if to give each their due reverence. "And Vanessa Lancaume. One discovered in Henryville, the other in Iberville, in the woods, each along the banks of the Richelieu. Clothed. Each strangled with something from their own attire. A long cord from the hood of Rochelle Beauchamp's sweatshirt. A bootlace for Vanessa Lancaume." The inspector closed his eyes. "*Méprisable.*"

Rath had not yet read a complete report for Jamie Drake but

wondered about her boot being put back on her foot when she was hanged. Was a bootlace missing?

"How old were they?" Rath said.

"Teens. Girls."

"Quebecois?"

"*Oui.* You doubt they are like your girl. We have, umm, *bogue dans le cerveau*—bug in brain—about it, yes. The border. Like it is a wall and no one can do a bad thing on both sides of the wall. But what is there stopping someone from driving back and forth to do the same things?"

The inspector was right. The border created a psychological distance that was illusion. There was not a damned thing to stop anyone from crossing the border, anyone with a clean record that was. So maybe that was a start, their man was clean. He'd killed numerous girls, but had not been caught. Was clean, officially. That might rule out Preacher. Unless—

"It is a border only on a map," the inspector said.

"Your girls and my girl have similarities. But—"

The inspector looked at Rath. His eyes were pale and tired. Haunted.

"Like I say, it is my suspicion your girl is hanged. Because of what the TV did not say. We are to report the same way about my most recent girl. We told CTV Montreal what to say, exactly. We have CTV say, 'The body of young girl is found in the woods along the Richelieu River.' We tell them *not* to say murdered, not to say hanged, not to mention anything. See. It was supposed to be reported today. So. When I am in my resort room and hear on your TV, on your WCAX channel, a report about your own girl, I think I was hearing a report of my girl on CTV. It is so same. *Exactement.*"

Rath had hung his hat on less. "And your new girl?"

The inspector sighed. "Hanged. See. It did not kill her right away. It was not the snap of the neck. Non. It was slow. Grotesque. Torture. And the rope. Is not just a rope. *Non?* Is a loop for killing animals. For the trappers. Yours, too?"

"Fuck," Rath said.

"Same then. Tell me of your girl."

"I need to see ID. You know who I am because you called me, but—"

The inspector smiled, retrieved a thin black wallet from inside his coat, and slipped an ID card from it.

INSPECTOR SERVICE DE POLICE

DE LA VILLE DE MONTRÉAL

INSPECTEUR EN CHEF

HENRI LA SALLE

RETRAITÉ

The ID appeared legitimate, though Rath had never seen a Montreal inspector's ID to know with certainty.

"*Retraité?*" Rath said. "Retired."

"Fifteen years."

"How can you be working recent murders if you've been retired for fifteen years?"

Was this guy a *nutter?* as Rachel would say. Maybe his ID was genuine, but he couldn't be working a new case if he'd been out of the game for fifteen years, unless he was a consultant of sorts, as Rath had been with the Mandy Wilks case. But Rath was twenty-five years younger, at least.

"Excuse me," Rath said.

The inspector, or whoever he was, nodded. "*Bien sûr.*"

RATH WALKED INTO the restroom, its greasy yellow tiled floor littered with leaves of toilet paper, stinking of and tacky with piss.

Rath took out his phone, brought up a browser, and googled Henryville, Quebec + Hanging + girl + murder.

Nothing about a murder came up.

He googled the same for Iberville.

Nothing.

He'd been played. Who was this guy?

Rath stormed out of the bathroom.

The inspector, *the stranger*, sat where he'd been left.

"Who are you?' Rath said. "What is this all about?"

"You misunderstand, *non*?"

"*No*. No. I *don't* misunderstand. Who are you?"

"I am exactly who I says I am: Inspector Gerard Champine, retired fifteen years. I call because of likeness for our cases."

"There are *no* cases. There is no mention of any murders in Iberville or Henryville, Quebec, this month, November, as you said, or any recent months, let alone involving hangings."

"*Mais non*. The most recent one, Lucille Forte, is not reported yet as I say. Should be today. Et Rochelle et Vanessa, they are not this month."

"You said November."

"*Oui*. November."

"This *is* November."

"*Non, non*, Detective. *Ma faute. Pardonnez-moi*. Rochelle Beauchamp and Vanessa Lancaume were murdered in November. *Oui*." The inspector smoothed the feather tucked in his fedora's band. "November of nineteen ninety-three and -four."

51

Ninety-three and -four?" Rath said.

"I should have made clear as crystal, the time line."

Rath took out his phone. Googled the names of the two dead Quebecois girls + murder + Iberville + Henryville. Not much came up, but enough to confirm what Champine claimed.

"Goddamn it," Rath said. If the killer north of the border and down here were the same, it meant Preacher, if involved, had to get a fake ID to cross the border as a felon. Extremely difficult, but possible, if he'd made the right contacts in prison. Rath and Test still needed to check out Timothy Glade and the other released convict.

"The girls from the nineties. Why the connection to the girls now, if they were not hanged?" Rath said.

"I see a connection to your killer back then. The Connecticut River Valley Killer. I see you in the news then. I remember you on TV for the CRVK case. And for your sister. I would say it is a tragedy, but, as police, we know murder is not tragedy. A tornado.

A flood. They are tragedy. They do not know what they do. A murderer. He *knows*. He is no tragedy."

"What else do you know about the CRVK?"

"A man suspected was killed in a fire. Killed himself and family. Your killings stopped. Ours, too. We only had the two, that we know. But. A lot of girls, they go missing but are not missed. You understand. From the city. The clubs."

"Were your girls from clubs?"

"*Non*. Families. Good girls."

"Did you ever contact us, the state police in Vermont, or in Canaan, about a connection?"

"*Mais oui*. A Barrons. I left many messages to him. And to Richard North."

"Barrons?" Rath and Barrons had worked closely, shared every fleck of evidence, every theory. So Rath had believed. "And what happened?"

"I never hear back. The man in the fire. I believed it was him, as you did."

"I didn't believe it, neither did Barrons."

"I did not know this. But. The killings stopped. But now. These two. Mine and yours of recent."

Rath needed to speak to Barrons. Ask him why he never got back to Inspector Champine.

"The case was yours back then?" Rath said.

"*Mais oui*. Mine. There is now the new one too for *us*, or for them, the Service de Saint-Jean-sur-Richelieu. She is not my case. *Évidemment*. But I see your girl on the news."

Three more girls, Rath thought.

The prospect exhausted him.

Sadly, more girls meant more evidence, a mistake made, DNA left behind, a pattern of behavior and motivation that would reveal an identity.

Even if DNA were found, without a match for it in the criminal database, or a suspect to swab, it was as unusable as a blind eyewitness. Preacher, though, he was in the database.

"You're retired, why not have the current inspector contact me?" Rath said.

"*En calvaire.* I am *pissed off.* These girls are mine. If this new girl is the same killer, she is mine, too. Should be. I have no, *traction,* in the force. *Mais!*" His index finger metronomed in the air to emphasize: "If I come to Saint-Jean-sur-Richelieu police with information, a lead American inspector, they may let me be more than a shadow."

"I see," Rath said.

"*Bon.* Can you get me your case files?"

"There isn't much. I can see. I want to know about your hanged girl. Forensic comparisons will establish certainty or not. Though with the snare . . ." Rath shook his head. A snare used to strangle coyotes along fence lines. "Officially. This. It may be for— I don't even know. FBI? I don't know." Coordinating with the Vermont State Police was a sinkhole of politics and tender egos itself; waiting for information and evidence to be shared through the bureaucratic chains was as slow as trying to run in water and demanded the patience of a bomb defuser. How would it be to work with a police force in another country, in a province whose people were schizophrenic over which language to speak? Rath didn't know. "Let's work it out between the two of us, for now," Rath said.

52

Nearly seeing double from driving in the fog, Rath made his way to Johnson.

In town, he texted Rachel to tell her he was parked just outside the inn on Main Street, too tired to even get out of the Scout. But he had her clothes. And coat.

She appeared from the inn a minute later and hurried to the Scout in the rain, hopped in.

"Whoa," she said, her nose scrunching like a rabbit's. "You really need to clean your car out. It smells like— I don't know what. An old bowling shoe."

"Smelled a lot of those, have you?" Rath said.

"It's putrid."

"It may actually be my jacket that stinks."

"Jeez, Dad. Burn it. And sell this heap. Get a real car. A reliable car."

"What, a RAV4? This rig is as reliable as they come. How many RAV4s will you see in forty years?"

Rath pointed to the Dress Shoppe bags in the backseat. "I think I did a good job," he said.

"You mean the clerk did?" Rachel smiled.

It was good to see her smile.

It was good to know Preacher was being watched by Larkin.

Rath's phone buzzed. GROUT. Rath answered.

"Hey," Grout said. "I read about a body of a young girl found in the woods, and with this thing with Rachel and Preacher, I—?"

"She's right here," Rath said.

Rachel wrinkled her brow, curious.

"She's OK then?" Grout said.

"For now."

"What are you doing about him, Preacher?"

"I can't say, right now."

Rachel's look of curiosity became one of suspicion.

"If any asshole messed with my daughter, never mind *Preacher,*" Grout said. "I don't know."

"I hope to nail him on new charges."

"You think he's the doer for the girl in the woods?"

"We detained him for questioning, and he's under surveillance."

"I heard you took my old gig."

Grout could not have masked his regret at leaving his position if he wanted to, so didn't bother trying. Not with Rath at least.

"I don't even want it," Rath said, making the same mistake he'd made with Test: speaking dismissively of a position others coveted. "Barrons had this idea that—"

"You don't have to get into it. It's good if it means you can pressure Preacher. It was me I'd *find* charges. If not, make him vanish. This girl you found? Is Preacher the doer?"

Rath could feel Rachel's eyes on him. The more cryptically he spoke, the more Rachel perked up.

"We suspect. Maybe teamed with someone else, too."

"He doesn't strike me as the sharing type."

"Prison changes a man. We also have a possible link that involves Abby Land—"

Rachel stared, incredulous.

"Why her?" Grout said.

"She and our girl in the woods were unlikely friends. Could be a dead end. But they were tight over a love for acting."

"Acting," Grout said. "That's fucked up."

"A lot of girls get the bug."

"Not the acting. Remember that lead from the Wilks case? It went nowhere, but . . ."

"Which lead?" One had to follow scores of leads that dropped off a cliff to nowhere if you wanted to find the few leads that took flight from the edge.

"You wanted to follow up with the notepad Wilks had from the Double Black Diamond Resort in Stowe," Grout said. "It was odd, a broke kid like her having a notepad from a five-star resort an hour-and-a-half drive from Canaan."

"I'm not following."

"I'm not done. Remember. A production company held *auditions* in conference rooms there. A crappy movie being shot in Boston. Affleck or some shit. Auditions for extras, whatever—"

Shit, Rath thought.

"Mandy Wilks wasn't on the list. But we didn't check for Drake or Land, of course. We were thinking maybe someone was running a scam that lured Wilks. But now . . . Land and

Drake. Actresses? *And* Wilks had a notepad from the Double Black Diamond? Maybe you want to check for Land and Drake on the list. It's weak as a well drink, but maybe you'd get a hit. That rich prig was there at the Black Diamond, too, the one I suspected for doing Wilks for a half a second."

"Who?"

"Boyd Hale Pratt *the Third*. He was there to meet that crazy old bitch about him and his wife adopting a baby. I dropped him as a suspect when Land was pegged. You got my wheels turning though. I miss this shit. We should meet. I wanted to talk to you about . . ."

Grout kept talking but Rath wasn't listening. His wheels were turning, too. In a direction he welcomed and dreaded. "Let's meet in person; what day do you have off from the mall?"

"Don't use that four-letter word *mall* with me. Tomorrow? Noon? I can take a long break. I'm the big chief of the mall rats."

"The old site along the river work?"

It did.

Rath hung up.

"What was that all about?" Rachel said.

"That was Harland Grout."

"I know. What was it about? What aren't you telling me?" Rachel said. "I have a right to know."

"The girl that was found in the woods. She was hanged. Tortured," Rath said.

"And it was Preacher?"

"I don't know."

"But you believe it. Is he going to try to torture me?"

He already is, Rath thought. "It may not be Preacher."

"*May not be?* The only reason he could be following me is to kill me. Hang me or torture me or— What other reason could a man like him possibly have?"

Rath couldn't say.

Rachel took the bags from the backseat and gave Rath a peck on the cheek and left.

Rath watched her walk safely back into the inn before he started the Scout.

On his way out of town his phone rang. Inspector Champine. Rath pulled over to the shoulder.

"Inspector," Rath said.

"Detective," Champine said. "Can you pay a visit tomorrow? At Service Saint-Jean-sur-Richelieu?"

"Name the time."

Inspector Champine named the time and bid Rath adieu.

53

Tuesday, November 8, 2011

The border crossing was quiet. Only one car idled ahead of Rath's Scout at the patrol booth. When the car accelerated away, Rath crept the Scout forward. His driver's window's crank hadn't worked since toothpaste came in a metal tube, so he cracked his door open to hand the patrol officer his enhanced driver's license.

"Roll down your window," the patrol officer demanded, motioning.

"I can't." Rath tried to open his door farther.

The officer marched out to the Scout. "Do *not* open your door," she said. "Roll down your window."

Rath gave her a helpless look. "The crank's broke."

The officer rested her hand on her holstered stun gun that she wore opposite her handgun. "Roll the passenger window down." She came around as Rath cranked down the window and handed his driver's license to her.

"Turn off your engine, put your hands on the steering wheel," she ordered then strode to the booth and ran Rath through the system. She walked back to the passenger window. "What's your business in Canada, Mr. Rath?"

"A meeting with the Saint-Jean-sur-Richelieu police."

"Nature?"

"A murder investigation."

She squinted at Rath as if he were putting her on.

"May I?" Rath glanced to his wallet on the seat.

"Go easy."

Rath slowly picked up his wallet and handed her his fresh detective's ID, the ink still wet.

The officer inspected the ID.

"Should have shown me this straightaway. Who are you meeting with in the police?"

"Retired Inspector Champine and Inspector Hubert."

"This is about the girl in Henryville?"

"I can't say. But, yes."

She smiled, handed Rath his ID. "Fix the window."

RATH DROVE 147 Nord, passing the currency exchange building, which was barely more than a hut.

As teens, Rath and his buddies had made the currency exchange their first stop after crossing the border. The American dollar was worth $1.50 Canadian back then, but businesses treated the American dollar as par, so if you didn't exchange American for Canadian, you got screwed.

After exchanging their money, Rath and his buddies would drive farther north and west to attend concerts in the now defunct Montreal Forum, and to hop from one Henryville and Iberville

roadside dive to another to drink Brador and Seagram 7, shoot
stick and throw darts until they had enough liquid courage to stop
at Chez Darlene or one of the other strip clubs patronized by local
farmers and laborers, American kids and businessmen. Rath re-
called the intense swell of anticipation as he'd walk into the clubs
about to see women strip for a cover charge of $2. Canadian. He
wondered if Chez Darlene still existed.

Rath drove 10 Ouest through one drowsy, agricultural ville after another, surrounded by dairy farms and cornfields. The flat
landscape's only meager elevation was the Montérégie Hills to the
north that broke the surface like humps of breaching whales on a
calm ocean. The hills were not visible today in the fog. Rath had
hoped the rain would turn to snow and the fog abate as he drove
north. It hadn't.

He passed split-level brick ranch homes painted pastel colors—
tangerine orange, mint green, Pepto pink—as if the palette were
restricted to those of a pack of Necco wafers.

It was hard to believe Montreal was now just a half hour north.

Just past a sign that read SAINT-JEAN-SUR-RICHELIEU 5 KM was
the classic old sign for CHEZ DARLENE, a twenty-foot silhouette of
a naked woman, her legs and fingers wrapped around a pole as she
leaned so far backward her long hair nearly touched the backs of
her stilettos. Rath was tempted to stop in on the way back, to see
if the place was the same.

Rath took the exit.

Saint-Jean-sur-Richelieu was not a farming ville. It was a bedroom community to Montreal, a vibrant small city of nearly one
hundred thousand, built up around a textile manufacturing in-
dustry that still thrived among what some folks considered the
northernmost finger of Lake Champlain and others considered

the headwaters of the Richelieu River, which flowed north a hundred miles to the St. Lawrence.

The self-proclaimed Hot Air Balloon Capital, Saint-Jean-sur-Richelieu had hosted the International Hot Air Balloon Festival going on thirty years. Rath had mocked the festival when he was a kid, dismissed it when he was a single cop in his early twenties, and embraced it as a father. He'd brought Rachel to the festival each summer from the ages of seven to twelve. She'd been giddy when she'd first laid eyes on the spectacular vision of a hundred colorful goliath balloons drifting in the blue summer sky.

In the several years that followed, Rachel had been raring to go again, talked about the festival throughout the winter and spring. He'd been proud of himself to find a tradition they could share for years to come and imagined her bringing her own children when she had them, his grandchildren; however, the winter Rachel was thirteen, she'd gone without mentioning the festival, and when he'd brought it up in the spring, she'd said, *Oh. Yeah. Are we going again this year?* In years prior the "again" was said with exuberance: *We're going again, right, we wouldn't dare miss it.* That morning, "again" was said with a sense of obligation.

Parenthood, at its best, Rath thought, is a perpetual recovery from minor heartbreaks, each leaving its own tiny scar. At its worst, it ended the way it had for parents of the dead girls.

Nearing the police department for Saint-Jean-sur-Richelieu, Rath drove down an avenue now home to a Marriott, a Riverview, and a Double Tree, new since he'd last been up this way. In the distance the prominent, jade steeple for the Cathedral of Saint-Jean-l'Évangéliste thrust skyward, above all else. He'd never been certain if the steeple was constructed of weathered copper, or green slate.

The Saint-Jean-sur-Richelieu Police Department was housed in a three-story building; its nondescript façade of square windows and gray brick screamed *municipal mundanity*.

The day was still foggy, but the drizzle was partly snow now. For a moment when he stepped out of his Scout, he let falling snowflakes land on his face and cool his skin.

54

Rath had barely stomped the slush off his boots and started to look for the welcome desk when Inspector Champine and a man perhaps in his midthirties, who looked like a teen next to the aged Champine, bustled toward him from a side corridor.

"*Bonjour*," the man said, smoothing his tie and working the bottom two buttons of his gray tweed sport coat. Rath imagined he'd just finished a midmorning snack at his desk and was pulling himself together for the meet. In one hand he held a green folder.

He extended his free hand and pumped Rath's hand with vigorous, dutiful haste.

"Inspector Rath, I am Inspector Hubert," he said, dropping the *H* and the *T*. *Ew-bare*.

Rath nodded, feeling no need to tell Hubert that he, Rath, was technically a detective.

"*Entrez. S'il vous plait*," Hubert said and powered down the hall away from Rath, Inspector Champine at his side.

Plaques of officers and Mounties in full dress decorated one wall. Another wall dedicated itself to photos of hot air balloons in flight. Hubert dropped his file on the table. "Lucille Forte," he said and sucked air between the slight gap in his upper front teeth. "*Quinze ans.* Fifteen. A solid family. Stable house, father a sociology professor at McGill. Her mother is a manager at one of the more reputable diamond merchants in Montreal."

"More reputable?" Rath said.

"Diamonds are dirty. Many connections to organized crime, heroine, trafficking. But the mother she is retail, not wholesale, where the dirt is. See. She probably thinks it's just the same as working at IKEA. We now have Forte's photo across the region. Asking for witnesses who see her last. That we know, she was not the kind to be in the area she was dumped. It is off a desolate road, *Nord-est* of here."

"Dumped?" Rath said. "I thought she was hanged." He caught Champine's eye, who nodded for Hubert to continue.

"*Oui,*" Hubert said. "She was."

"I was made to believe she was hanged in the woods."

"*Non,*" Hubert said.

"Then our girls are not that similar," Rath said, trying to conceal his anger.

"They are same," Hubert said. "Hanged slowly. This is what counts. Tortured. With that snare. Your girl, same, this is what Gerard said. No sex assault. She did have sex recently. But not forced. We have taken DNA from semen inside her. But not forced. Just torture by the hanging. That is not common up here. To have girls tortured but the sex left alone? Is it common in Vermont?"

"Of course it's not common," Rath said. Hubert had a point. Indoors or outdoors, the snare was a lock for the same perp.

"Ours, maybe she is done inside out of it being convenient. Maybe the woods are convenient in Vermont," Hubert said.

"We have a feather that shows she was tortured inside," Champine said.

"Feather?" Rath said.

"Goose down. From a pillow. Or duvet. Bed covering," Hubert clarified.

"Why not from a jacket? A sleeping bag?" Rath said. "Or a wild bird?"

"Our lab says *non*," Hubert said, put off. "They will check all. They say now it is pillow or duvet. There is difference I am told. They will do more. Get exact. Brand. Manufacturer. Store sold. They are like magic these days. No one can hide. No one can get away with anything for long."

"What else tells you she was killed indoors?" Rath asked.

"The side of body that was against the earth in the ditch is muddy and has debris of the woods, fields. But not her side that was up. She was shampooed, skin washed with a scented soap. We will find out about this soap and shampoo, too. We will. Our team. She had been dead for twelve hours but her body had not been exposed to the elements more than three or four hours before she was discovered. It did get cold that night and snow some. There was not enough snow on top of her yet. For one. And her skin did not show the signs of exposure. That was clear."

"Who discovered her?" Rath said.

"Snowplow driver. Salting the road. This is another sign. He'd been through two hours earlier, and there was no sign of the salt from his previous trip being scattered on her as it would have been."

"And you had two strangulations from the nineties you think are linked? Inspector Champine said you'd explain the link, even though the MO was different."

"We *know* they are linked," Hubert said.

"How?"

"Fingerprints." Hubert smiled.

"You have fingerprints?" Rath said. Did these inspectors not believe in full disclosure up front? They seemed to enjoy teasing out critical information.

"Partials," Hubert said. "Enough."

"How many points matched?" Rath knew that with each passing day forensics techniques previously seen as infallible were being questioned. Bite marks in flesh, fingerprints, even DNA, or the processing of it, in some cases, were all being viewed as far from indisputable. Some techniques were no more reliable than eyewitness accounts, which had long been known as dubious. As with any science, forensics evolved, changed, learned from mistakes. Mistakes that put innocent people in jail and allowed the guilty to escape. Many scientists in other fields did not see forensic *science* as science at all.

"*Je ne sais pas,*" Hubert said. "We leave it to lab to tell us: match or *non.* They know."

"How did you get fingerprints?"

"One from a broken piece of a victim's eyeglasses. Valerie Lancaume. From nineteen ninety-one. The new one from Lucille Forte's brass belt buckle. Same."

Rath licked his dry lips. Fingerprints? This was a revelation.

"Do you get an ID match in a database?"

"*Non.* Just between the two." Inspector Hubert said grimly. "If he was in database, we'd have arrest. Or know who we are looking for. *Non?*"

"I'd like the prints. Electronically."

"Do you have prints for your hanged girl?"

"No. But we can run them against our own database. Maybe he has a record in the States."

"*Bon.* Maybe we get him then."

"I'd like nothing more," Rath said. If it was Preacher, they had him.

"The border. It is nothing. It is easy to hide one side from the other. On purpose. With Lucille Forte there is no sign of struggle. She is at her after-school activities with friends, as normal the day she disappeared. No one sees her with anyone strange. She does not act odd or show worry. She seems her excited self. Excited for it almost being the weekend. She maybe was 'selected' only for how she looked. Like much girls. We do not know. But. She was hanged, slowly. Given air, then choked. Over and over. Gruesome. She is fifteen. Your girl, she is fifteen. Is she from what kind of family?"

"A good one," Rath said.

"Two parents, you mean?"

"That's not what I mean," Rath said. He'd grown up in a house with both parents until he was ten, and his mother had finally put his father out for his infidelity. The house had been far more calm afterward. And, he hoped, he'd done a fair job raising Rachel in a stable and nurturing home, by himself, just the two of them. "But, yes, both parents. Present. Involved. No financial hardship. Successfully employed. Active in the community."

"An only child?"

"She is," Rath said.

"As ours. A good family, active in community. And an only child."

Curious, Rath thought. Was someone purposely targeting only children, from good families? Was that a reason? "Your two girls from the nineties. They were strangled, but not hanged."

"*Oui,*" Hubert said. "Not quite the same modus. But the fingerprints connect them, no doubt. Let us trade files, all info, *oui?*" Hubert said.

"Is your file in French?" Rath said, "because—"

"The original, *oui. Mais,* we have it translated just for you. Let us each dig into what the other has. See what is what. What is not what." Hubert handed the files to Rath. "You brought your file, *oui?*"

Rath reached into his bag and brought out copies of the file on Jamie Drake, set them on the table. There were certain protocols that needed to be followed in an international exchange of information. Protocols that took time. Far too much time. Ignoring these protocols would not damage the case, but it would damage Rath's detective career. Fortunately, he did not have or want one.

"Let us meet again or speak on the phone. If we feel we are closer," Hubert said.

"Let's hope we are," Rath said.

As RATH WAITED behind a line of cars to cross back into the States his phone buzzed. Grout. Shit. He picked up. "You stood me up, you Sally," Grout said.

"I'm in Quebec, working something hard."

"A pole dancer."

"Tomorrow." Rath was too tired to hear about Grout's wanting back on the force. He wanted no part of it, really, getting between Test and Grout. But he could at least hear out a man he'd once mentored as a green patrol officer straight out of the academy.

"Tomorrow," Grout said. "Eight? Gives me time to get in for nine. And don't stand me up for a Frenchie stripper with bad teeth."

55

At home, ready to collapse from the excruciating drive in the rain and fog, Rath spread the contents of the Saint-Jean-sur-Richelieu police file out on his kitchen table.

Outside in the dark night, coyotes yowled.

Rath scoured Lucille Forte's short file and biography. A decent student, the U.S. equivalent of a B- average. No siblings. Parents made comfortable money. A four-bedroom home at the end of a cul-de-sac. No friends or teachers witnessed or sensed anything amiss the day of her disappearance and death. She had gone to after-school tryouts until 4 P.M., then headed for the bus stop to catch a bus to bring her a few blocks from her home. A CCTV camera picked her image up when she got off the bus at her stop. It captured no one else. After that, she was out of CCTV range. She seemed to be a social, upbeat teen, active in sports. Friends said, in part: "She was her usual bubbly self at tryouts. She looked forward to the dance Friday, and more tryouts Saturday and Sunday."

Rath made a note to find out what sports she played. Being

November, it might be basketball or skiing. Perhaps a girls' hockey team. Whatever it was, sports meant travel to other schools. Opportunity for predators.

He picked up the file photo of her. She was, or had been, a cute girl, in a plain way. Curly black hair, feathered with bangs that reminded Rath of the '80s. Her skin pale, her smile gargantuan, an irrepressible shine to her brown eyes. The translator had neglected to change the metric system to the U.S. system and had the girl down as weighing 45 kilos and standing at 152 centimeters. Rath figured the conversion. The girl stood about five feet even and weighed a hair under a hundred pounds. Petite. Perhaps her sport was gymnastics, or figure skating. Canadians cherished their ice skating.

Rath returned to the same question. Why would a killer risk going over the border, ensuring that a vehicle's make and license plate number were caught clearly on camera? Of course it was only a risk if the murders were put together. Those odds were slim. Perhaps Quebec provided new hunting grounds, close to home, but off the radar of law enforcement and media.

He could not get his head around it. He needed another perspective. Test's. He'd put off looping her in on the Quebec lead long enough.

Rath phoned her work cell.

"Hey," Test said upon answering.

"I have a lead, in Saint-Jean-sur-Richelieu. There's another—"

"Wait, what?"

"A Quebecois inspector approached me, so I ventured up to see if—"

"You went to Canada without saying a single word to me?"

"I wanted to see if anything was there before I wasted your

time. They have a murdered girl. Hanged. Tortured. The MO is exact except their girl was killed indoors."

"What's her name?"

"Lucille Forte. I wonder if she knew our girl down here, somehow. But I can't figure how."

"Social media. Facebook. Instagram. Mutual friends."

Rath knew as much about social media as he did about needlepoint.

"The Quebecois girl. She's into sports. Maybe our hanged girl was too, as well as acting. Look into it. Quebec has prints from her murder and from a victim from the nineties. They match. No match to a database though."

"There are *other* victims? From the nineties? Are we talking the CRVK? How the hell am I just hearing this?"

"Because I *just* got back from a long, long day and was processing before bringing you in on it tomorrow. Saint-Jean sent the prints electronically, and I had Larkin log them into IAFIS to see if we get a hit for priors down here. Should hear back soon."

"Both sides of the border," Test said. "Nearly twenty years apart."

"Check social media for Lucille Forte. See if there is any link, however slight, to our girl, or to Vermont." Rath's phone buzzed. "That's Saint-Jean. I'll call you back." He killed the call with Test and took the call from Inspector Hubert.

"*Bonjour,*" Rath said, feeling foolish for using one of about nine French words he knew offhand.

"Hello," the inspector said. "I am calling to see if you have run our prints in your FBI's fingerprint system." He sounded anxious.

"I should know any time. I haven't gotten into the files as deep as I want yet. I have a question. What kind of sports was Forte into?"

"Sports? *Non*. She does not participate into the sports."

"Her file says she was at tryouts, practice."

Rath heard a shuffling of papers. "*Mais non*. Tryouts. This means for us, uh, rehearsal. For a play. She was in the plays. Very good at it. A very good young actress."

"I need to make a call." Rath hung up and phoned Test.

"She was an actress. Lucille Forte."

"That's not coincidence. Not a third girl. Maybe there's a production they were all in, or an international program for theater, like with sports, the Burlington International Games. Something to bring kids from Canada and the States together. I'll ask the Drakes."

"The acting ties them together. But how does Preacher tie in? How does he know Drake was hanged? And the time? He had to have something to do with it. Except how would he get into Canada as a felon?"

"The state police are scouring Jamie Drake's computer and phone. I'll get a full report on her texts and e-mails, social media. If Forte is in there, I'll find out."

"If you still have those lists from the Double Black Diamond Resort, sign-ups for the acting auditions, look into them, I was talking to Grout and—"

"*Grout?* Why?"

"I was telling him your theory about Land and Drake and Wilks and the acting connection. Grout reminded me of the list of names for wannabe actors who attended the auditions at the resort."

"You shouldn't be talking to a civilian about open murder cases."

"He's hardly a civilian. And we talk to civilians all the time."

"Not about tenuous links or information not made public."

Rath wasn't going to debate how he got information. "It's your *lead*, the acting angle. Grout gave it merit."

"It had merit before."

"It gives you something concrete to search," Rath said. "Check it."

"Soon as this call ends," Test said and ended it.

56

Test dug the Mandy Wilks file from her backpack, set it on the kitchen island. She respected Rath, even liked him personally, to a degree, but to have to report to him *and* have him conferring with Grout behind her back, it was hard to stomach. She didn't appreciate Grout nosing in her case. He'd chosen to be a mall cop, let him be a mall cop. She especially didn't need her old superior getting the idea he could strut back into his old post as if his resigning were a temporary distraction.

As a superior, Grout had been dismissive and haranguing, not respectful of her work. Personal and philosophical differences were one thing. Test did not have to be chummy and have barbecues with other cops' families to work well together; but there did need to be respect for the work.

If Grout ever cajoled Barrons into rehiring him, Test did not know what she'd do. She was not a quitter, but she would not brook such disrespect.

Test opened the file.

From the living room, Elizabeth shrieked, "Get up off me!"

"Then tell me where you hid my car!" George shouted.

"You two stop it in there," Sonja said, wondering where Claude had gone off to in the house that he wasn't hearing the kids. She needed him to referee so she could work.

"Then tell her to stop hiding my cars!" George shouted.

"Don't shout at me," Test said.

"He has a hundred cars!" Elizabeth shrieked. "I only took one."

"And quit shrieking," Test said.

"She took my favorite!" George shouted.

Of course Elizabeth took his *favorite*. It was his favorite *because* she took it. If she'd taken a different one, that one would have been George's favorite. It never ended.

"Where's your father?" Test said.

"I don't know, upstairs," Elizabeth said.

"You two need to go upstairs in five and tell your father to start your bath," Test said, returning to her work.

At the back of the file, she discovered the list of attendees for Keep at It Casting's auditions held at the Double Black Diamond.

There were eleven sign-up sheets. Forty names per sheet. Nearly 450 names. No, twice that. The sheets were double sided.

Test took an apple from the bowl on the island and took a bite. It was one of the last apples from those she and the family had picked in September. It had gone soft and mealy. She was tempted to toss it, but was too hungry.

"Ow!" Elizabeth shrieked.

Jesus, Test thought. How was she supposed to get any work done? Where was Claude? If he couldn't help out when she needed him to, so she could find a balance, she'd have to take all her work to the station.

"Tell me where it is!" George shouted.

"Enough! There is no shouting in this house!" Test shouted, cringing as she said it.

"You just shouted!" Elizabeth shouted.

"I'm allowed, believe me," Test said.

"What's going on in here?" Claude said.

"Where've you been?" Test said.

"Upstairs, in the bathroom."

"Didn't you hear them?"

"Of course I heard. It wasn't going to do any good to shout from upstairs when I couldn't back it up." Claude pointed at the kids. "Upstairs, both of you. Let's go. Bath time."

"But she hid my car," George said.

"And instead of sharing, you torture her? Upstairs. Come on."

With the kids stomping and muttering their way upstairs, Test took another bite of the apple and was about to return to studying the list when it struck her.

Jesus.

She picked up her phone and called Rath. When he picked up, she said, "Why do we torture?"

"What?" Rath said. "What are you saying?"

"Why do we torture?"

"To get sick kicks out of seeing a person suffer."

"You're seeing it wrong. Like I was. Why do *we* torture? Entities? Governments? The mob?"

"Shit," Rath said.

"Right. To extract information. Maybe Jamie Drake and Lucille Forte were targeted. Because they knew something?"

"What information could teenage girls have?"

"No clue. But maybe he targeted them specifically. Because

they knew something. About him. Somehow. He tortured them not for kicks or pleasure. For information. Maybe Dana Clark is being held somewhere and— "

"But both girls are so far apart, different countries, can both have the same important information? And the same info a woman in her forties would have? Where does that leave us with the Quebec girls from the early nineties? And Preacher?"

"I don't *know*. But it doesn't exclude Preacher, necessarily."

"True. Keep after it. Dig and find the girls' common ground, if there is any, and we may get an idea about who they knew in common and what they might know."

Test hung up.

She returned to the files in peace, underscoring each name with a ruler as she went so as not to miss any.

She searched for Abby Land and Jamie Drake.

Halfway through, she found both. Jamie Drake right above Abby Land.

Test's breathing slowed. Both names. Right there in black ink.

The two girls had befriended each other over acting, so why was Test surprised to see their names on this list? Why *wouldn't* the girls travel a couple hours to audition for a *movie*?

The two names did not give her as much pause as the notepad from the Double Black Diamond Rath had found in Wilks's bedroom. Wilks might have acquired the notepad anywhere—Test owned plenty of pens and notepads from places she'd never visited. That theory didn't float anymore. It could not be coincidence that Mandy Wilks had a DBD notepad, and both her killer and a friend of her killer, now murdered herself, had been to the same resort.

In the file, there was one more person of interest mentioned linked to the resort at the time Mandy Wilks's case was being investigated.

Boyd Pratt.

Grout had run into Pratt at the DBD when there to interview staff about Wilks's notepad. Pratt had later proved he was at the DBD to meet a woman about a private adoption he was trying to arrange for him and his wife. The adoption agency was under investigation, but Pratt was dropped as a suspect.

Test opened her laptop and typed in notes.

MANDY WILKS: DBD notepad. No witnesses put her at DBD.
   Murdered by Abby Land.
ABBY LAND: Attended audition at resort October 12.
   Murdered Mandy Wilks.
JAMIE DRAKE: Attended audition with Abby Land. Oct 12.
   Tortured and murdered by hanging. Murderer unknown.
   Suspects? Ned Preacher? Luke Montgomery????
BOYD PRATT III: At DBD Resort for adoption. Not a suspect
   for Wilks's murder.
LUKE MONTGOMERY: no connection to DBD. He is Abby
   Land's supposed "motive" for killing Mandy Wilks. He
   claims he doesn't know Land or Wilks.

What did any of this prove?

Not a thing.

Test looked deeper into Grout's notes about the Double Black Diamond.

What was this?

Boyd Pratt had been at the DBD at least three times: the day

Grout had run into him, as well as earlier on September 26 and October 12.

The day of the audition.

Pratt, Land, and Drake were all at the DBD on the same day? And Mandy Wilks had a notepad from the resort.

Test took a bite of apple. Its punky flesh had gone brown and nasty where it was exposed to the air. She tossed it in the trash and did what she thought inconceivable just minutes before: she called Grout.

"I DIDN'T TRUST that prig from the start," Grout said when Test asked him about Pratt. "But I chalked my prejudice up to disgust for all pricks born with a silver spoon up their ass."

Test had to admit part of her missed Grout's unvarnished takes, even if she disagreed with him most of the time. He was irascible, even more so than Rath, who somehow managed to remain cool while simmering. Not Grout. His evisceration now of the wealthy, and his jealousy of them and insinuation that money scrubbed life of all problems, was naive. Its parallels to Abby Land's jealousy over Mandy Wilks's beauty were not lost on Test.

"What made you suspect Pratt, besides the spoon up his ass?" she said.

"Besides the fact he was at the resort that matched Mandy Wilks's notepad, a resort nearly a three-hour drive from his estate, a long drive for a big step down in luxury and privacy from the estate? The way he *is*. Arrogant. Entitled. Superior. A wolf in creep's clothing.

"He and his wife lost their only child, a young teenage daughter, a year ago and were desperate to have another, but couldn't. So they sought adoption. Pratt didn't want to adopt just *any* baby. He *demanded* a white, *American* male from 'good stock.' After losing a daughter to leukemia? It was as if he finally had a chance to correct the mistake he believed his daughter was."

"But you had no evidence?"

"If I'd had evidence, I'd have brought him in for questioning, if not arrested him. I interviewed him at his *estate*. The family's estate—thousands of acres on the lake, guest houses and cabins. Technically I guess half of it is his, though Pratt himself seems to have no job. He'd probably be homeless if he hadn't won the parent lottery."

"You really like this guy," Test said.

"He's a catch, if you like a pompous ass in tweed and moleskin and Chameau boots who looks like he just got back from a driven shoot in the Hebrides."

"A what? Where?"

"Skip it. Why call me? It's all there."

"Abby Land and Jamie Drake. They were on the audition list. The same day Pratt was there. That's not coincidence."

"I agree."

"That's a first."

"As your boss, I took the other side to keep you thinking of theories other than your own. On your toes. I don't have to bother with that shit now. You'll want a chat with him. How I'd love to grill him like a cheap steak. I miss that part. I miss most of it."

Test wondered if Grout were being more agreeable the past five minutes than in the previous five years because he wanted back in.

"What should I expect from him?" Test said.

"Arrogance, deflection. BS and subtle threats."

"You found no one who could ID Mandy Wilks? No indication she'd been there at all? You have no notes speculating if you thought Wilks was at the resort or not."

"I had no evidence. I suspected. With the notepad from the resort. It's not a place she could afford. But no proof to suggest she'd been there. Now, though, with the other two girls being there, same day as Pratt, I think it's a lock she got the notepad from the resort herself. She was there."

"Were the pads available in the rooms or out in common areas, or only at the concierge? Only for employees?"

"They're called *team members*. But the notepads are in the rooms."

"All of them, or just business suites?"

"You have a lot to look into. I wish I could help more." Grout sounded forlorn.

"I wish you could, too," Test found herself saying, despite her self-interest.

57

Test decided to surprise Pratt. Catch the target unaware. She thought about doing it alone. Decided against it. She'd agreed to work together; she needed to honor it, even if Rath did not.

She phoned Rath and informed him of what she'd discovered, and her plan to surprise Pratt.

"Tomorrow?" he said. "We *need* to meet with Preacher's other prison buddy, Glade, in Concord. We can't sit on that."

"We will, first thing, day after. And I'll put Larkin and another officer on alternating shifts on the main drag out of Forgotten Gorge Road. Preacher won't be able make a move. I expect the affidavit to be processed and Preacher made an official material witness any time. When it is, we haul him in and keep him for seventy-two."

"What time do we hit the road for Pratt."

"Before first light. This fog is a bitch."

58

Rachel lay awake, unable to sleep as Felix snored beside her. It was not his snoring that kept her awake. It was every other noise. Each tick of the radiator, rattle of wind at the window, or footstep outside in the hallway made her suck in her breath in the dark, afraid to move, certain she and Felix were not alone, that the sound of her very next heartbeat would incite an intruder to leap from the shadows and prey on her.

It was insane, of course. The door was locked. She had a *gun*. They were safe. That's what she told herself over and over, her new mantra: *You are safe. You have a gun.*

Rachel sneaked out of bed and sat perched at the edge of a chair at the window table, feet lightly drumming on the floor and fingernails tapping on the track pad of her laptop as the laptop warmed up.

She opened her Internet browser. She checked the site she'd checked a hundred times in two days.

There. There it was. Finally.

She exhaled with the kind of relief she had not felt since receiving her acceptance from Johnson State the previous spring. In fact, it was a kind of relief she had never known. It left her exhilarated and washed out all at once.

Preacher's picture and rap sheet were up on the sex offenders website.

Preacher. And his address.

Her skin itched as she considered what she was going to do now that she had his address.

She wanted a look at his location. She used Google Earth to zoom in the satellite image. Preacher had chosen a remote, private spot to live. The house was barely visible through the screen of trees at the end of a trickle of a dirt road in the woods. Mud now, with this rain. She had no car, and even if her Civic were running, she'd need four-wheel drive to get up there in these conditions.

Rachel took the revolver out of her backpack, checked that it was loaded. It was. She'd known it was; she'd loaded it herself and checked it at least a dozen times already since breakfast yesterday.

She zoomed in on Preacher's residence.

She did not know what she was going to do, exactly. But she *was* going to confront him. She had to do that, at least. Blindside him.

If she were able to disarm him with surprise, and was literally armed herself, she felt confident whatever needed to happen, whatever was destined to happen between them, would. She could not just hunker and hide. Wait it out. Expect Felix or her father to *do* something.

Why should everyone else act on her behalf?

She looked at the satellite map of Preacher's lair once more. The nearest house was two miles away.

Rachel tucked herself back under the bedcovers and fell asleep wondering if a gunshot could be heard from that distance.

PART IV

59

Wednesday, November 9, 2011

Test and Rath watched the entry gate of the estate from Test's Peugeot wedged between two luxury SUVs in the visitor lot of the estate's Farm Stand Gift Shop. The estate was, for tax purposes Test supposed, not officially called an estate but an "agricultural education center." Put a few cows and sheep in a field, make some maple syrup and cheese, and presto, a family who can afford fifteen hundred acres and five miles of premier lakefront that sells for twenty grand a square foot is now a nonprofit with no property taxes.

Test sipped coffee from her Thermos as Rath ate a nasty-looking sandwich smelling of pickles. She hoped the scent of pickles cloaked her car's ripe odor that had proved to be a pair of old running shoes after all. She'd cleaned out the car of kids' toys and gear, crayons and coloring books, as best as she was able in a hurry. Found a few crayons that had melted in the summer, then hardened to globs that she'd need a chisel to remove. So be it. Rath looked like he'd showered, but a certain queer stink rose from that awful Johnson wool jacket of his.

"I can't believe there's fog here, too," Test said. She and Rath had not spoken most of the long drive, except to strategize about who would ask Pratt what. It was decided that Test would lead.

"It's following us," Rath said. "The fog."

Test had not known fog to ever be so widespread, so seemingly permanent. The weatherman, *meteorologist,* had explained it was a rare phenomenon due to a rainy mild front stalled over northern New England, combined with all the snow melting from the cold ground.

A wind hammered out of the west, off the nearby lake, thinning the fog, enough to make out the massive, stately oak trees along the stone drive that led through rolling hills to the heart of the estate.

A Range Rover appeared at the crest of the road, working its way toward the gate.

Test screwed the cap back on her Thermos and started her car.

The Range Rover raced through the gatehouse at a reckless speed.

Test checked the license plate number. It was Pratt's. Test caught a glimpse of the driver. Boyd Pratt III. A woman rode shotgun.

Test pulled out and followed at a distance.

The vehicle rode south along a road bordered with oaks not nearly as impressive as those of the estate.

Pratt drove fast, too fast. Fifty miles per hour in a 35 zone. In the fog.

Test could have pulled him over, but that would have gone against her plan.

The road took a lazy bend out of the trees, passed a school, and crossed railroad tracks to bring Test to a red light, just behind the Range Rover. The town center. An inn with Adirondack chairs aligned on its massive porch occupied the near corner out of Test's window. A stone building whose sign announced WINE & COFFEE sat across the intersection.

The light changed. The Range Rover charged across straight into the parking lot of the wine shop.

Before the Rover was settled to a stop, its two front doors were slung open.

Pratt stepped down from the vehicle and pulled on a tweed driver's cap, giving it a contrived cockeyed angle over one eyebrow. He peeled leather driver's gloves off his fingers and tucked them into his Barbour coat's pocket. He wasn't wearing the moleskin trousers Grout had described, but his wide-wale cords, of a goldenrod hue, ballooned absurdly, tucked into Le Chameau rubber boots. He looked like he should have a pair of spaniels leaping at his heels, a shotgun broken over his shoulder. Test wondered where his pipe was. Surely he smoked a pipe.

"Fucking dipshit," Rath said.

Victoria Pratt, tall, fit, and statuesque, looking a good fifteen years younger than Boyd, was dressed, unlike her husband, in line with the fashions of the present century. She pulled the collar of a Marmot jacket to her throat, the jacket's fit impeccable, as if custom tailored. She was the rare and reviled type of woman on whom any article of clothing fit precisely, effortlessly, like the riding jodhpurs and the leather riding boots she wore now with a casual grace absent any of the haughtiness with which anyone else wore such attire. Her hair could be a mess, Test mused, but it would be a glorious, perfect mess. Tousled. Her hair was not a mess now; it was slung back in a long sleek ponytail of a magnificent blond shade that, if not natural, had cost her hundreds of dollars to look as if it were. Test stamped out a hot ember of jealousy as she got out of her car between the shop and the couple, Victoria Pratt striding toward the store as Pratt reached for her elbow but missed it.

Rath got out of the Peugeot just as Pratt and the woman approached and Test said, "Excuse me."

The couple ignored her.

"Excuse me," Test said, louder, and stepped in the path of Pratt. "Boyd."

Victoria Pratt eyed Test with the leery look of a wife whose antennae are raised by a strange woman who addresses the husband yet pays no mind to the wife.

Rath hung back, as discussed.

Boyd Pratt glowered at Test. *What is this? Who is this woman in a baggy, pilled EMS fleece jacket, shouting at* me?

His wife studied Test with eyes as green as the Caribbean.

Pratt started to power around Test and charge inside, as if the store were about to close and if he didn't get inside he'd lose the deal of the century.

"Mr. Pratt," Test said.

"*Boyd*," the wife said. "*Hale*."

Test thought for a moment that Victoria Pratt had said "heel," and in fact was not certain she hadn't. Whatever the case, Boyd Hale Pratt III heeled as his wife shot Test an apologetic look of futility. Husbands.

Pratt stopped. With a huff, he pivoted to face Test and Rath. "Yes?" he said.

"I'm Detective Sonja Test."

Pratt raised an eyebrow, doubtful. "I know the police in town. I don't believe you're one of them." Pratt made to turn away.

"And this is Detective Rath," Test said. "Canaan Police."

"I see."

"I'd like to speak to you," Test said.

Pratt sized up Rath. "You, I know. I've seen. On television."

"What is it, Officer?" Victoria Pratt said with the faintest shadow of an accent Rath could not quite place.

"I've never been to Canaan," Boyd said. "What could you want a word with me about?"

Test spotted a picnic table on the shop porch. "Let's sit. I'll explain. I won't keep you more than ten minutes."

"I don't have ten minutes," Pratt said.

"Yes, we do," said his wife.

Test and Rath sat on one side of the picnic table, Victoria Pratt on the other side. Boyd remained standing. He pulled back his coat sleeve and glanced at a gold watch gaudy with diamonds and gems. "Nine and a half minutes."

"Do you know Abby Land or Jamie Drake?" Test said, coming straight at him.

"Who?" Pratt said. Test wondered if he was trying to buy time by asking her to repeat herself, a technique politicians and manipulators used to gather their thoughts, gauge the enemy, and prepare a mollifying answer instead of a truthful one.

Victoria Pratt looked at her husband, then back to Test. The mention of female names had touched a nerve.

"Abby Land and Jamie Drake," Rath said.

"Never heard of them."

"Perhaps not their names." Test took out photos of each of the girls. "How about their faces?"

Pratt glanced at the photos. "No."

The wife looked at the photos more closely, with at least feigned respect for Rath and Test.

"Look at them closely," Test said.

Pratt gave a petulant sigh and gaped. "No."

"Why are you asking my husband about these girls?" Victoria Pratt seemed to sense this was important in a way to which Boyd was oblivious, or pretending to be oblivious. But the wife's concerns were likely pedestrian, suspicion of an unfaithful husband, compared to why Rath and Test had paid this visit.

"Mandy Wilks? Did you know her?" Rath said.

Pratt licked his lips. "Her? Again?"

"Who?" Victoria said, more than suspicion in her voice now. Worry. Perhaps anger. Maybe even fear of not so much wondering how well she knew her husband, but that she knew him all too well. His philandering. The look she gave her husband could have melted iron.

"I didn't know her," Pratt said. "I told the officer that weeks ago. From what I gather you've resolved all that mess up your way."

"Who are these girls?" Victoria said, as if trying to defuse the rising tension.

Pratt glanced at his watch. "Seven minutes. I suggest you lay out your reason for being here."

"You'll speak to us for however long it takes." Test was not playing this game. She was not abiding by his schedule or exposing her reasons for being here. Pratt knew the girls. Somehow. He knew them. All of them.

"What was your reason for being at the Double Black Diamond Resort on October twelfth?" Rath said.

"I've been over this." He took off his cap and put it back on, more snugly. "I met about a possible adoption."

"It's true." Victoria Pratt slipped a pair of sunglasses out from her jacket pocket and put them on. They were the colossal, retro style à la Audrey Hepburn that swallowed half the face and seemed absurd on most women, in a way that reminded Test of an insect. On Victoria Pratt they were, of course, impeccable, their light pink frame coordinated exquisitely with her French manicure.

"You wanted a boy, a son, American, white, from good stock, is that correct?" Rath stared Pratt in the eye.

"How did you acquire personal information?" Pratt said.

"Nothing is personal in a murder investigation," Rath said. "About the adoption."

"Your own daughter is adopted, if I read recent stories correctly," Boyd Pratt said.

"Murder investigation?" Victoria said. "How does that have anything to do with us? Our pursuit of adoption? You can't just ask my husband willy-nilly questions and expect—" Her anger had taken a turn, directed now at Test and Rath. Her husband may have been a heel or a cheat, but murder? One had to draw the line.

"If you think I left my home at four this morning to ask willy-nilly questions, you are mistaken. My questions have very specific reasons, none of which you need to know," Test said.

"Five minutes," Pratt said.

"Abby and Jamie. Both were at the Double Black Diamond when you were there October twelfth," Rath said.

"Small world," Pratt said.

"Too small for our liking," Test said, "and for your own good. Abby Land is in jail for murdering Mandy Wilks."

"What are you implying?" Victoria said. Test could not see the woman's eyes behind her sunglasses, but she could feel them on her; she was giving Test her undivided attention. Unlike Pratt who looked off toward the store, affecting superiority through boredom.

"I know all this," Pratt said. "It's old news."

"And Jamie Drake was found hanged," Test said.

Victoria Pratt went so stiff she looked as if she might shatter. "*Suicide*. What could that possibly have to do—"

"Murdered," Rath said.

That got Pratt's attention, though he tried to conceal it. At the word *murder*, he'd just managed to stop himself from jerking his head to face Test. Had he done it? Killed Jamie after torturing her to get information from her? But what information? What could she know? And Pratt's flinch seemed one of surprise. Or was he just as practiced an actor as he was an ass?

Pratt glanced at his wife. He then fixed his eyes on Test. "It's got nothing to do with me."

"You see our concern, though," Test said, nodding at the wife whose eyes remained hidden behind her sunglasses. Test wanted to swipe the glasses off the woman's face, so she could read her eyes, see if there were fear of her husband in them, fear of ideas formulating in her mind about her dear, rich hubby. "Both these girls were at the resort at the same time as your husband."

"He and five hundred other guests. It has nothing to do with him, as he just stated." She removed her sunglasses, her eyes set on Test's. Ice cold. She'd protect her husband. Protect her way of life. "The time my husband has granted you is up. This is rather ridiculous, you ambushing us like this."

"I'll need to know your whereabouts this past Saturday," Rath said to Pratt.

"Will you now?" Pratt said. Test could see him straining not to smile. "You'll have to *know my whereabouts*? You're something. The both of you, driving all this way for nothing in a car that looks like it might disintegrate any second. Doesn't the Canaan Police Department provide vehicles?"

The wife raised an eyebrow at her husband. They were on the same team now. "Tell her," she said to him.

"I was here, in town," Pratt said.

"Anyone who can verify this?" Test said. "Besides your wife?"

"He was breaking ground for the new town library he's building. Half the town was here," Victoria Pratt said.

Test's confidence flagged.

"You can confirm this?" Test said to Pratt.

"Google it," the wife said. "It made the front page of the *Free Press* and was aired on the local news. Maybe if you'd checked into that *first,* you'd not have wasted our time. Now, please. We'd like to have our day back."

60

Back home after a long day, Rath was too keyed up to sleep.
He took out his .30-06 Springfield 760 rifle and laid it on
the kitchen table to disassemble it as he drank a beer or three.
Breaking down the weapon was an annual ritual he usually per-
formed in October to prepare for rifle season. He'd not found
the time this year, but now, tonight, he needed to take on a task
natural to him, to the season. Do something for himself, something that concentrated his focus on the minutiae at hand, and
nothing else.

There were seventy separate parts to his Springfield pump action 760 carbine. Rath knew each one by feel, blindfolded, from
the action bar lock and the bolt assembly, to the hammer spring
trigger pin and rear-sight aperture.

He aligned his tools and rags and snake bore cleaner, solvent
and oil.

He had it all set up, ready to go when his phone buzzed. He
ignored it.

The first time.

Not the second time.

Not at this late hour. He feared it could not be good, so could not be ignored altogether.

It was a Quebec number by the looks, though unfamiliar.

Rath answered. "Hello?"

"I have something for you, Inspector."

"Who is this?"

"Pardon, Inspector Hubert. Champine has arranged for you to meet the owner of Chez Darlene."

For a moment Rath thought he was being played by Grout. Except Grout had no idea of Hubert's or Champine's names, nor could he fake a Quebec number.

"What is it?" Rath said, "Why?"

"We have checked deeper. We have learned despite Lucille Forte being from a what you say, good family, she worked at this place. This Chez Darlene."

"Are you shitting me?" Rath said.

"*Excusez-moi?*"

"Nothing. Sorry."

"*La mise en place est sur cent trente trois Nord.* Champine visited the owner. Alex Poitras. Champine got nothing, but thinks perhaps if it is linked to an American crime, too, one that will make bad news for American customers, well, perhaps a visit from an American inspector. If you want to see this owner *a midi,* noon, Champine will—"

"I know the place," Rath said.

"*Mais oui. Bon. Bonne nuit.*"

As soon as Hubert hung up, Rath realized he was in a jam. He and Test needed to get down to Concord, New Hampshire, and get the jump on that Timothy Glade.

They needed to do it together. Glade was a violent, unhinged sort; Rath did not want Test approaching him alone.

If he had time after Chez Darlene, maybe they could make the run. He texted Test and explained. He knew she'd be miffed about his not making it to Concord, and she'd want to hit Quebec with him. She'd be even more ripped when she read that he wanted her to take shifts out on the road by Preacher's place. Tail Preacher if he so much as slithered on his belly from the place.

He didn't look at her text when she shot back an instantaneous response.

61

Thursday, November 10, 2011

At 11:30 A.M., Rath pulled off 133 Nord, just past the twenty-foot silhouette of the naked woman and into Chez Darlene's parking lot. The sign was sooted grimy and gray with road grit and exhaust fumes from generations of passing vehicles. A smaller modest sign, black with soiled white lettering read: DAN-SEUSES NUES OUVERT 24 HEURES TOUS LES JOURS. Nude Dancers 24 hours every day.

A lot of girls, Rath thought. Around the clock like that.

The one-story, cinder-block building, windowless and painted black, had a flat roof that must have been a bear to shovel after a heavy snowfall.

He drove the Scout around back. It was 11:34 A.M. on a weekday morning, mid-November, and the spacious back lot was nearly full with pickup trucks and sedans. The lot was not visible from the road: local family and businessmen did not need their vehicles seen by passersby.

The lot abutted a foggy cornfield. To the north, a dairy barn and three towering grain silos. Just south, on the roof of a shuttered, roadside donut shop circa 1950s, perched a gargantuan orange donut that Rath believed used to spin in a slow, drunken manner, though perhaps it had only been he who had spun slowly and drunkenly.

He trod to the metal door at the back of the club.

His phone buzzed. Grout. He left a voice mail. Rath gave it a quick listen. *You're blowing me off again. Rain date, tomorrow, same time and place on the river. We need to talk.*

Rath hauled open the solid door and was clobbered by the Lenny Kravitz cover of "American Woman" detonating from down a hall as dark as a rat tunnel, at the mouth of which strobed gaudy red and green lights. Rath wondered if the color of the lights was Chez Darlene's nod to the coming Christmas season.

Out of the dark stepped a bald bouncer with a goatee and a serpent tattoo curled around the edge of his left eye. His white button-down shirt lay open at the neck to display a gold chain as thick as a jump rope. "Three," he said with a French accent. He knew an Anglo-American when he saw one.

Rath dug out a five from his Carhartts and handed it to the bouncer who stamped the back of Rath's hand with a female silhouette much like the sign out front. He did not offer Rath change.

Rath walked down the dark throat of the corridor toward the flashing lights and din. The perfumed air almost, but not quite, cloaked the greasy, bodily odors lurking in the place, which would have been as dark as a shut tomb if not for the red and green strobe lights fracturing the darkness every millisecond.

Rath had the sensation of being trapped in the complete dark, and that the schizophrenic lights, and the images revealed to him in this close space, were in his mind alone, part of a macabre and base hallucination. The deafening music assailed his eardrums.

The walls of the dark, low-ceilinged room, made up of solid mirror, reflected the images of themselves back to themselves infinitely, so at first Rath thought the place was more expansive than he'd remembered, that there were dozens of girls performing on as many cramped stages. But no. There were just four girls, working their bodies in rote gyrations meant to be erotic, or at least raunchy and titillating, but left Rath cold. He did not know which inspired greater pity, the young girl nearest him, closer to sixteen than to twenty years old, or the dancer pushing a very hard fifty. The young girl, in blond pigtails and a Santa's elf getup, was white as milk; the older woman, black as coal.

The few spaces not dedicated to mirrors were given to flat-screen TVs playing varied hard-core pornography scenes. Orgies, threesomes, women on women. With the TVs sound muted, the faces on the screens looked distorted with anguish instead of the ecstasy for which Rath supposed they were striving. The TVs had not been here years ago.

Anger at the owner Alex Poitras, and disgust at himself for ever having set foot in here years ago, edged out Rath's pity for the dancers.

At tables circling the stages, half occupied by women, patrons stared with blank eyes at the dancers and TVs, lips slightly parted.

To the left was the bar. Lit in a red, liquid, lava lamp glow.

A tall woman in an electric blue wig and brutally kohled eyes stood behind the bar and served a drink to a man whose eyes were riveted to the climactic scene playing out on the TV behind the bar. The Money Shot, Rath and his buddies had called it, no second thought. No thought at all.

The place was claustrophobic, stifling, the air dead.

Rath tried to plant his eyes somewhere so they would not be beset by the images of flesh, but had trouble doing so. He supposed this was the point.

Beyond the bar, behind the drawn black curtains, were the VIP stages, and the private booths.

The bartender walked up to him as "American Woman" faded and "Shook Me" started up. The music was not new. The music was old and unchanged.

"Yes?" the bartender said. She saw through Rath. She was not sure if he was a cop or not, but she knew he wasn't here for what the place offered.

"I'm here to see the owner. Alex Poitras."

The woman laughed. "I sincerely doubt that, honey."

"I was told to meet him in his office. It's about a girl who worked here."

"It's always about a girl who works here."

"Not up there," Rath said, referring to the dance stage. He nodded to the kitchen door behind the bar.

"Her? She didn't show for her shift for two straight days. No call, no text, just left me hanging. Shocker. Teenagers these—"

"She's dead. Her body was found twenty kilometers from here. So maybe you could cut her some slack."

The woman washed a glass in the sink at her hip.

"Alex is expecting me," Rath said. "It was set up."

"Alex's office is not on-site."

"I'm a cop."

"Again. Shocker."

"From the States."

"The shocks just keep coming."

"A Chief Inspector Hubert set up the meeting. They must have thought I knew the office was separate from this place, or Inspector Champine and I would sort it out."

"Tightly run ship."

"Can you reach Alex, let him know."

"Yeah. Sure. I'll do that." She pulled a cell phone from her apron pocket and texted. Waited, clicking a long, fake fingernail on her teeth.

She looked up from her phone.

"Alex says you're late. If you can get to the city inside thirty minutes, you can have a half hour."

"Where?"

"Hotel Gault. *Quatre cent quarante* St. Helene. Old Montreal. The penthouse apartment. Third floor; look for the red door."

Outside, even the degraded light of the gray day forced Rath to squint and blink. His skin was oily and hot, as if he'd had a plastic bag over his head while inside.

How had he ever come here? Not just as a stupid teenager, but as a man, a cop?

In the Scout, Rath tried to breathe as he watched three young men and a woman stagger out of an SUV laughing as they cavorted to the door of the club.

The thought came hurtling to his mind before he could drive it away: *You'd still be coming to places like this and never have changed if you hadn't had to raise Rachel. She saved you.*

She had.

Because Preacher murdered her mother.

Rath shook his head to try to rid the thought that plagued him most: that good had come of Preacher's murders. Yet, it was true. Rath was a better person because Preacher had murdered his sister.

62

In Montreal, Rath exited 10 Ouest onto the ramp, the La Ronde Monstre, the tallest wooden roller coaster on earth cresting in the distance on the banks of the St. Lawrence.

Rath had never been to Old Montreal, and instead of heading straight into downtown as he'd done on every other visit, he veered right, North onto Rue Notre-Dame. Luxury sedans and SUVs swam and powered past, making the rattling Scout seem as anachronistic as rabbit ears.

The four-story Hotel Gault, with its gray stone and terraced top floor, stretched from the lobby entrance at the corner down the twin blocks of Rue Sainte-Hélène and Rue Récollets. The grandeur of its architecture felt like a different world from the Chez Darlene, but it was the same world, where one business bank-rolled the other.

Rath drove past a valet out front, parked on the street, but had no Canadian coins to feed the meter.

As the doorman held the door, Rath realized the smallest bill he had was a $10. It didn't matter. His mother had survived on tips for two decades; he knew its toll.

In the hush of the stylish lobby with its blond wood accents, modern furniture, high ornate ceiling, and a wall of exposed brick as a gesture to its past, Rath handed a ten-spot to the doorman who took it with a nod and a *merci*.

Rath rode an elevator to the third floor. Its rise was so silent and rapid, he thought for a moment he was still on the ground floor when the doors opened.

He stepped into a quiet hallway, his footfalls silent on the silver carpet as he walked to a red door as described by the bartender.

He knocked on the door, alone in the empty hallway.

The door opened, and an Asian woman, perhaps in her sixties, stood before him, her hair white as snow, her silver metallic eyeliner flickering so much at first Rath thought she was about to cry. *"Bonjour. Monsieur Rath, entrez."*

Rath stepped inside.

The woman closed the door behind him. Her silver toenails matched the carpet into which her bare feet sank as she minced across to the French windows that looked out to what would have been a view of the St. Lawrence if not for the fog.

The suite featured more blond wood, the kitchen all stainless steel and hard edges, opening to the living area where the sharpness softened to sculpted colorful furniture and the requisite exposed brick wall. Flames jigged in the fireplace. A gas fire. On and off with a switch. No calming scent of wood smoke, no dancing sparks or snap and hiss and sigh of sagging logs as they burned down and collapsed. No ashes. Just clean orange flames tinted blue at their roots. The woman stared at him from across the room in her black tailored suit. "What can I do for you?"

"I'm here to see Alex."

"Yes."

She continued to stare at him, still as a deer, one eyebrow arced as if to prompt him to say more.

"He was expecting me," Rath said.

"No, he wasn't."

"He was. It was set up by Inspector Hubert, but wires were crossed as to where to meet. Alex told a woman at his . . . establishment, to come within a half hour and—"

"Hmm. There is no he. I am Alex."

Rath's confusion cleared.

"My parents did not possess forethought," Alex said, as she'd likely said a thousand times. "What do you want?"

"To speak to you about a girl."

"*Mai oui.* Always. *Les filles.*"

"Not girls. A girl. She worked at your club."

"Hmm. Which club? Not that it matters. I don't know the names or the faces. I don't hire them. I pay people to do that, operate, oversee. Hmm. I *own* the business so I do not have to *run* the business. You understand."

"How does a woman end up owning a place like that?" Rath said before he'd thought better of it.

"A place like?"

He should have known. Whatever justification she'd encased herself in to operate a place like Chez Darlene was impervious to banal questions from the outside; her stock defense was in ready supply. And who was he to ask, a guy who'd once coughed up thousands of dollars for lap dances over a half-dozen years at

Chez Darlene and a dozen clubs like it, never a thought where his money went. His justification was the same as Alex's: the clubs were legal. The girls were adults. No one forced them to do what they did. Excuses. And lies.

"I know what happens in those places," Rath said.

"*Mais oui.*"

"It's one thing for a man to operate a—" Rath said.

"*Oh?* Is it? Is *it* one thing for a man, and another thing for a woman? What would you know about being a woman? Hmm. You're a man, you can't know what it is to be a woman. Even if you were one of those poor confused trans darlings I keep for certain clientele, you still could not *know. Feel?* Perhaps. But *feeling* is not *knowing.* You can't *know* what it is to be something if you are *not* that thing."

"I mean, how did you come to own Chez Darlene."

"I own it, and many others, because it was my husband's. He was shot in the back of the head. Three blocks from here, three years ago, along the banks of the river. They suspected me, for a while. Of course. I took his businesses over. I used to dance. Formally trained in ballet. But that kind of dance leaves you with broken-down ankles and a broken-down bank account. Hmm. Now look at me."

She looked around the penthouse that had to run a grand a day. "It's not all sob stories. Girls come. Girls go. Some are alcoholics. Some addicts. Some abused. Raped. Some make horrible, immature, *infantile,* decisions. Are their own worst enemies. Date dicks. Some have their shit together. Save money. Stay straight. How does that make them any different from other girls their age?"

She had her spiel down all right. Hermetically sealed against argument, she supposed.

"You think the girl who works in a bookstore or a coffee shop has no booze problem or pill problem or coke problem?" she continued. "No strange kinks? She's never been abused or raped or made bad decisions, dated dicks. No daddy issues? She's a square, straight-A saint destined to live happily ever after. Is that it? Is that the drivel you're pushing?"

"I'm not pushing anything. I want to know about one specific girl. Lucille Forte. She worked at Chez Darlene."

"If she worked there, she isn't a girl. She's eighteen, minimum, a woman."

"She didn't dance. She was fifteen; she worked in the kitchen. I can't get anywhere with the people who *oversee* your place. She was found dead alongside the road. Hanged. Tortured. Like someone wanted to get information from her."

"*Maman.*"

Rath wheeled around to see a teenage girl, a *young woman*, as Alex would have it, shuffle into the kitchen from the hallway that must have led to the bedrooms. She stood at the slate counter, palms pressed on its surface as she stretched her neck to work kinks out of it. Her long black ribbed turtleneck draped down to the top pockets of baggy pants of the kind Rath had not seen since Lake Placid hosted the Olympics. Cargo pants. She was barefoot. Like her maman. Her eyes and cheeks were puffy with sleep, her face bare of makeup. She chewed on a strand of her straight black hair as she looked past Rath at Alex. "*Avez-tu vu le chargeur de mon téléphone?*"

"*Vérifiez la prise près de mon bureau.*"

"*J'ai fait.*"

"*Votre sac d'école.*"

"*J'ai fait.*"

"*Je ne sais pas.*"

"*Oooph. Puis-je utiliser le tien?*"

"*Il est dans mon sac Longchamp bleu. Dans ma chambre.*"

"*Merci.*" She shuffled back down the hall without a glance at Rath.

Alex rolled an eye. "You have kids?"

"A daughter about that age," Rath said. "She was my niece. Her parents, my sister and sister's husband, were murdered when she was a baby. I adopted her."

Alex Poitras stepped from the window and flipped a wall switch. The fire in the fireplace died. "This explains your need of saving girls and your distaste for my business."

"I don't have to have a daughter to have a distaste for your operation. And I think the person who killed Lucille Forte could be the man who killed my sister. Or he's at least may be involved, somehow. I think he intends to harm my daughter if I can't get a reason to put him away again."

"Why don't *you* put him away? My husband would have put him down like a dog. Never let him walk around. Free."

"I can't risk getting caught, my daughter—"

"Don't *get* caught."

"Criminals always get caught."

She laughed. "I hope you don't believe your own lies. So many girls killed by perverts who are *never* caught. Never pay. How many girls were ruined at the hands of your man? And you do nothing."

"I'm here to do something. To build a case. I can't risk the shame my daughter—"

She laughed harder. A bark. "You'd rather your daughter be killed by the animal who killed her parents than have her live with petty *shame*? You are only shamed if you let yourself be shamed."

"That's not it."

"No. You are afraid. *That's it.* Afraid of prison. Afraid of your conscience. Afraid to pay for your daughter's true safety. You'd rather she die than go to jail for her. You are *un lâche*. Hmm. A coward."

Rath felt dazed, enraged. How had he let the conversation spiral into this cesspool?

He took out a photo of Lucille.

Alex looked at it. "Never met her. I'll take it, see that staff sees it. You sure she worked for me?"

"She did. Maybe under a different name."

"Not with us. Hmm. Everyone, dancers included, is legitimate. Taxes. Specific hours. Citizen or immigrant. Proper papers, work visas. If she worked for me, she worked under her real name, unless she got fake papers she can pass off to a place that can sniff out the best of fakes. I don't need to be shut down for hiring the paperless. Do you have a photo of this man you fear?"

"I don't fear him."

"Hmm."

Rath handed her a photo of Preacher.

"Good looking," she said.

Rath bit back his anger and handed her a piece of paper on which he'd written his name and phone number. He didn't have a card yet, wouldn't be getting one. As soon as this case was closed, he was done. He'd escape into the deep woods to find some peace, track a big buck on the snow, if any snow ever fell. If the case went beyond the end of deer season, maybe he would hop that plane to

the Bahamas and try his hand at bonefish and Kaliks, as Barrons
had proposed.

Alex took a cell phone from her hip pocket, snapped a photo
of the scrap of paper, balled up the paper, and tossed it in the fire
place. She hit the switch and the flames leapt up and turned the
paper to ash. "Where is this Canaan, Vermont? Near Burlington?
I go to Burlington many times."

"It's not anywhere near there."

Alex twitched an index finger toward the door, to indicate it
was time for him to leave.

"Your daughter," Rath said. "She work at Chez Darlene?"

"She works for another business I run."

"Why not a club?"

"Hmm. It is not what you think. That I think she's better than
that, the clubs are beneath her. No. It would not be right for her to
take a shift from girls who *need* the money. And she dances like a
water buffalo."

"What's this other business you own?"

"*Run.* It's mine. Not my husband's. I'm late now to meet with
my buyers and sellers."

"What do you buy and sell?"

"Many things. But mostly books."

"Books?"

"We tend to sell a lot of books at a bookstore."

63

The world was watery and opaque with fog in a way that reminded Rachel of the jars of water in which she'd rinsed watercolor brushes when she was a girl.

The rain pounded, wearying. Rachel had slept in all day, too wiped out from being awake all night after finding Preacher's address. She'd told Felix to go to his earlier and midday classes and she'd meet him on campus for her 4:15. Not to worry. The campus shuttle shelter was fifty feet from the inn. She could manage it. He'd insisted on staying for a while. Missed his two morning classes. But when Rachel still hadn't left bed for so much as her ritual coffee, he'd reluctantly headed out for his midday class.

Rachel had a back-to-back 4:15 English Comp and a 5:30 Soc 101 class. She didn't intend to stay for her 5:30 Soc; she wouldn't have time. She'd meet Felix dutifully before the 4:15, and let him see she was OK. Then, after it, she'd come back to town. Her handgun class was at 5:30. What was more important: a class on sociology, or a class that could save her life?

Ahead on the corner, the shuttle was pulling out from the curb. Rachel ran, too late.

"Damn it," she muttered.

Now she was going to be late. The next shuttle wasn't due for twenty minutes. It would be quicker to hoof it up the steep hill to campus. She might meet Felix in time if she hightailed it.

As she hiked up the hill the box of ammunition rattled and the heavy handgun thwacked against her side.

The trek was perilous in the fog, the shoulder a spit of gravel the width of a bicycle tire. The few cars that drove past were unable to see her until right upon her. She kept pinned to the roadside brush.

She was halfway up, sweating and chugging breaths, when a car slowed beside her. She glanced at it as her hand rested on the zipper of her backpack. The car was an old job. Something her dad would like.

She could just make out enough through the fogged windows that the driver of the car was a man.

The car's window lowered with a squeak.

"Would you like a ride up the hill?" the driver said.

"No," Rachel huffed without giving him a second look, increasing her pace.

"This hill's a killer."

"I'm good."

"Enjoy," the driver said. The car accelerated out of sight. Rachel's heart rattled. *If that man had been Preacher, and he'd wanted to hurt me, he could have done it and no one would have seen it. And I'd never have had a chance to get my gun.* The gun was as useless as a brick in her backpack.

She pulled her jacket collar up tighter to her neck. Not long ago she'd have trusted the stranger and hopped in without a thought, been on campus by now, in time to meet Felix and allay his own fears. No more.

She trudged up the hill as fast as she could.

Toward the top, her cell phone burbled in her jacket pocket; Felix's text tone. She did not take her phone out in the rain. She was all of five minutes late and he'd be after her: WRU? U OK?

Rachel tramped across the muddy green, saw Felix on the steps of Dibden as he searched for her in the crowd of students hustling for the doors from the rain and fog.

She ran up the steps to him, against the flow of students exiting Dibden and put on a smile as she tapped his shoulder. She expected a smile in return, but did not get one. Felix's face was strained with worry and agitation. It pained her to see it, but she did not know what to do to relieve it. If she let him in on everything she was feeling and planning, he would try to stop her, or, worse, try to solve it for her. One trait that attracted Rachel to Felix was he never interfered. Never tried to solve her problems for her. He trusted she could take care of herself. Now. Now, she sensed his wanting to help too much, save her. Make all her worries go away with a magic wand.

As many books as she'd read and movies she'd watched about depraved killers, she'd never read any serious, academic, scientific literature about men of Preacher's nature. It had all been true crime books, pop culture and exploitative, she realized now. Her interests prurient, entertainment. Now, she sincerely wanted to know, *needed* to know, the real, latest science behind what made men like Preacher tick. What drove them to do what they did?

She needed to know so she could prepare herself. Do background research before she went ahead with her plan.

Even now she doubted she could do it, see her plan out to the end. It chilled her. She doubted she was brave enough, or dumb enough, to do what she had in mind. Fear knotted in her gut and left her blood cold at just the thought of ever facing him. But she had to face him. She felt compelled to confront him, to know why he had been in the pet shop. She had gone over and over it. If he'd wanted to hurt her that day, or since, he could have. He would have. Wouldn't he? She could not help but think he had another reason that day other than to hurt her, or even to frighten her. Part of her—the part that was brain-dead, obviously—sensed Preacher wanted to tell her something, in person. Did he want to apologize? It made her sick to think it. What he'd done was far beyond the reach of apology. An apology would cheapen his crime. Still, she wondered, what did he want? What did he have to tell her, or was she simply delusional because she was so exhausted and distraught? And why did she have such a fascination with depraved men like Preacher? Was her obsession a coincidence or born out of her being just upstairs while Preacher murdered her parents and raped her mother? Even if she had no conscious memory, she'd heard it all, what must have been savage screams of pain and fear. How terrified her mother must have been. For herself, and for her baby. Had she died believing her baby was Preacher's next victim?

Rachel wondered now if she was doing exactly as Preacher had hoped, letting him consume her thoughts? Until a few days ago, Felix had been the person other than herself she'd thought of most. He'd been the most important person in her world, the one with whom she'd been most honest. She'd become remote, and deceitful by way of omission. She'd bought a gun without his knowing, was carrying it in her backpack, had been researching Preacher and her parents' murders, making plans, all while pretending she'd been going about her day as she always did. She'd become someone else.

She could not continue the deception. Did not want to continue it. It was not fair to Felix. It was not fair to her, or to them, as a couple. It was not right.

There was only one true way to overcome fear and take away the hold it had on you. That was to face it. To face him. That was Rachel's plan—to confront the man who'd murdered her parents and ask him: *Why?*

She'd borrow a friend's car, take the gun with her, she'd follow him from his home, and take him by surprise in public. And—

"Why are you soaking wet?" Felix said. He did not lean to wrap her in his arms as he always did. "I texted you."

"I missed the shuttle," she said. "I didn't want to take my phone out in the rain."

"You hiked up the hill? Alone? You could have—"

"I wasn't alone. Two other girls missed the shuttle. The damn thing was early. Again. You know how that driver is. Never waits a second."

"Tell the truth."

"I am," she said.

"You're not."

"So I'm a liar?"

"Come on. Don't be like that. Are you depressed about all this business, sleeping all day? Or pissed off? I don't blame you. I *am*. It's messed up. I'd be freaked out. I *am* freaked out. But mostly by you. How you're acting because of it."

"I'm not acting like anything."

"Yes, you are."

"I'm not."

"You suck so bad at lying."

"OK. I'm freaked. Maybe depressed. Hurt. Pissed. OK. It messed me up. I'm sorry."

"You don't have to be sorry." He hugged her but for the first time since she'd met him two months ago, his hug did not melt away her worries. Eight weeks. That's how long she'd known Felix. How well did she even know him? She'd never even met his parents, or his childhood friends. *Stop thinking like that,* she told herself.

"You don't know what it's like," she said, "to have someone watching you, someone who's done what he's done. Who could do it to you. You're a guy. If someone were watching you, you wouldn't have to worry. You're six foot three."

"And all of a hundred and ninety pounds soaking wet."

"That's *eighty* pounds and a foot more than me. You don't get it. Most any guy that tried to hurt you, you could defend yourself. If even a regular guy, five foot eight and a hundred and fifty pounds tries to hurt me, I'm *going to be hurt.*"

"Not if you stick by me. Like we planned. Stick close. For now. That was the agreement. Go to class. Meet after class, and hang out with your boyfriend even more than usual, so you're not alone. That's not so bad, spending more time with your boyfriend, is it?"

"We can't be around each other twenty-four seven. You have your work-study and class schedule. I have mine. They don't match."

"Hang with your friends. And. Screw work-study. We'll explain to them—"

"*No.* I don't want people *knowing.* I don't want a pity party, or *OMG that's like so creepy* from girlfriends who can't relate. No one can relate. And it's no one else's business."

"So we lie," Felix said. "Tell work-study there's something else going on and we can't work for a while. No biggie. They won't care. When this is over, we'll just work more hours."

"And when will *this* be over, exactly?" Rachel said.

Felix shook his head. "I don't know. But you can at least be where you say you're going to be *when* you say you're going to be there," he said. "Every time you make me wait or don't text back right away, my stomach drops. I think the worst." He was right. It was reasonable to have her at least show up when she said she would.

The streams of students filing in and out of the building had dwindled to a few loners pushing through the rain to make it to their next class.

Rachel and Felix stood alone on the steps.

"I gotta get to class," Rachel said. "So do you."

"Meet me here after, OK? Before all this crap, we met after every class anyway. Now this happens and you seem to want to spend less time with me. I don't get it."

Rachel did not get it either. She wanted to spend time with Felix. Of course she did. So why wasn't she? Why was she retreating? "Sure," she said, "I'll meet here after class." She turned to go inside.

Felix reached for her to give her another hug, his fingers grabbing at her backpack. The ammunition rattled and the revolver shifted.

"What's in your pack?" he said.

"Nothing. My tablet."

He took hold of the straps and lifted the backpack. She pulled it back to her.

"It feels like a rock," he said.

"It is, it's a rock for my dad, a hunk of quartz I found a while back. You know he's into geology. Finally going to give it to him. I gotta go." She left Felix standing there and pushed through the doors of the building.

Inside, she climbed the stairs to a window that overlooked the steps and watched her boyfriend who stood with his back to her. He stared out at the rain and fog, his hands jammed in his coat pockets, then looked up toward the sky though there was no sky to see in the fog; Rachel could barely make him out in the mist.

He hunched his shoulders and stepped into the murk.

64

Rath drove south on New Hampshire Interstate 93, the fog hampering progress.

New Hampshire was a peculiar state, the joke being that Vermonters were forced to drive through it to get to Maine and back. The Granite State had a lot of, well, granite, so its trout streams, though cold, clear, and dazzling to the eye, also tended to be devoid of the insect life brook trout needed to thrive, the trout scrawny and stunted. *Racers.* The motto, Live Free or Die, was a bit hyperbolic, too; yet what did one expect from a state that for decades had strapped its identity to a rock outcrop, the Old Man of the Mountain, and slapped the Old Man's image on any tchotchke that took ink. Five years ago, the Old Man had crumbled into the forest below, and the populace had mourned as if for a beloved grandfather. The state's license plate still bore his image.

Rath took the next exit.

Timothy Glade lived with an elderly aunt. Hopefully she

wanted him there; Glade wouldn't be the first violent ex-con to *persuade* an elderly family member to *offer* room and board.

Rath turned left into the Old Man of the Mountain apartment complex.

Most of the vehicles in the lot were at least a decade old. A bulb in one of the parking lot lights was out, the glass fixture shattered.

No one was around, at least not that Rath could tell in the dark and fog.

From out on the highway, an eighteen-wheeler's horn blared.

Rath walked to the door of 64A and knocked.

A dim light shone inside, visible through the shade. From the way it flickered, the light was from a TV screen.

The aunt was likely asleep. A risk of dropping in at random was you might not find your target as planned. Rath knocked louder.

A brighter light flicked on inside.

The door opened.

An elderly woman answered, as brittle and jaundiced looking as dried summer grass, fingers gnarled with arthritis, barely able to work the storm door latch.

"What'd he do?" she said.

She knew.

Yet she helped her nephew anyway. Or abided him. Perhaps abetted him. Old age did not equate to innocence.

"Nothing," Rath said.

"You're not here for nothing," she said.

Yes. She knew. Rath wondered how many generations of this woman's male kin had been in and out of *scrapes* their entire lives.

"Is he in?" Rath said.

"You could find him sleeping on the couch at noon, if you tried then."

"Expect him back anytime soon?"

"I don't expect anything from Timmy. He left four hours ago to run to the drugstore ten minutes away for me."

"To pick up a prescription, or—"

"I know better. Lady nighttime diapers."

The throaty growl of a rotted muffler rose behind Rath.

"Speak of the devil," the aunt said.

A car with a headlight out sped into the lot, rocked over the speed bumps, its underbody grinding and shooting sparks despite the damp asphalt.

It whipped in next to the Scout. A Ford Escort. Late '80s.

Its exhaust backfired, a flame blasting out the tailpipe.

Timothy Glade got out twirling keys around his finger, took the steps two at a time, his head down.

He stopped fast, as if he'd scented Rath.

His head jerked up. At the instant his eyes caught Rath's eyes, he turned and bolted.

Rath chased as Glade fled across the lot toward the woods on the far end. Woods that stretched for miles. If he made it, he'd be gone. Maybe for good.

Rath dug in, gaining fast; too fast.

Glade had stopped and now wheeled around and swung his arm, catching Rath square in the windpipe.

Rath hit the pavement hard, his knees and palms scraping on the asphalt just as his face struck the pavement.

A boot kicked him in the lower back.

Rath reached for his sidearm. He should have drawn it at the start. Been ready.

The boot kicked him again. Rath rolled away, grabbing for Glade's ankle. Rath's throat felt collapsed, as if he were breathing through a reed.

Glade's eyes went wide as he saw a pile of bricks a few feet away. He lunged and grabbed a brick, stood over Rath with it and reared back.

Rath crabbed backward, trying to scurry under a car, but the car was too low for Rath to use to protect himself.

Glade swung the brick down hard. Rath kicked Glade's knee. The knee buckled and the brick struck the car's bumper and glanced off Rath's head.

Rath was pinned against the front of the car.

He reached for his sidearm again.

Glade straddled him, the brick raised, ready to bludgeon.

"Timmy! He's police! Timmy, please!"

Glade glanced behind him.

Rath pulled back his leg, his knee to his chest, then drove the heel of his boot into Glade's ankle.

A bone cracked. Glade howled. Rath drove his boot into Glade's shin and ankle again.

Glade collapsed.

"Timmy," the old woman cried.

Rath found his feet and pounced on Glade, flipped him over onto his stomach and drove a knee into his back, cuffed him. Yanked him up.

Glade wailed as he limped in place. "You broke it. You broke it."

I'll break the other one, too, Rath thought as he shoved Glade up to the top apartment step and pushed Glade down to sit.

"I didn't know you were a cop," Glade whined. "My fucking ankle."

The aunt stood near, gaping.

"Go inside," Rath said. "It's cold out here."

"I'm fine."

"Go inside. Now."

The aunt disappeared into the apartment.

Rath looked down at Glade. "Who'd you think I was?"

"People."

"I'm not people. I'm one guy."

"I didn't know if there were others."

"Who?"

"People that want to hurt me."

"That you owe money or—?"

Glade shook his head and stuck his leg with the wounded ankle out straight, winced and moaned. "I wish. No, I don't owe nobody nothing. I don't even know who it is. But they know what I done and where I live. They call the house, they leave notes, they break headlights on my aunt's car and the streetlights, one took a shit on our porch and left a copy of my mug shot splattered with blood. What looked like real blood, with my face all hacked up."

"Because of what you did?" Rath said.

"I got no control over it," Glade said. "No. That ain't true. Most times I do. Like ninety percent. But I'm like a alcoholic. Gotta keep temptation away. I don't own a cell phone or a computer or nothing, because then it's all right at my fingertips, man. I gotta keep busy, keep my mind busy, keep my body busy, off tempting thoughts of that shit."

"Of boys."

"And girls. I need to do the meetings. That's where I was. Way over in Nashua. They don't have enough meetings 'round here. I need to go like once a day. I need *support*. I don't *want* to hurt no one else. But they come and trash my aunt's car. Break her windows. Vandalize her place she worked hard to retire here. I brought this shit. Disgraced her."

Rath crouched beside Glade. "I don't give a shit about your sob story about broken windows after what *you* broke. I don't give a fuck if you need to go to meetings. All I need from you is to know the relationship you had with Ned Preacher while you were inside."

"What? Are you crazy? Preacher? I didn't know the guy. Didn't want to know him."

Rath took Glade's ankle in his hand and cranked it sideways so it made a popping sound.

Glade went rigid with pain. "*Jesus.* What the fuck?"

"*What the fuck?*" Rath said. "Two minutes ago you want to cave my skull with a brick. Murder me in your aunt's parking lot, in front of her, a police officer, and now you ask *me* what the fuck? You knew Preacher. You shared his cell block for three years."

"That doesn't mean I *knew* him. I didn't even talk to him. We weren't girlfriends, that's for sure. I broke the asshole's nose because he wouldn't stop his bullshit praying after lights out. You want to talk to someone who knows the guy, talk to Shelly."

"Who's she?"

"Not she. Man. Shelly. Sheldon. Clay Sheldon. Those two were tight as a ball of snakes. They had some shit going on I'll tell you what. You want to talk to someone who was close with Preacher, really fucking close, Shelly's your guy."

"Get up," Rath said. "I'm going to uncuff you. Try anything, I'll break your other ankle."

"I need medical attention. I need to get to the hospital."

"Then go."

"My ankle's busted."

"Call an ambulance." Rath leaned close. Glade was rank with stale sweat. He could have stood to have some namesake air freshener sprayed on him. "I suggest you tell doctors you slipped on the wet walkway. Unless you want to be charged with assaulting a police officer and head back into the joint. If I had time to waste on you, that's what you'd do, but I don't have time to waste."

In his Scout, Rath dialed Test. "We need to get to the North Star."

PART V

She is exceptional. An exception. Close to the bone. Too close? Perhaps. A grave, grave risk. There is no doubt. But a titillating risk. That is how he likes it. How he wants it. Needs it. More and more, the greater the risk, the greater the satisfaction. What is life without risk? Death. A long slow, pale death. The kind he'd been forced to live for too long, imprisoned: a life of death. No more.

To be unable to be who he truly is, to live his life as intended, to have to suppress his true self, smother it, strangle it, choke it down for so many years, it nearly killed him, even while another part of himself, the Good Boy, the Good Man, had begun to think, had begun to believe, that his dormancy, the forced hibernation of his urges, might be for the better, for all concerned. He'd almost convinced himself of it. Convinced himself he could live that way. Kill his true self. But that was to live a lie.

And how times changed. Look around. Look around. Everyone was entitled to be true to themselves now. True to their identities, true to how they identified. The voices who spoke up and said no. You can't be like that, you can't LIVE like that, you can't be YOU, those voices were trounced now, stifled, belittled. Silenced.

Could he get away with it? That was where the thrill came, the risk of getting caught. Would he be caught and judged by those who did not understand? Those who were less . . . sophisticated. Would he be punished for being who he was? For how he came into this world?

Care would be needed. Care would be taken.

The Right Girl, the Right Girls, needed to be selected. He needed mature, grounded, reasonable girls.

Girls like Jamie. He could not trouble his mind now with what had happened with her.

There were other girls to appreciate what he offered. What he did. Girls who did not get greedy. Did not get cute. Did not get stupid. Like that other one. That could not be tolerated. Was not tolerated. An example had to be made. He'd been clear, painfully clear, on that point.

He watched the new one now, the smart one, the clever one, as she came out of the fog.

Yes. Care was needed for this one.

Care and luck.

She was a smart one.

He watched her now on the steps.

The old ecstasy awoke, the sensation that he was about to step barefoot out on a razor wire stretched high above a pit of crude spikes. One misstep and he would plummet and be gored, impaled, bleed out.

On the other side of the pit stood his reward, his treasure. Her.

He shuddered at his end of the wire. The ecstasy did not come from the fear of walking across the wire, high above the pit, trying to reach the other side to claim her without falling and being skewered.

No. It came from crossing halfway across the wire and stopping, poised above the fearsome spikes and seducing her into wanting to step across the wire to meet him halfway.

The seduction. That was the reward: to see her come to him of her own free will.

Oh.

He watched her go inside the building.

In the sixteen years of dormancy he'd thought about what to do when, if, his freedom came again. He had decided it would be much sweeter if they came to him, met him halfway to do to them what he did best. He knew these girls existed. Had learned that years ago, but then found himself caged. The girls, they have their own fixations, obsessions, kinks. Needs.

His last girl, the one he'd thought would be his last, forever, who had opened his eyes so many years ago, made him understand that some girls liked what he liked, needed what he needed. Loved what he loved. She was a miracle, until he found himself in prison.

No more.

Unchained now, he knew his power. He knew there were girls hungry to step across the wire to him when they caught whiff of his supremacy on the breeze.

What was this?

He straightened up, watching the new one. The smart one.

She came back out of the building. Oh, the sneaky whore. What was she hiding from her boy, that insect boy, the praying mantis, what duplicity was at work? His mouth watered at the proof of what he already knew: no one was without secrets, without alternate lives they kept in the shadows until someone came to shine the bright light of truth upon them, set their world on fire and scorch it to ash.

He was that bright, hot light.

And he knew the shadows. Thrived in them. He knew about alternate identities. The car he sat in now not registered in his real name. A terrific, thrilling risk that made him hard.

He got out and watched as she descended the stairs and walked directly toward him, their encounter preordained.

She was not paying any attention to where she was going; she was going to run directly into him, her first step out on the razor wire.

Yes, this one was special because of who she was.

Special because she was the daughter of that fuck who dared challenge him and press him, tried to trick and expose him. He started all of this. Frank Rath.

He deserved it.

65

Rachel gasped as she bumped into a man.

She fumbled for her backpack zipper to get at her handgun. She was too slow.

"Apologies," the man said.

He looked vaguely familiar. Handsome. Sort of. For an older guy. His eyes had none of that bright spark that quickly glazed with lust when men his age realized they were unexpectedly in the presence of a young woman and had her undivided attention, if only for a nanosecond.

Maybe he was gay. He didn't give off a gay vibe, though.

Why did he look familiar?

"Were you hiking up the hill earlier?" he said.

Rachel did not answer. She needed to get moving. She could not be late for her handgun class.

"I offered you a ride," he said.

"Oh. Right."

"You still look in a hurry. I'm heading downhill." He nodded at the vehicle nearby. "If you care for a lift."

She did not *care for* a lift. Not from him. Not from any stranger.

"I understand," he said and walked toward his old car.

Rachel was running even later now from standing around and talking.

She'd accepted plenty of rides to and from campus when she'd missed the shuttle. Rides from strangers. Most from girls, a few from guys her age, students; though guys her age, in some ways, were worse than older men, their motivations so obvious, their attempts at double entendre coarse and juvenile. *Give yah a* ride. *A* lift? Pathetic.

The stranger was opening his car door now, not looking back. Rachel's fear of Preacher had made her so paranoid she trusted no one; before Preacher, she'd have taken this guy up on his offer. He seemed perfectly normal. And there was something about him. A confidence. Not swagger, just a sort of *take it or leave it* aura, not flip like young guys whose apathy was just another tired ploy: the more they pretended they didn't care for her attention, the more desperately they wanted it. This guy. He just *was*. It seemed he'd asked if she needed a ride simply because he saw she needed a ride. He reminded her of how Felix might be when he was this guy's age, no ulterior motive. Except, Rachel had to admit, a bit guiltily, this older guy had probably been more handsome than Felix in his day.

"Hey," Rachel shouted as the guy shut his car door.

Rachel jogged up to the car. The man, startled, cranked his window down a piece. This man was not Preacher. She could not let Preacher inform her every decision, cripple her everyday freedom. Could she? She might as well stay locked inside or flee to Florida.

The ride down the hill would take two minutes, tops, and she had a gun in her backpack. Her fear was misplaced. If she could not accept a normal ride, how could face Preacher?

She unzipped her backpack a bit, slipped her hand inside it to get her fingers around the butt of the revolver.

"Change your mind?" the stranger said.

Rachel considered getting in the car with a frisson of inexplicable high excitement and apprehension, as if she were about to step out onto a high wire.

"It was nice of you to offer," Rachel said. "But I'll walk."

The man nodded amiably.

"Hope you don't mind," Rachel said.

"Why should I mind?" the man said, seeming confused by her apology. "Be safe." He rolled up the window and drove away without a hint of hesitation or regret.

66

The door to Clay Sheldon's unit was open a crack.

Rath unsnapped the holster of his M&P45 and approached from one side of the door as Test approached from the opposite angle, waved him to move in on the door. She slipped her hand on her own weapon, at her hip.

Rath rapped a knuckle on the door. "Sheldon," he said through the crack. "Detectives Sonja Test and Frank Rath."

Test nodded for Rath to push the door open.

She did not like the door being open. No one left a motel door open, unless they were moving into or out of it. And if Sheldon were packing up to split in the night, they'd hear him inside; unless he'd heard them and had taken cover because he knew why they'd returned.

Rath pushed the door open and stepped inside, weapon drawn, sweeping the unit that was lit by one pale bedside table lamp.

Test entered behind him, sweeping her own weapon across the room.

There was nowhere to hide, except the bathroom.

Its door was shut. Light leaked from under it.

Test covered the closed bathroom door with her sidearm.

A ticking sound came from the kitchenette, like that of a clock hand pinging away each irretrievable second.

The place appeared the same as when Test had last questioned Sheldon. Almost. The bed was unmade. Normal enough. Enter Test's bedroom any given day and you'd find her bed unmade too.

The nightstand drawer hung open a few inches.

Test smelled burnt coffee. An empty coffeepot sat on a hot plate, its bottom charred black as it ticked, as if about to explode.

Test nodded for Rath to open the bathroom door.

He pushed the door open.

The reek of bleach burned in Test's nostrils and eyes.

Water dripped behind the plastic shower curtain, dribbled from the sink's faucet.

Test nodded to Rath. He pulled back the curtain.

"Nothing," he said.

No.

Not nothing.

Test knelt. Along the bead of caulking where the turquoise tile met the ceramic edge of the dated tub, a dark spatter. Not even a spatter. Five or six specks.

"Blood," Rath said from behind her. "The sink, too." A wafer of melted white soap sat beside the faucet. Except the soap wasn't quite white. A film of pale pink coated it, the foam in which it sat a shade brighter.

On the floor beneath the sink, a few drops more.

"I'll call New Hampshire staties," Test said.

67

W ho are you two again?" New Hampshire state trooper Lawrence Pines said as he stood outside the North Star Motor Court and rubbed a thumb absently over a nasty mark on the back of his hand. The ragged flesh a livid pink against his dark skin. *It's not a scar,* Test thought, *it's too fresh. A wound.*

"Detectives Test and Rath," Test said. "Canaan Police."

The trooper stared at them. Test and Rath showed their IDs.

"What are you *doing* here, is probably the better question," Pines said.

Test explained the previous interview. Sheldon's connection to Preacher and thus perhaps to the hanged girls and possibly to Dana Clark's disappearance. "We left feeling squared with him. But came back based on an interview that revealed Sheldon had lied to us."

"Will wonders never cease," Pine said. "You should have been in touch with us the first time."

"It was an informal inquiry, being right across the river," Test said.

"Save it. Law enforcement needs to work together."

"We are. Now," Test said. "If we'd looped you in the first time, you'd probably have bitched we were wasting your resources."

"We'll never know."

"Let me show you what we have," Test said.

Upon being shown the blood, Pines said, "So?"

"We need forensics here," Test said.

"It's a bathroom. Looks like someone got cut shaving."

"You shave in the shower much?" Rath said.

"Could have nicked himself and kept bleeding. You know how a nicked chin bleeds like a sliced artery." He considered Rath's unshaven face. "Maybe not. More likely a woman friend cut herself in the shower, shaving her legs, kept bleeding at the sink." He scratched at the ruin of flesh that was the back of his hand.

"The door was open," Test said. "The coffee burned to a black crust. His clothes are still here but he's gone."

"Let's speak with the manager," Pines said.

THE MANAGER, a middle-aged woman wrapped in a sari the color of a plum, told them Sheldon had paid for the two weeks, in advance. "He not trouble. Quiet like the mouse."

"Have you seen him today?" Test asked.

"Not for couple days. But that does not mean he is not round. I don't see everything. I am busy. I guess he is inside because he asked the maid not come."

Rath looked at Test.

"This is not unusual," the manager said. "Many who lives in efficiency do not have maid each day. It is extra cost."

"Do you have CCTV?"

"I do not know this."

"Video cameras. Security?" Test said, looking around at the ceiling corners of the lobby.

"Too much of the money. Is broken. My husband, he has a gun instead."

"Where is your husband?" Test said.

"Maine. We have other motel. That one it has the cameras," she said. "They not break."

"Can we see Sheldon's registration card?" Test said.

The manager gave a wary look, but dug around in a tin box of index cards. "Here." She handed the card to Test.

Test looked at it. "Did you see him driving the car listed on here? A black Civic?"

The woman nodded. "Is something happening?"

"We will need to take a closer look in the unit. If that's OK."

"If it is a must. I hope nothing happens to him."

Test thanked the woman and turned to leave.

"His poor wife," the manager said.

Test turned back. "He's not married," she said.

"Girlfriend she is maybe then."

"Who?" Test said.

"The woman who is crying."

"When was this?" Test said.

Rath and the state trooper exchanged looks with Test.

"She was here," the manager said, "the night we got all the first fogs and rains. She was, it's not my ways to gossip. But she was very drunks. I saw him helping her from car, holding her upright, I heard her making sobs."

"What did she look like?" Test said.

"I do not knows. It is dark and all the fogs."

"But it was a woman?" Rath said.

"I see this, yes. I am going from a room to office, a family need a crib. I brings it to them. I am coming back when I sees him pulling her from backseat of car. She could not stand on her owns, and was, she was getting sick. I said something but he had car parked right in front and was inside quick like cat."

"And you didn't ask what was going on?" Test said.

"I see many much worst things here, a motel, many, many things worst than a drunks wife."

"Why do you think it was his wife?" Rath asked.

"I sees him next day. He is getting ice from machine."

The trooper scratched at the back of his wounded hand, but his focus was on the manager.

The manager bowed her head slightly, looked up from under her eyelids as if she'd talked too much and feared repercussions.

"I ask if his wife is OK, and he say fine. Fine."

"Did you see her again, the wife?" Test said.

The manager shook her head. "I heard car late at that night. Woke me in office, the engine and headlights."

"Did you see her get in?"

"I see only the car drive away."

"What time?"

"Late. Next morning. Three in morning or more."

"And when did it come back?"

"I don't knows. I sees the car is back sometime, but not sure when it got back. I am busy."

"Have you seen her, the wife, since?" Test said.

"Not ever since."

68

I'm going to be late," Test said to Claude, speaking to him on her cell phone as she stood outside Clay Sheldon's taped-off efficiency, members of the NH State Police crime scene forensics team scrambling in and out of the unit.

Test sensed Claude wanting to ask *how late,* but he didn't. There was no point. They both knew that even if Test estimated when she'd be home, she'd likely be as accurate as a ten-day forecast in January.

"Sorry," she said. "When this case is over, you'll get some time for yourself."

"It's not time for myself I want. We have to talk, too, about the visiting artist position."

"We will." She'd forgotten all about it.

"I need to give them an answer."

"I know."

"By tomorrow noon."

Test paused. She wanted Claude to take the post, but they needed time to figure out what they would do with the kids those two weeks.

She'd be able to handle them *if* her caseload allowed, and she could take a few PTO days. She'd not taken a day since July; doubted she'd take any more until April. But if she got a crazy couple weeks when Claude was gone, what would she do with the kids then? The sitter was for evenings, date nights, not a nanny who could watch them at all hours. Neither she nor Claude had family nearby as many of her friends did, grandparents itching to watch their grandkids for free. "Just tell them yes," Test said. "We'll make it work."

"You sure? What if they want me to take the fulltime position next fall?"

Rath stood in the doorway of the efficiency, paper booties on his socked feet, paper hat on his head, blue surgical gloves stretched over his hands. He looked like a mad baker. He had no wife. Besides Rachel, in college, he had no obligations other than to himself, and Test could see in his eyes, his appetite for police work surging with each step in this case.

"You sure?" Claude said again.

She wasn't sure. But he wanted it and it was only two weeks. They could negotiate the fulltime position later, if it were offered. "Take it. I gotta go."

"I don't want to just—"

"*Take* it."

Test ended the call and walked over to Rath. "Any prints?"

"It's a fleabag motel, they don't exactly scrub each surface clean between visitors," Rath said. "Going to take forever to sort them out. We need to get prints from Dana's home, for a comp. Her iPad maybe, or a brush with a hard handle. A remote control. Something only she used."

"You think she was the woman the manager thought was his wife?" Test said.

Rath nodded.

"Where the hell is her car?" Test said.

"Out there." Rath looked out toward the parking lot. Route 145 was a hundred feet away, yet invisible in the fog.

Trooper Pines stepped out from inside the unit. He did not look well. He looked as if he'd just been diagnosed with a terminal illness.

In his hand, pinched between his gloved fingers by its corner was a photograph.

A Polaroid.

69

The Polaroid was of Dana Clark. A younger Dana Clark. Not that anyone other than Rath and Dana Clark's daughter would ever be able to identify the bloodied body so cruelly cut and brutalized as being Dana Clark, or even being female. Rath doubted Dana Clark's husband or closest friends would be able to ID her. Rath and Tammy Clark had an advantage, a disadvantage. They'd both seen this photo before, or one like it. And witnessed the woman herself, left for dead in her flower garden.

"Fuck," Rath said.

"There's more of them inside," Pines said. "Dozens."

Rath looked out toward the highway hidden in the fog, listening to the sound of cars and trucks swoosh past in the rain.

"Dozens," Rath heard Test say. "How long would that take?"

"At least a minute for each photo to develop, I'd think," Pines said. "He'd have to place the photos somewhere, not just let them fall facedown on the grass, get ruined. He'd have to change film, too."

"He brought boxes and boxes of film with him. He knew he

was going to take all those pictures?" Test said. "He attacked Dana Clark back then. He gets out of prison and . . . finishes what he started. He moved right across the river, has a vehicle. Unlike Preacher."

"It makes no sense," Rath said, turning to them from looking at the fog. "He has no prior. He robbed a store and killed a kid. I bought that he was suicidal about it, that he's never forgiven himself for that."

"Bought a bill of goods, sounds like," Pines said.

A woman in forensics garb and eyeglasses with thick blue frames stepped outside from the unit. She held up a sealed evidence bag. "A hair from the bathroom floor. Near the droplets of blood. Long. Gray. Likely belonging to a female."

"Dana Clark's," Test said.

"We'll see," the woman said and marched off across the parking lot into the fog.

"We wondered if Preacher and Sheldon were tight, that's why we visited Sheldon the first time," Test said. "Sheldon convinced us otherwise. But maybe he and Preacher *were* tight. Are tight. Maybe Sheldon opened up to Preacher about his own dark past that no one else knew about, and no one would *understand, appreciate,* except someone like Preacher. Sheldon is the perfect age for the CRVK. He lived within twenty-five miles of most of the murders."

"If we buy that he and Preacher were tight," Rath said. "If we believe Glade over Sheldon."

"Pick your convict," Pines said.

"We're *here*," Test stressed, "because *you* visited Glade, on your *own* and *believed* him. And now you question it? It led us to a gray hair, blood, an abandoned motel room, and these photos. To

Sheldon. It doesn't mean Preacher's not involved just because it doesn't lead straight to Preacher; and it doesn't mean it's not good police work on our part. Your part. If Sheldon shared his plans with Preacher, it explains how Preacher knew about Jamie Drake's hanging. But we follow evidence. If Preacher's not our man for this he's not our man. We'll get him on something else eventually"

"Where's that leave our Quebec girls?" Rath said.

"I don't know," Test said. "Where'd you find the photos?" she asked Pines.

"Plastic baggie hidden in the back of the minifridge. Not inside in the back, but between the minifridge's plastic shell and its interior body."

"God damn it," Rath said. "We had him and we let him get away."

70

Bleary but wired, Rath sat at the kitchen table with Preacher's envelope in his hand.

One DNA test. He could have it done by an old friend in forensics with the state police. He'd know in a week. Easy.

He put the envelope in his pocket and stood and looked at his .30-06, still sitting on the table from the other night when he hadn't gotten to it.

He set to breaking the rifle down to clean it.

By 11:07 P.M. he'd managed to drink two beers but had only taken apart and laid out the carbine's barrel, action tube assembly and action bar lock, the walnut forend and slide action when his phone buzzed.

Grout.

Shit. Rath kept forgetting.

He picked up. Before he could say hello, Grout said, "Come clean, you're breaking up with me, aren't you? Found yourself a—"

"I had a shit day."

"She was that ugly, eh?"

"Pretty ugly. How about we meet tomorrow? Noon?"

"Promise?"

"Swear."

"Good, because we need to meet. I need to tell you a few things. Express myself. Bring chocolates and roses. I'm pretty pissed."

Rath ended the call.

He was on a second Labatt Blue and had his .30-06's trigger assembly and safety taken apart, and was looking on the kitchen floor on his hands and knees under the kitchen table for the damned sear spring that had sprung out from between his fingers, when his phone buzzed. Test.

It was 11:54.

Rath answered as he checked for the spring between the cracks in the floorboards.

"The blood from Sheldon's unit bathroom is contaminated by bleach. Of no use," Test said. "Prints will take a while. The hair was easy, got one of Clark's from a brush at her daughter's. NH put a rush on it. It's not Dana Clark's. She wasn't gray."

"Damn it," Rath said. "Her DNA has to be in there somewhere. That 'drunk wife' Sheldon 'helped' inside. And those goddamn photos. That locks it. Maybe we'll get a match of prints. Let's hope."

Rath spotted the spring on the floor, reached for it. No. It wasn't the spring. It was just a coil of dark thread. "Damn it," he said.

"What?"

"Nothing." Rath searched along the base of the kitchen counter. How did things just disappear like this? Where the hell was that spring?

"NH's forensics got a good sweep. Other fibers and hairs. If she was there, we can match her. Speaking of prints, Larkin wanted me to pass along we got no match in the FBI system or any system for the prints from our Quebecois *copains*. There's an APB out for Sheldon and his vehicle across New England. The motel manager will call immediately if Sheldon returns."

"That's not going to happen," Rath said.

"It could. He doesn't *know* we know. We came the second time because of what Glade said. It's likely Sheldon killed Clark *before* we interviewed him the first time, yet he was still there. His clothes and belongings are still there. We put the place back in order. He paid for the whole week."

Rath's back and knees ached from searching for the spring. He stood with a groan and searched from a standing position, a new, wider perspective.

Still, nothing.

"Where the hell is he then?"

"Maybe he's working on his next victim. Maybe you're right and he's long gone, in Milwaukee or Anchorage or Biloxi. Maybe he's lost in this fog. But maybe, just maybe, he'll be back."

"Anything else?"

"Larkin did a complete background on Sheldon, his ex-wife, and his daughter. Sheldon's tattoo, there's something to it."

"Which tattoo?" Rath said. "The guy had more graffiti than a hick town water tower."

Rath gave up looking for the spring and sat at the table.

"The one across the top of his chest," Test said. "It said Angel. His daughter's name is Angel. It was his daughter's name."

"So he's one of a million ink junkies who thinks getting a tattoo of his kid's name, or worse, a hideous rendition of his kid's face, proves how much he loves his kid instead it reeking of insecurity and bad taste."

"If anyone can justify having his daughter's name tattooed across his chest, it's Sheldon," Test said. "His daughter was murdered. Raped and murdered. When she was fifteen."

"What?" Rath said. "When?"

"Years ago. Before he robbed that place and killed the clerk. No one was ever arrested. But a neighbor who was a suspect killed himself soon after. No note, though; so no telling if it was actually him or not. There was no DNA to match. The rapist had doused the daughter's entire body in *bleach*."

"Bleach? Like in Sheldon's bathtub?"

"I hate to even think anyone would do that to his own daughter. But we both know that's not the world we live in. Sheldon's life unraveled. He got divorced, lost his job. He told us he robbed that store out of desperation. That was true. He was broke, angry, suicidal, living in slummy digs."

"You think he killed his daughter? Maybe she was one of many?"

"I don't know anything. Except Sheldon had the Polaroids. No one else could have them except Dana Clark's attacker. My guess is he had one seriously dark, secret life. And maybe he shared it with Preacher inside, and now they're on a tear together."

"Larkin stay posted on Preacher all day?"

"All day, poor kid. Preacher never moved. Mailman came and went. Neighbor. No Preacher."

"That it?" he said.

"For now."

"Get back to your family."

"Are you kidding? They were all sleeping three hours ago." She hung up.

Rath stood and stretched, and felt it. He lifted his bare foot off the floor. There it was. The spring. Right underfoot.

71

Friday, November 11, 2011

The Lamoille River, a torrent of mud, gouged at its banks as Rath and Grout sat on a rock outcrop. A massive chunk of earthen bank across the river calved and was claimed by the current. One wrong step into the water and you were dead, as sure as if you stepped in front of a logging truck going 100 mph.

"So what is it?" Rath said. "I can't help you with Barrons, getting your old gig back. Test deserves—"

"Forget that. For now. I was digging around into our friend the prig, Boyd Pratt *number three*," Grout said, "and mucking online regarding the Double Black Diamond. It's a Starmont operation. That's the parent company."

"I'll take your word for it," Rath said. He'd never stayed at a luxury hotel or resort, and he'd not been in a motel since before he'd adopted Rachel.

"Starmont's majority holder is Champlain Enterprises," Grouts said.

"OK."

"I asked myself, back when I first ran into Dipshit the Third at the Double Black Diamond, 'Why is he here?' I mean, the resort is pushing three hours from his estate on the lake. And a big step down to boot."

"Privacy," Rath said. "He's well known in his area and didn't want to have the discussions at his estate."

"I chalked it up to that."

"But?"

"Like I said, a major holder of Starmont, which owns Double Black Diamond, is Champlain Enterprises. And guess which prig's family is behind Champlain?"

"That's why he did business there? It's his resort. What am I not getting?"

"Starmont owns a lot of resorts. Care to guess where their newest resort is?"

"Jay Peak?"

"Go north, my friend."

"You can't go north, without—Canada."

"You win the big teddy bear. And not just anywhere in Canada. Guess where th—"

"I'm not guessing."

"Quebec. *Saint-Jean-sur-Richelieu*. The Riverview. And one in Montreal. Old Montreal."

"Which one?" Adrenaline charged through Rath.

Grout told Rath, though he didn't need to; Rath knew.

72

Felix had just taken the shuttle up to campus for his morning work-study when Rachel ducked into the Lovin' Cup for her caffeine fix and saw the man.

He sat near the window, sipping tea and reading a book as she came in for a coffee before heading up the hill again. She needed a jolt to kick-start her. She was running on fumes.

The man did not see her, immersed as he was in his book.

As she moved ahead in the short line she watched him. She could not make out the cover of the book, a hardcover with a sort of foil wrap. The fingers of the hand in which the book rested were long and they stretched to cover most of the book's spine. What was he doing here, in a college coffee shop on a weekday? Didn't he work?

"Go ahead," a girl's voice said as Rachel felt a nudge at her backpack, the handgun shifting.

The line had moved forward.

"Clare. Clare?" a barista said. A girl came and got a coffee and muffin at the end of the counter.

Rachel stepped forward, her eyes on the man near the window.

He was not that attractive, not really. But there was an air to him. Her earlier impression had been correct. A man of his age sitting in a coffee shop run and patronized by undergrads was out of place. If he were any other man, Rachel would have had one of two impressions of him: he was a poseur wannabe coffee shop artist who suffered delusion and did not recognize his age difference to those around him, saw himself as one of them, mentally and philosophically; or he was a creep. She got neither impression from this man. He was simply enjoying a tea and a book before he headed to wherever his day brought him. *Which is where?* Rachel wondered. Was he a visiting professor, a salesman? No. He was dressed too casually, worn jeans and a flannel shirt, although the shirt did have suede patches at the elbows.

"Patrick," a barista said. "Patrick. Order."

"Go ahead," the girl behind Rachel said.

Rachel stepped to the counter and ordered her Red Eye to go.

She watched the man near the window as the cashier, a classmate of Rachel's, said, "Fueling up before the lecture later?"

The man peered up from the pages of his book. Instinctively, Rachel gave a slight wave, but the man seemed not to recognize her and went back to reading.

Rachel felt slighted, and moronic. What did she expect, the man to leap out of his seat for a girl he'd offered to give a three-minute ride? If men of his age all seemed to look alike to her in a vague way, what must students Rachel's age look like to him?

Rachel went to the end of the counter to await her coffee.

The man glanced at her again. Or did he? His eyes showed no

recognition. Perhaps he was merely gazing at the menu above her, a blackboard scrawled with colorful chalks.

"Your daily Red Eye," her classmate said. Rachel took the cardboard coffee cup and slipped a corrugated cardboard sleeve onto it.

When she turned to leave, the man was gone.

73

Outside, Rachel sipped her coffee, savoring its dark intensity as the caffeine revved in her bloodstream. It made her feel as if she were about to lift off her heels. As much as she mocked Felix for his beer obsession, Rachel was just as much a sucker for the dark hot brew.

She headed to the shuttle shelter and spotted the man looking in a shop window up ahead.

As Rachel passed by in the fog, she caught the man's eye in the window reflection.

He noticed her this time, no doubt about it.

"Hi," she said.

The man turned from looking at backpacks and mountaineering gear in the Precipice Outdoor Shop.

"Oh." He squinted, as if mining his memory. "Apologies. I'm in a cloud."

"Cloud?"

"Research."

"Are you a scientist or a professor or—"

"Hardly. A layman."

"What kind of research?"

"Of no consequence to anyone but myself, and perhaps my few subjects."

Rachel looked toward the shuttle shelter. She only had a few minutes to spare.

"I'll let you grab your shuttle." The man started away.

"What kind of research?"

"It's not appropriate to discuss with a young woman I don't know; and certainly not something your boyfriend would be comfortable with me sharing."

"How do you know I have a boyfriend?" Rachel said.

"I don't *know*. I presume. You're young. In college. And— You ought to catch your shuttle."

"And what?" Rachel said. "I'm young, in college, *and*—what?"

"It's of no importance. We don't know each other. My research is private. Not a subject to just divulge to strangers outside coffee shops. It could be . . . misconstrued. And gauging by your answer, you do have a boyfriend, which would make my sharing doubly taboo."

Taboo? What in the world was this man researching?

Whatever it was, Rachel's pushiness was inappropriate. If a man were to press her when she clearly did not wish to be pressed, she'd have stalked off by now.

"There's the shuttle," the man said and brushed past her, his arm just grazing hers as she saw the book in his hand, *Deviants: Interviews.*

Rachel felt a rush of heat as she watched the man go.

She hurried toward the shuttle, eager to see Felix.

But she found herself peering after the man in the fog for a heartbeat more.

74

I believe I have some insightful updates, if I may?" Larkin said as he reported to Rath and Test in Rath's barren office.

"That's why we're here," Rath said.

"Right. So. The update. We thought Preacher didn't have a car. Or he had one hidden. Perhaps stolen. But he does have a car."

"What the hell, where?" Test said.

"Right there, under our noses. The truck."

"That truck is registered to an Andrea Diamond."

"Right," Larkin said. "Well, sitting there in the cruiser like that watching his road, I got itchy looking at the fog and that massive rock with the lone rose on it memorializing a car wreck. So. I started thinking about how Preacher got to Johnson, or across the border, if it's him. I started searching deeper into this Andrea Diamond. I dug social media, checked her criminal history. The usual. She's clean, as we found initially. But, then I hit it. A *relative* of hers is anything but clean. Her cousin. Clay Sheldon."

"Preacher is driving Sheldon's cousin's fucking car?" Rath said.

"I didn't see him drive it, but it's sitting in his yard."

"Damn it," Test said. "We need to check a lot deeper into her."

"I did," Larkin said. "Immediately. I did not want to leave my post, so I tracked her down by phone at her work, Connecticut Valley Bank, she's a teller. She says the car is in her name but the car is actually Sheldon's. He'd asked her to register it in her name, as a favor. Gave her some line about not wanting two cars in his name, and he was going to trade it to a friend, anyway, so it would only be in her name for a week or so. She thought maybe it was sketchy, but she and Sheldon were those close cousins as kids, the ones tighter than siblings in some ways. She was his daughter's godmother. She wanted to do something to help him out. Classic enabler, I suppose. Said it didn't hurt her any."

"Trade the car for what?" Test said.

Rath thought he knew. "We have reason to go pick Preacher up," he said to Test. "He lied to you about the truck."

"Technically, he didn't," Test said. "He told me he didn't *own* a car. He doesn't. But. His MW affidavit will come through today. We'll get him and haul him in."

"I did a deep dive into Pratt, too," Larkin said. "His alibi checks out for Jamie Drake's murder. He was at the library groundbreaking. No doubt. Airtight."

He brought up a local online newspaper on his laptop to show the photo of Pratt in requisite hardhat, pushing a shovel into the dirt with the heel of his Le Chameau as a small crowd of citizens circled round to witness the event.

"And the time frame for the Quebec murder, he *was* at a conference in his hotel up there, with about a dozen other investors and business partners."

"The wife?" Test said. "She's not in the photo for the groundbreaking."

"Probably just didn't make the frame," Larkin said.

"Find out. Find out if she was up at the hotel with her husband when he had that conference, too. Look into her background. Dig. She's a good fifteen years younger than Pratt. They've been together at least since they had their daughter who died, so Victoria was young when they met. Very young." Test glanced at Rath just as a thought slipped through his mind, something to do with Victoria Pratt's age. Or the age of her daughter. He could not seize it before it escaped.

"Find out all about her and Pratt," Test continued, "how they met, and where. What she did and who she was before she met her not-so-charming prince. Thank you, Officer Larkin. Check on her maiden name, too, as quick as possible," Test said.

"Won't take a minute." Larkin left Test's office.

It was more like a half hour before Larkin returned, but he was practically gamboling when he did. "Victoria Pratt. Maiden name: Legault."

"French," Rath said.

"French *Canadian,*" Larkin said. "She's from a small town outside Saint-Jean-sur-Richelieu."

"Shit," Rath said. Her accent, French Canadian, diluted from years of disuse in the States.

"I need you to find out if she still has family up there. Old friends we could speak to," Test said.

"Done."

"You're good," Test said.

Larkin nodded in a deflective manner. "Once I found she was from there, I did a quick search. Worked backward. Found her maiden name. From there, where she was born, parents, childhood hometown, schools. Her parents have lived in a small town a couple hundred miles north of Ottawa for twelve years. Her sister, Charlotte, lives in the house they grew up in. I have the address."

"Good, we'll need it," Test said.

75

An hour north of the border, Rath drove slowly through the fog, down a dirt road that ran through harrowed fields. Test had thought her car stank, but this old rig of Rath's needed an olfactory exorcism, the stench ungodly. She'd had her window cranked down most of the way, despite rain coming in and the raw temperature.

At the end of the road, a Chevy Blazer sat parked out front of an old log cabin. Rath nearly hit a horse that trotted out of the fog toward a barn that looked about to keel over in a pile of timber.

Kids' plastic riding toys, wagons, and bikes sat in the slush of the yard, apparently left where they'd been last used in the summer.

Chickens and guinea fowl scattered as Rath and Test headed to the steps of the cabin.

Before Rath could knock, a woman opened the door and stood out on the steps, wiping her hands on a blue apron cinched around wide hips. Her purple dress fell to her ankles and had a high collar, like a doily, reminding Rath of Quakers, or the Amish. Of the Gihon River Inn. She squinted as if unsure of what she was seeing.

"Charlotte Collins?" Test said.

"*Oui,*" the woman said.

"Detective Sonja Test and Frank Rath from the States."

"It's Vicky, isn't it?" Charlotte Collins said. "Is she dead?"

"Nothing like that," Test said.

"Then, what's she done?"

Is she dead? What's she done?

"We'd just like to speak to you," Test said.

Charlotte Collins looked at the Scout, then at Rath and Test. "I'd like to see identification first."

THE HOUSE SMELLED wonderful, of freshly baked bread. It was warm, *toasty,* too; tidy, open, and spacious. Test had envisioned small rooms as cluttered as the yard.

A braided rug lay on the living room floor in front of a fireplace where a fire roared.

In the kitchen the woman picked up a bread pan and turned it over and tapped it so a perfectly golden loaf tumbled out onto a cooling rack.

Test bet this woman cooked a moist Thanksgiving turkey, though Canadians had celebrated their Thanksgiving a month earlier.

"What's Vicky done?" Charlotte said as she washed a plate at the sink.

"We don't know," Test said.

"Her husband hurt her?"

"Why would you think that?" Test said.

"People don't change. Not for good. None I've known, anyway."

"He hurt her?" Rath said. "When?"

She set the plate in the dish rack, paused as if unsure how to begin, or if she should begin at all. "Back when he first got his hooks into her, and *hers* into *him*, too. To be fair. I'd see bruises and be terrified. She was only fourteen. I was eighteen. We shared a bedroom, so not much privacy. She told me he'd done it, but that she'd *wanted* him to, she *liked* it. I didn't believe her. Not for a second. This wasn't the sister I knew. And. No one *likes* that, to be *hurt*. At least that's what I believed then. I know I sure didn't, and don't. That much I do know. He worried me. Worried us. He was more than twice her age. My father, he was homicidal about it for a good spell."

"Where did they meet?" Test said.

"A club."

"A strip club?" Rath said.

"I wish." She sighed. A sigh, it seemed, not of pain or disappointment but of longtime sorrowful resignation.

"It was worse than a strip club," she said. "It was of a, as Vicky described it, more private, upscale nature. Club *Pègre Imaginaire*. Underworld Fantasy. It was like the club for, um, swappers, but, much, much more. That was only a small, innocent slice. She would tell me stories, stories she had to know I never, ever wanted to hear, even if they didn't involve her, my baby sister. And she'd smile when I'd tell her to stop; she'd laugh, tell me I should join a nunnery. The things, if she did half of what she said she did, if she was subjected to even a fraction of that ugliness, *that darkness*. It was like a cult, a sick, brainwashing cult, except the religion was sex, or so-called sex, more like dehumanization. Torture."

Rath and Test exchanged looks at the word *torture*.

Charlotte sat on a stool at the kitchen counter, as if suddenly too tired to stand. "As she told me, the club catered to extreme, uh, tastes. Everything from . . . well . . . *Extreme*. I don't even want to say. It upsets me and makes me so sad to think about it. Something happened to her. When she met him. It was like her brain changed. Like he'd stirred up the chemicals in her brain. She was not the same. She'd been a good girl. Not perfect. By a long shot. But decent."

"She told you about this, torture?" Test said.

"She'd come home nearly catatonic and manic all at once, like she was high on all kinds of stuff, though she swore she wasn't, that she didn't *need* drugs. And she'd just start in on her stories. She saw *nothing* wrong with it. She said she wasn't taking money, wasn't being forced or drugged, it wasn't prostitution or pornography. It was fun. It was pleasure. It was love. I told her I was going to tell our father all about it. He'd put a stop to it. And she laughed at me again. Like she'd been waiting for me to threaten to tell and could not wait to spring the cold facts on me, that the age of consent was *fourteen*. She told me this like she was repeating it, like she'd been told it by someone else, by him, to use as an excuse, to justify it. I didn't believe her. I thought what was being done to her, it had to be rape. *Had* to be. I called the local police, while she sat there and watched me, right from the chair in that living room, rocking, rocking. The police officer I ended up finally getting an answer from probably thought I was loony, a teenage girl calling to ask what the legal age of consent was. But Vicky was right. The age of sexual consent was fourteen. Back then. It was raised all the way to sixteen a year or two ago," she said bitterly.

Test's stomach churned.

"So you didn't tell your father?" Test said.

"Nothing my father would have said or done, short of killing Boyd, would have stopped her. And she'd just keep at it and I feared she'd taunt him, too, or my mom. I was scared my father would kick her out and she'd be at even greater risk. And it would have broken his heart, and my mom's. At least she came home afterward, had a home, a safe bed. Me."

"Does the place still exist?" Test said.

"It was raided not long after she told me, luckily. I thought that would be the end of it. A sad dark phase."

"Raided for prostitution?" Test said, "Or pornography, or—"

"Tax evasion or laundering money, something like that, but the other stuff, it was all legal, no prostitution or criminal forced behavior or abuse or sex slaves, no *unwanted* abuse or unwilling slavery at least." She did not look at Rath or Test while she spoke. She'd opened a recipe box and arranged and rearranged recipe cards. "I don't doubt my sister participated of her own free will. It's always made me far more sad. That she did it willingly. Or *believed* she did."

"I still don't see how no charges were ever filed for sex with . . . a child?" Test said.

"Like I said. The age of sexual consent in Quebec was fourteen. Believe me, I *researched*. I followed her a few times and I saw Pratt, the monster. Twice her age. All his money, pomp and filthy ways. The way he talked to her. To my father. Mocked his being nothing but a fur peddler and a dirt farmer."

"You met Pratt?" Test said.

"Of course. Eventually. She married him. After he got her pregnant. I got to say, it shocked me."

"What did?" Test said.

"Everything. The marriage. The baby. And how they seemed to genuinely love each other, in a perverted, abnormal way. And then there was the change."

"How so?" Test said.

"He did an about-face. When my sister told me she was pregnant, I thought it was going to wreck her, all her good fun ruined, all her adventures, and I thought Boyd was going to force her to get an abortion. But she wasn't upset, she was over the moon. She said this was all she ever wanted, to have his child. She loved him, that's why she did all the things she did, she loved him, didn't I get that, how did I miss that, that what I saw as depraved and filthy was beautiful to her, a show of love, a show of what she would do to please him, anything, everything. To get his love in return. It scared me. This talk. It was so strange, radical. Desperate. And she was so young. To hear her say those things. I didn't even have a boyfriend. She said she would do anything for him, to keep him. He was tall and handsome and rich. She sounded mad, imbalanced, more manic than ever. But happy. And he came around. He seemed different when he visited with her later to announce their engagement. Promising to take care of her and love her and the child they were expecting. Yet I didn't trust it. Him. He was wealthy, yes, but jobless. He lived off the family money, as far as I could see, and had no real ambition or goals. No reason to *grow up*. I hoped the child would make him grow up. It did, I guess, as little as I have seen him since. He seemed to change from being the selfish deviant who tricked my sister into being a husband of sorts. He took her to the States and I've only seen her and her daughter a few times, and the last time I saw her was for her daughter's funeral, a year ago. It crushed her. Just *shattered* her. All she wanted was another chance, another baby. That's all she talked about. She's only thirty-one, but he's fifty. I got the sense that the baby was the glue that kept her marriage together, kept her together. And him. It's that case with other people, other, normal marriages, besides hers, of course. Children holding the couple together. But without a child between her and her husband, their world together, and her world and his world separately, would fly apart. The baby kept him on the straight and narrow; however straight and narrow that was compared to other people, I don't know. But I'm afraid, and I think she's afraid, he'll return to his old ways. Go off the rails. With someone else. That's why I thought something had happened to her when you showed up, that he'd done something to Vicky. Started up again with his old wickedness. Hurt her in ways he did when she was fourteen, a child, but can't any longer now that she's a woman."

"When did she become pregnant?" Rath asked.

"Ninety-five."

"ALL THIS TIME," Rath said as he and Test sat in the Scout, "we thought the CRVK stopped because he died. Went to prison. Moved. Grew ill. No. He stopped because he got *married*."

"No," Test said. "Because he had a child. A daughter. *That* kept him at bay. Kept his urges in check. Far as we know. His daughter dies, the adoption didn't work out. He's *free* again. Except, he has an airtight alibi for Jamie Drake. And for Lucille Forte. Which leaves—"

"Victoria. You think a fourteen-year-old girl was the CRVK?"

"You heard the sister. Victoria would do anything for his love. Everything," Test said.

"They did it together? Psychosexual homicidal kink?"

"There's precedent. Some of the most heinous crimes are committed by couples that would never have so much as shoplifted as individuals. But. I don't know. What do you think? Could she be our girl for Jamie Drake.?"

"It's a stretch," Rath said.

"It is. But if she did it, she may be worth a look for the Quebec murders, too."

"What about Dana Clark?"

"Sheldon's our guy for her. The Polaroids lock it. But he and Preacher are hooked up with something sinister, somehow, with Preacher owning Sheldon's truck. Either the Pratts or Sheldon or Preacher are the CRVK. But I couldn't say which."

"It takes someone strong to hang Jamie," Rath said. "Someone like Preacher or Sheldon."

"Victoria's fit. And, if she and her husband did it together . . ."

"Her sister mentioned the father peddling furs. That means a familiarity with traps, and snares."

"We need to find her," Test said.

"Call in an APB. Get someone to their estate. I want to go drag Preacher in, tell him we know about the truck and his link to Sheldon. Hold him as a material witness."

"Let's go get the bastard."

76

Before the evening lecture, with Felix at his lab, Rachel browsed the third-floor stacks and found the three books she'd wanted: *Interviews with Violent Criminals, Criminal Sociopaths,* and, *The Criminally Deviant.*

As she emerged from the stacks, she saw the man at a Xerox machine.

He peered up to see her as he snatched sheets of paper the machine spat into the paper tray.

He lifted the top of the copier and yanked a book from under it, tucked the book under his arm.

Rachel walked over to him.

"Research?" she said.

He nodded, secreted the book in a canvas bag at his feet. She'd startled him; his breath was short. She made him nervous. Is that why he was so quiet? Was he not confident and assured after all, but shy? She could not figure him out.

"You too?" he said. He nodded at her books in her arms.

"Killing time in the stacks before a lecture."

"An art lost to the iPhone. What do you have there?"

"It's of no real consequence to anyone but me," she said in a rush of sarcasm that immediately made her blush.

The man did not seem to notice Rachel had parroted his earlier words.

"And to the professor who'll read your paper, I imagine," the man said. He cocked his head at the books. "Why the interest in violence?"

"It's private," Rachel said. She felt awkward now. The reason she'd picked these books *was* private, painful. "Why your interest in the criminally deviant?"

"My interests aren't in the criminally deviant."

"I got a glimpse of your book on the street and—"

"I'm interested in the sexually 'deviant.'"

"Oh," Rachel said.

"Your look is exactly why I didn't share earlier, despite your prying."

"I didn't pry."

"Of course you pried. Curiosity killed the cat. Satisfaction brought him back. Or her. It underpins my research. Curiosity. And lies. Denial of self truths. But. You don't have to lie to me. I'm a stranger. Lie to family and friends, but no need to lie to me because I don't care what your bent is. The premise of my research is that we lie about what we are most curious about, sexually and otherwise, to friends and families, ourselves. We let shame or fear or judgment keep us from being honest about our true nature. Our fantasies. Our desires. We don't dare share them. We cling to them so tightly out of fear of judgment that they become anchors that prevent us from being our truest selves."

Rachel's blood warmed, both with uneasiness and a certain

freedom. No one had ever spoken to her like this. She would have been repulsed if this man had pressed these views on her, but he hadn't. She'd prodded him.

"In fact" he said, "what is called deviant is being revealed more and more as the norm. What adults do for pleasure that has long been labeled taboo is far more 'normal' than the prurient suppose."

Rachel did have certain . . . scenarios she'd never shared with Felix. With anyone. She worried what he'd think, that he'd see her differently. So she forgot about them. Tried to.

"This liberation is due to what I call *ready exposure to the possible*. As a boy I had to hunt for my father's *Hustler* issues to sneak a glimpse of what life offered. Now? Now, you can type in any taste and up comes video of whatever you want to see, acted out for your pleasure. No generation before has had that . . . luxury. Still, we view in private, ashamed. I bet you haven't shared your deepest desire with your boyfriend out of fear of it driving wedge between you, convinced yourself your desires aren't worth upsetting the status quo. Guess what? He's doing the same. Keeping his secrets secret. Not sharing. Imagine if you two both just shared."

Rachel swallowed. The stranger's candor teased her curiosity, as if she were walking down a hotel hallway and heard certain hedonistic sounds as she passed an open door. Did she walk past without a peek? Could she resist?

How could she fault him for telling her what she had asked to hear? Yet how could she have expected to hear *this*? No one spoke this way to strangers. The man was right. Once or twice, out of curiosity, Rachel had searched online to sate her curiosity, and not been disappointed. Fueled was more like it.

Again, as she had before, she had the sensation she was about to step out onto a high wire.

The stranger stuffed his printed copies into the canvas bag then slung the bag over his shoulder. "I've wasted your time," he said. "Good luck with your research. Fascinating in its own right."

"I'll see you around," Rachel said.

"I doubt that. I stopped in town on a whim. Though I may stay for dinner. Is there a place to get a bite, besides the coffee shop, in town?"

"The Wild Panther Inn," Rachel said. "They have a pub thing going on. Great comfort food. I was going to grab a bite there later." She actually had no such plans, but she was hungry for one of their burgers now that she thought about it.

"Join me," he said.

"I can't."

"I understand." He started to walk away again.

"I have a lecture I need to go to later," Rachel said.

"I understand."

"Maybe," she said, "you could give me a lift? They've got great burgers and I'm starving. I'll grab one to go, and shuttle back up."

77

The front seat was just that: one seat. A bench. Black. Leather, she gathered by its odor. Chrome and wood trim. A pack of gum sat on the immense dash, and a few food wrappers and loose receipts littered the bench seat.

Rachel pulled the seat belt across her, a lap belt, not retractable. She pulled the extra length of belt through the buckle, snug. If the car stopped fast, she would slingshot forward and smash her face against the dash. She pulled her backpack tight to her side against the door, the weight of the handgun reassuring.

The man started the car. The engine roared to life with a dangerous and romantic growl that new cars didn't possess. Rachel glanced sideways to catch his profile. If he noticed, he gave no indication as he backed the car out of its spot, palming the enormous steel steering wheel.

"I'm famished," he said. But he said nothing else as he drove down the hill through the fog. He did not glance at her, but minded the foggy road. He did not try to steal a peek at her or make small talk. It was a relief. Old guys always asked about her studies and immediately launched into how much they *loved* and *knew* about the subjects. Lame.

The silence was exactly what Rachel always wished for when in circumstances with a man of his age, on a bus, or train or plane, a doctor's waiting room. When a man mistook a random glance from her as an invitation to speak to her, speak *at* her, and continue to speak at her even when she answered his pestering questions with a flat yes or no and refused to meet his eye again, turned back to her cell phone or her book, all her mind screamed was: *Stop. I am not sleeping with you because you ask me my name and where I'm from, if I have any siblings. Just. Leave me the fuck alone.*

Which is just what he was doing.

Leaving her the fuck alone.

He was beyond that. It was as if he knew that's exactly what she wanted. Needed. Knew women enough, respected them enough, to know they wanted respect, not come-ons, and if they did want a come-on, there would be no mistake about it.

He tapped an index finger on the steering wheel and looked out the windshield as Rachel took in the old car's metal ashtray, the buttons to the AM/FM radio jutting out like black teeth. The massive green metal glove box door in front of her knees.

The wipers crept across the windshield.

He piloted the car surgically around a nasty curve.

In town, he parked across the street from the Wild Panther. The rain had picked up, a deluge. He grabbed an umbrella from the backseat and strode around and opened the passenger door, holding the umbrella for Rachel. As they dashed across the street, they were nearly struck by an SUV as silver as the fog itself, its horn blaring before it sped off. It gave Rachel a start, and the man, too. He escorted her into the inn, the slight pressure of his hand at her lower back.

Inside, Rachel laughed and shook the rain from her hair and went to the bar to place an order for her burger. The man followed, ordered a scotch, sipped it.

"What's your name, anyway?" Rachel said.

"What would you want with my name?"

"So I don't have to keep thinking of you as *The Stranger.*"

"Maybe I prefer you think of me as *The Stranger.* Much more mysterious." He held out his hand. "Bryant Hale."

Rachel shook his hand. It was smooth and cool.

"And you're Rachel," he said.

Rachel pulled her hand away, out of his, her heart knocking hard in her chest. How the hell did he know her name?

"The girl at the coffee shop called out your name, when your coffee was ready," he said, and smiled.

"Right," Rachel said. "Of course."

The bartender brought Rachel's boxed burger to her. Rachel could barely lift it, she was so weak from fear. No one at the coffee shop had called out her name. Her friend had said. *Your daily Red Eye.*

Before Rachel could get her money from her backpack, the man broke out his wallet and handed the bartender a $100 bill. He seemed to want Rachel to see the money. He turned back to her. "Sure you have to go to that lecture?" he said.

"I need to go," Rachel said, furious and disappointed with herself for engaging this stranger. *You imbecile,* she thought. All she wanted now was to see Felix, get home as soon as possible after her lecture and get into bed and let her sweet boyfriend hold her.

As Rachel started away, the stranger's fingers grazed her fingers.

THE NAMES OF DEAD GIRLS

She yanked her hand away and headed straight for the closest exit at the side of the building.

Just before she headed back into the fog, she turned quickly and, with the stranger working at his scotch in profile to her, snapped a quick photo of him on her phone.

Ten minutes later, she was still shaking when she boarded the shuttle and sent her father a text with the stranger's photo. U know him?

She wanted to cry. The heft of the gun in her backpack felt like an anvil. Like the one in her stomach. What had she been thinking? *Buying a gun?* Taking lessons? *Planning to meet Preacher?* Engaging with this stranger? Trusting him? She could barely trust herself, her own thoughts and instincts. She'd see if she could sell the gun back to the shop owner. Then she'd tear up her parents' murder file. Tear it up and burn it and never look at it again and try to scrub her mind of what she'd read and seen. Had she lost her mind? It felt like it. No. Not quite. Worse. She'd lost herself. No more. She wanted no part of it anymore. Any of it. Especially the gun. It was of no use in her backpack. It was a danger.

Rachel hurried to the Gihon River Inn, shivering as she climbed the stairs. She ducked into her room, where she took the gun from her backpack and hid it under the bed, sighing with relief to be rid of it. It was of no use unless she had it in her hands at all times. If that freak stranger came anywhere near her, she'd scream her god damned head off and kick him in the balls.

She texted Felix: Headed 2 lect B home str8 away Promise XXX

RACHEL WAS STILL shivering as the shuttle climbed the hill. Not from being damp or cold. She shivered wondering, *How did he know my name?*

78

Preacher sat at the table. His blood roared in his head as he waited for the knock on the door, his eye on the pink stationery, the cursive with its loops and curls as feminine as a woman's curves or the scent rising from the paper itself. He read the letter, again and again.

Smiled.

In his darkest fantasies he'd never imagined one of *them* coming to *him*. Reaching out to him in such a manner. Believing she could understand him. That she knew him. Could save him. Yet, in prison, he had received letters from many of them. Dozens. Women wanting to help him. To be with him.

Save him.

He stared at the book on the table. The *Bible*.

Words.

Words words words.

Yet more.

Salvation.

Freedom.

He'd read the words. Learned them, recited them, behaved in the way they instructed, the good ways.

There were many terrible ways in this book, but these passages, he believed, showed how weak some of us were, how we had to fight to resist the terrible ways. He did not have to fight. He was stronger than that. He had always been stronger than that.

How easy it had been. They all thought he was a fraud. That he was not truly saved. They saw him as the beast, the monster, saw him as they saw fit. Even when he did them favors and told them the truth, gave it to them straight, like he had on the phone with Rath, they did not want to accept the truth. The unforgiving bastards. He smiled. He had to keep his old temper in check. Be better than that. Be godly.

Before, he'd thought to be godly was to use his power, like the God of old, vengeful and spiteful and merciless, wielding a power of violence and ruin.

He'd learned.

He was not sorry for his past sins. He was saved. Forgiven.

Real power was to resist those urges, rise above them. Power was the truth.

The truth.

The book was the truth. Yet people did not want the truth. Franklin Rath did not want the truth about the type of woman his sister had been. Franklin Rath did not want to hear the truth about who his daughter was, and he did not want his daughter to know the truth.

But she would. And soon. Preacher had given Rath enough time to tell his daughter the truth, and Rath had failed.

Now, Preacher would tell her. How good that would feel. To lay it bare. How freeing. To see what the truth did to them both.

It was up to them to face it. Accept it. Learn from it. Or let it crush them. If Franklin Rath and his daughter were destroyed by the truth, it proved only that they were weak. He could not help that. Even if they wanted to kill the messenger.

Preacher hoped Rachel would eventually accept the truth. He dreamed of it. Dreamed she would come to him as his daughter one day.

As soon as this visit was over, he would go visit Rachel, go visit his blood child, and tell her who she was. Who he was.

The knock he'd waited for came at his door.

He stood, his pants down around his ankles, erection straining. He needed to gain control of his terrible self. Demonstrate real power.

He tucked himself in and pulled up his pants, left his shirt out, to drape and conceal himself, and went to answer the door to receive his Love.

HER EYES SHONE when she looked up at him, shone just to be in his presence. She did not look how he'd imagined, and he had to fight to hide his disappointment. He'd hoped she'd be more . . . tempting. Harder to resist. She was his first test.

"I've looked forward to this more than I can say," she said, her breath shallow, wanting.

She would do. For his first test. But first he needed to find out if anyone knew she was here. Anyone knew she'd been in contact with him, had planned to come here. He'd not heard a car pull up. Had she walked all this way? Or been dropped off? Knowing they were alone would make it harder for him to resist. Test him as God would have him tested.

"Come in," he said.

He let her go up the stairs in front of him. Her long raincoat hid her body, and he clenched his teeth against the temptation of his Terrible Self. There was time for all that if that is how it went. If he failed this first test. Proved weaker than he thought. He might need to be tested many times. There was time to get it right.

He had all the time in the world.

But he needed to be safe, make sure the sorry thing had not told anyone. If she had, the test would be too easy, and he would need to let her go. A loss, but a small one. There were others.

"Through here," he said at the top of the stairs, pointing at the kitchen's swinging doors straight ahead.

She went through the doors.

He felt sick at his living conditions, three chairs that did not match one another, and a table that did not match any of the chairs. He had swept the place, though, washed his few dirty dishes, and put a tablecloth on the table. A paper tablecloth, but still, a tablecloth.

All for show—she'd not be around long, either way—but still the disgust was there.

"I apologize for the state of things."

"The Lord does not judge us by material worth," she said.

He pulled the chair out for her and stood behind her, breathed in the scent of her hair. His erection strained, and she had not even taken off her coat yet. They had not even begun.

"Take off your coat, be comfortable."

"I am," she said. "Very." She lowered her coat off her shoulders, draped it over the back of the chair as she looked back at him, her eyes on him, unable to hide the lust even as she pretended she was here to do the Lord's work. Let her pretend. Let them both pretend and play the game. Play their roles. Let the Lord test them.

His cock leaked.

She had to know what she was doing to him. How she was testing him. She knew. She knew. They all knew. He was not mistaken. Was she leaking, too? She had not come for the Lord.

Her breathing was deep and unsteady, her chest rising and falling beneath her dark blue dress.

She sat.

He sat opposite her.

She gave him a shy smile, but her eyes were hot with wickedness. He knew the look. Knew her mind was hot, too, with nastiness. He knew.

This was going to be good. Still, he needed to know if anyone knew she was here, if she'd told anyone about him, about this. He'd hate to have to let her go and not be truly tested. But how could he ask her and not scare her off?

She gazed at him, drank him in, his face. Her breathing grew heavier. It was not his imagination.

She unbuttoned the button at the throat of her dress.

"I came alone," she said as if she knew his thoughts. "I came alone in the trust of the Lord. And to prove my trust to you."

He could smell her sweat. It disgusted him even as it aroused him. This was good. A real test. The truth would come from it, and that was all he could ask. Was he man or beast?

"No one knows I'm here," she said. "Only the Lord. And the

Lord will keep me safe. I know you will not harm me. You are not a beast. You are a man. A real man."

His pant leg grew damp. His erection fierce.

He could smell her sex from across the table.

"You know I want to be good. I do not want to sin. And I know you are good. You do not want to sin," she said. "But." She swallowed, unbuttoned the next button of her dress. A hint of dark red revealed. Her bra. Or an underthing. "It's hard. Isn't it? Isn't it hard?"

Yes, yes it was hard. Hard. Painful. Torture.

"Yes," he said. "Yes. It's hard."

"Hard to be good. Hard not to sin. Hard to control yourself."

He nodded, swallowed. The slut. Coming here all alone. Teasing him knowing who he was and what he'd done. She was sick. Filthy, And she was his. All his. She deserved whatever she got. The tease. He'd make it slow. Make up for lost time. All that lost time. *He'd eat her fucking alive.*

"I want to do things to you. With you," she said, her voice shaking, a whisper, trembling. "Things I know I should not do. I must not do. Awful. Sinful acts against my nature. But with you . . . I cannot help myself. I cannot stop myself."

"Don't stop yourself," he growled.

Yes, he'd eat her fucking alive. He'd tear her hot living flesh with his teeth. He'd go further than he'd ever gone before; he'd cut her and slice her and then he'd chop her into fucking pieces and bathe in the pieces in his tub. He'd dump her remains in the woods to feed the coyotes. Grind up her bones.

She stood.

He flinched, not expecting this.

She was a brave one.

Dumb as mud. But brave.

She walked over to him.

Stood before him, undid a third button.

The scarlet showing.

For a moment he thought—

She touched him.

His shoulder.

Softly.

He recoiled.

No one touched him like that.

Ever.

No one.

Who did she think she was?

Who did she think was in charge here?

"Shh," she said. "I know what you need. I know what the beast in you needs to do to me." She whispered as if she couldn't breathe. "But I need to get what I need first."

She came around behind him, fingers trailing the flesh under his chin, his throat, to the back of his neck, his skin hot where her fingers touched him, as if lit on fire. She pressed her thumbs deep into the flesh and muscle back of his neck.

Fuck. It was good. She was good. She was evil.

He'd not been touched like this in—forever.

Never had he been touched like this in his life.

Never had he known this.

He was going to—

She bit his neck.

He felt a hot quick pain.

No.
She bit again.
No.
He wasn't being bit.
He was being stabbed.

79

That guy's sort of a creep, isn't he?" the woman sitting next to Rachel said as they filed out of the lecture hall.

The woman wrapped a blue wool headscarf around her tousled hair and tucked its end down into her coat. She wore no makeup but still had a striking, powerful presence.

"Some people might think the material is creepy." Rachel laughed. "But the lecturer himself seemed dull. I was disappointed."

"No." The woman laughed, too, and touched Rachel's arm. "Not the lecturer. I agree. Zzzzzz. Boring. I meant the man from earlier, the one pestering you. The old creep."

Rachel didn't know if the woman was talking about the stranger or how she'd know about him.

"Sorry," the woman said. "I was in the SUV that honked at you, the one you crossed in front of, before you and that creep went into the hotel together."

"That was *you.*"

"Tah dah." The woman smiled. "Though sorry I startled you earlier. The fog. I didn't see you at first."

"Why do you call him a creep?"

"He is, isn't he?"

Rachel paused. "How do you know?"

"Oh boy. Let me tell you."

They exited with the throng to stand under the overhang of the lecture hall. The rain was blowing sideways, in sheets. The woman snapped her umbrella open. Rachel pulled up her wet coat collar.

"Share my umbrella to your car," the woman said, hoisting the umbrella over them both. "I'll tell you all about that bastard."

"I take the shuttle."

"Please. That's insane. You'll float away before you reach the shuttle. It's the least I can do for nearly running you down earlier. We make a mad dash on three."

Rachel looked out at the rain.

"Ready," the woman said. "One. Two. Three."

THEY WERE SOAKED by the time they got to the SUV. But at least the vehicle was comfortable. As the woman waited for the windshield to defog, Rachel's seat warmed right up. It sure beat the shuttle.

"So. Why's the guy a creep?" Rachel said.

The woman started the car and backed out, drove out of the lot toward Campus Hill. "Let me guess. He played Mr. Remote. Mr. Aloof. So much so you started to find it, if not attractive, mysterious, alluring."

"I guess, yeah, how—"

"And you kept bumping into him at odd times in odd places. Turn around in the coffee shop and, poof, what do you know. There's Mr. Aloof. Again. And surprise, he's *still* being aloof.

Pretending he doesn't recognize you. Pretending he doesn't see you. Pretending you don't exist. The Great Pretender. Except. It never struck you he was pretending, because he's so good at it and you're—"

The woman was driving too fast, dangerously for the dark and the fog.

Rachel wondered if the woman were drunk.

She was acting like it. Or like she was on something. *Erratic.*

"Can you slow down?" Rachel said. "Please."

The woman slowed the SUV down. "Sorry. Guys like that. They get me worked up." She laughed.

Rachel took her phone out and texted Felix: Home in 5

Felix: cant wait 2 C U

Rachel: same

"Guys like what?" Rachel said.

"Who pretend."

"How do you know he did all that? Do you know him?"

"Who you texting?"

"My boyfriend."

"Ah. Got to check in?"

"Hardly."

"Your generation, it's so different from mine. Can't ever be alone, out of contact. Check in constantly. No trust or independence. Texting replacing loyalty."

Rachel did not understand what the woman was going on about, but her tremulous voice edged close to hysteria.

"I have loyalty," the woman said. "I do what it takes to keep my man instead of betraying him, even if he is a betraying bastard himself."

"You can let me out here," Rachel said.

"Did he pull all that crap about kinks and taboos and how normal they are," the woman said. She was angry now. Enraged. "Did he feed you the one about the rest of the world being so uptight, judgmental, hypocrites? Did he give you the bullshit but only after he manipulated *you* into asking about his 'project,' his fucking research. Is he still using that bait?"

The woman was scaring Rachel, even more than the man had scared her earlier.

"You can let me out here," Rachel said.

Her heart pounding, she sent a text to her father and Felix: silver suv range rover? lexus? woman, 30s?

The text came back: Undeliverable.

"Please, stop," Rachel said. "I'll be all right to walk."

"Stop here? Stop now? In the middle of the road in this storm, in the dark? You're just full of smart choices, aren't you? Like falling for his shit. That shit. A married man. Did you know that? Did you ever consider that? Did you bother to ask if he *belonged* to someone else? Did it ever enter your pea brain to ask what an older guy like that was up to? How he just showed up wherever you showed up? Or how he might be trying to trick you? Like he tricked me. Like he *ruined* me. At least I had a fucking excuse. At least I was a stupid fucking hick fourteen-year-old. You're what, *eighteen*? In *college*. Your dad's a *cop*."

"How do you know—"

"And you have a *boyfriend*. And *still* you go to an inn on a weekday afternoon to fuck my—"

"*What*? I didn't—"

"*Don't interrupt me*," the woman screeched, waving her hands wildly. The SUV swerved, teetered, crossing over the centerline around a curve. Headlights of an oncoming car raked through the windshield as the car blared its horn and the woman yanked the SUV back on her side of the road, just missing the other vehicle. "*I'm* talking here. *I'm* the one talking."

80

Preacher's house sat dark among the trees and fog as Test pulled the Explorer into the yard.

The Subaru was gone, but the old Ford pickup truck sat in the yard.

"No way to squirm out of this, not with him having that truck here," Test said as she and Rath crossed the wet yard and took the steps to take Preacher into custody. Pieces of the broken porch still lay scattered in the muck, though the snow and ice had melted.

Test knocked on the door.

Rath sensed Preacher inside, lying in wait.

Test knocked again.

Rath stepped off the porch and knelt at a low basement window and cupped his hands to see inside.

It was too dark in the basement to see anything.

"We're going in," Test said.

Rath drew his sidearm as Test drew hers and took hold of the doorknob. The door was unlocked.

It opened with a creak.

Rath smelled the odor from out on the steps.

"What the hell?" he said as he and Test stepped inside, his handgun trained up the stairs, Test's trained on the basement stairs.

The odor bloomed, potent.

The house stood silent.

The place was gloomy with shadows.

Rath hit the light switch beside him, and the chintzy fixture above him lit the stairway.

The top three stairs were darker than the rest. Nearly black.

Rath looked at Test and climbed a few steps.

Blood had spread over the lip of the stairs from the floor and run down the risers to pool on the top three treads.

Rath stepped over the blood-blackened stairs and followed the blood through the swinging doors of the kitchen, at the center of which Ned Preacher sat in a cheap folding chair, his body slumped forward onto the table.

The chair and table were caked with black blood, as were Preacher's clothes and body. A lake of the blood had spread from beneath the chair to the stairs.

Test stepped up behind Rath.

"Let's check that it's clear," she whispered.

She and Rath combed the residence, upstairs and down, finding no one.

Back upstairs, the two stepped carefully around the dried blood to stand in front of Preacher.

He'd been dead for some time.

His body had been slashed and torn and gored so many times there seemed to be no flesh untouched by the knife.

So much blood.

"I'll radio the state police and ME," Test said. She did not care if she were first on-site, first to investigate. She was tired of this shit.

Rath and Test backed out of the house, mindful of surfaces and the blood.

Outside, Rath watched Test walk to the Explorer. When she was out of sight behind the screen of hemlocks, Rath stepped off the porch to the trees.

The birdhouse was still there.

Rath put on a surgical, crime scene glove and lifted the birdhouse lid.

The trail camera sat inside.

Rath needed the SD card. Images of the killer had to be on the card. But there were images of him on it, too, pictures from fishing and hunting. He'd meant for whatever images the camera took here to be for his private use at the start. Now, he needed to erase the pics of himself. It could not be known that he'd put the camera up. It would complicate matters of evidence, even though he'd put the camera up as a citizen. He'd erase any images incriminating himself and send the SD card in the mail. Anonymously.

He was about to lift the camera out and snatch the SD card when the Explorer's door slammed shut. He'd run out of time.

He closed the birdhouse lid and hurried to the porch without the SD card.

Test had a camera slung over her shoulder and held a box containing crime scene coveralls, hoods, booties, and rubber gloves. She looked at the gloves on Rath's hands. "Raring to go, huh?"

They put on the garb and went inside.

Rath searched the kitchen as Test scoured the living room. There was no evidence of a struggle, nothing obviously out of place. Rath opened drawers, the refrigerator, cupboards, and a pantry, all of them nearly bare. He flipped through a pile of junk mail and bills on the table, checked the trash can under the sink and found nothing but a glop of pasta. Something nagged him. Something was missing; he could not think of what it was. The more he forced himself, the more it eluded him.

It would come; he needed to trust his subconscious.

He returned to the living room. Test looked up from where she was standing in the far corner of the spare room.

"Anything?" Rath said.

"How does someone stab Preacher in a chair without a struggle? It has to have been someone he knew. Trusted."

"Clay Sheldon."

"Sheldon visits, maybe under the pretense to share what he's done with Dana Clark. Or maybe to do just this. Kill the one person who knows what he's done. After we visited him at the North Star, he knew we were circling and that Preacher was a loose thread."

"Maybe." Rath's mind was working. "Who else could come to Preacher's home and lull him?"

Rath stared at Preacher's corpse. It strained against the ropes that bound it, as if Preacher were trying to get free. This was it then. The end of him.

"I need to call Rachel as soon as I'm back in cell service," Rath said.

"About her," Test said, her tone grave yet conciliatory. "She called me. The first night she stayed at your house. After Preacher was watching her. She wanted copies of the police report for her parents' murders."

"I hope the hell you didn't provide them."

"She has legal rights to the files."

"You didn't have to be the one to give them to her. You kept that from me? If you'd made her come in and make copies, she may have balked. Who knows what seeing all that shit might—"

"Trigger." Test looked at Preacher's body.

"I won't honor that with a response," Rath said, but he felt chilled, knowing what Rachel had read and seen about her parents. He knew the anger it spawned, the compulsion to *do* something.

He needed to get that SD card more than ever.

"We'll see if forensics can find anything we can't," Test said.

"They usually do."

81

Rachel tried to send the text again. It bounced back. As she checked the door handle to see if the door was locked, the woman snatched Rachel's phone, smashed its screen on the steering wheel until it blinked out, then tossed the phone out her window and into the woods.

"Let me out!" Rachel shouted, her mind spastic. "Let me out of this fucking car!"

The SUV sped up, careened.

At the bottom of the hill, the woman drove through the red light and through town. The fog forced her to drive at twenty miles an hour. Rachel tried to open the door. It was locked. She tried to power down the window. Locked.

She watched, helpless as the vehicle drove past the Gihon River Inn where Felix sat waiting. Where her gun sat in her backpack.

Rachel yanked on the door handle.

It was no use.

She pounded on the window. She needed to break the window and scream out for help or climb out, fall out, if she had to, risk cutting herself on broken glass, risk breaking a leg or cracking her skull on the road.

Because if the woman got out of town and headed into the wilderness before Rachel could get out—.

Rachel pounded her fist on the widow.

"Stop it!" the woman screeched. "Stop it! Stop it stop it!" She grabbed at Rachel, but Rachel elbowed her and the car swerved.

Rachel considered attacking the woman or the steering wheel and making the vehicle crash. If it were just Rachel and the woman who might get hurt, she'd do it. But she had no idea who the SUV might crash into if she did.

She pounded her fist on the window. It splintered. She unlatched her seat belt and raised her fist to finish the job and felt something touch her hair, slide over her face and around her neck. A rope or a cord or—

It pulled tight as a noose around her throat.

She gasped. Her hands flew to her throat, clutched at the cord.

She couldn't breathe. It felt as if she'd swallowed her tongue as a pressure swelled behind and in her eyes, as if her eyes might pop.

She clawed at the cord.

She tried to fight the woman, but the grip the cord had around her neck was too tight, seemed locked, and her hands instinctively would not leave her throat.

The vehicle drove out of town and jounced as it turned down a dirt side road into the woods.

Rachel tried to dig her fingers down between the cord and her throat but couldn't.

She couldn't breathe. She'd pass out soon. She'd die.

The vehicle rocked to a stop. The driver's door opened as the cord tightened around Rachel's throat and Rachel was hauled backward across the seats, out on her back onto the muddy ground, the rain falling in her face, running into her nose. She flailed, tried to turn over, tried to get to her knees. The woman stood over her, yanked on the cord as the rain cascaded in sheets. "Did you fuck him in that nasty hotel?"

The rain drenched the woman's hair. Her black eye makeup streamed down her cheeks. She looked wild, mad.

The cord released, just enough for Rachel to sip a breath, to gag and vomit.

"Did you?" the woman railed.

Rachel gagged. Shook her head no. Sobbed.

"Did you!" the woman shrieked.

The cord slackened.

"No!" Rachel blurted, gasping as the cord tightened again.

She kicked at the woman's feet but the woman pulled on the cord and stepped around to stand by Rachel's head, peering down at her, so she looked upside down from where Rachel lay on her back. She needed to tell the woman she'd left out the side door of the place. Had not stayed.

"Liar," the woman said. "What'd he do to you? Did you like it? Like being choked? Like being abused?"

Rachel shook her head crying.

Her eyes felt so hot and strained and engorged it seemed she would start crying blood.

"You liked it, did you?" the woman screamed. The rain was nearly blinding Rachel, filling her nostrils. Her skull seemed to be cracking. "You loved it," the woman railed. "Thought you could do more for him than me. His wife. The mother of his child. I'll do anything for him." She yanked on the cord, her eyes bulging as if she were the one being choked to death. "*Any thing.*"

She brought her face close to Rachel's, her head cocking to the side as if she were a child merely observing, confused as this madwoman before her choked to death, unaware it was she who was tightening the cord. Her black eye makeup ran down her face and her soaked hair, straggly and wild, hung down in Rachel's face.

The cord tightened.

82

Forensics found nothing of worth in Preacher's place. Not at first blush. The state police forensics team lifted prints, but found no signs of struggle, no sign of forced entry, no stray hair that might belong to anyone but Preacher. Not a trace of a footprint in all that blood.

Rath was searching Preacher's bedroom, looking through the clothes in the closet—six white button-up shirts, six pairs of black jeans, one black belt, two skinny black ties—when Test came to the doorway and said, "You need to see this."

Rath followed her back to the living room where a forensics technician from the state police held a cell phone in his gloved hand. Test went to him and took the phone. "Look," she said to Rath.

Rath stood near Test and looked at the phone's screen display of typical icons.

"How'd you access it without a password?" he said.

"Didn't have a password set up."

"Where was it?"

"Between the couch cushions."

"Is it his?" Rath said.

"You tell me."

Test pointed at an app icon that looked like the face of an old radio.

"So?" Rath said.

Test tapped a gloved finger on the app.

As soon as the app opened, even before the audio started playing, Rath understood.

"Simple Wi-Fi app," Test said.

"A *scanner*," Rath said. "A fucking scanner?" His mind tripped. "He knew Jamie was hanged because he heard it on a fucking police scanner? He told me: 'I hear things.'"

"That's why he was so smug. While we were at his house with the warrant he was at the station, phone in his pocket. He—"

"What?" Rath said.

"He was reaching for his phone as I told him he had to come to the station. I told him to put it away. I think he was going to show me, then saw a chance to toy further with us. He was probably hoping we'd charge him, let us get as far along as he could stand before rubbing it in our faces how he knew about her being hanged."

"He was never involved," Rath said.

"What?" Test said.

"Sheldon acted alone in killing Dana Clark."

"Then who did this? Why does Preacher have Sheldon's truck?" Test said.

Rath looked around at the nearly empty drawers and cupboards. The junk mail on the table.

The mail.

He looked through the stack of mail again.

"What is it?" Test said.

Rath checked the garbage can under the kitchen sink. Nothing.

"What is it?" Test said.

"Nothing," Rath said.

But it wasn't.

He walked out to the living room to find the state police detective. "You find a letter. On pink stationery?"

The detective called an underling over and asked the question of the woman. "No," she said.

Rath peered out the window. Several scene workers were outside. There was no way to get to the camera. *Where is that pink letter I saw you read that day I watched you get the mail on your porch?* Rath thought. *What was on it?*

"The trash outside in the bin," he said. "Has it been hauled for the week or—"

"Hauled yesterday."

"What's this about?" Test said.

"Nothing," Rath said.

83

You can't have him!" the woman shrieked. "He's mine. Despite what he is, what he does. He's *mine*."

She leaned her face in close to Rachel's face, bared her teeth as if she'd bite Rachel's face. Rachel reached up and grabbed the woman's hair in both hands and yanked savagely. Kept yanking. The woman howled. Rachel tore at the cord. It loosened. Rachel heaved for a true breath, her throat raw and burning as she hauled on the woman's hair, torqueing the woman's head sideways, back and forth, back and forth until she rolled the woman over onto her back.

Rachel jumped up, coughing and wheezing, vomiting, and stomped her boot in the woman's face. Stomped harder. Heard bone break. Stomped again. Kicked the woman in the side. Kicked her knees and ankles as hard as she could, as her father had once taught her, to hobble an attacker.

Then, she ran, tugging loose the cord.

She stumbled in the dark and fog, falling and crashing into trees at the roadside, getting up again and carrying on.

Her breaths came as heaving, joyous sobs as the cold rain cooled her flaming skin, the gulped oxygen miraculous as it filled her lungs.

She ran toward the diffuse lights of the town visible ahead in the fog, until finally she came out onto pavement, crying with relief.

She ran down the sidewalk and shoved through the doors of the inn where she ran straight into Felix.

"Where— God. What happened?" Felix said.

"Call my dad call my dad call my dad," Rachel said, as she collapsed into him.

84

As Rath drove the Scout onto the pavement from Forgotten Gorge Road, a flurry of texts and voice messages sprang up on his phone.

All of them from Rachel or Felix. All of them urgent, some confusing and cryptic. What alarmed him most was the photo with the text Do u know him? Boyd Pratt.

Rath yanked the Scout to the side of the road and phoned Rachel. He got no answer, not even voice mail. He called Felix's number. Felix picked up first ring.

"What's going on?" Rath said. "Why isn't Rachel picking up, why—"

"She's here. With me. She's OK. Well, not OK. Shaken. And—"

"What are you talking about? Let me *talk* to her."

"She can't. Her voice. Her throat is too sore, weak."

"What the hell happened? *Tell* me."

Rath's blood drained as Felix explained.

"Stay put," Rath said. "I'll be there as soon—"

"No," Felix said. "We're borrowing a friend's car. She wants to come home."

Rath let out a long breath. "OK. OK. Good. Good. But first, you need to get the police there. Call nine one one and—"

"We did. An hour ago. We spoke to them, they got all the information. They got the woman, they got the crazy lunatic. She was right where Rachel left her. Rachel *trounced* her."

Rath wanted this news to bring him comfort, or a warped sense of pride. But it didn't.

"Rachel needs to see a doctor," he said.

"The EMTs checked her out good. Her throat looks really, really bad. And it's raw and sore. But they found no internal damage."

"She needs to see a real doctor."

"Tomorrow. She promises. She just wants to go home."

"See you there."

He called Test. Voice mail. He texted her: PULL OVER AND PICK UP. He called again. She picked up first ring.

"Listen," Rath said, and filled her in.

"Where's Rachel now?" Test said.

"Coming home."

"I should have never sent her the files," Test said. "I should never have caved, even if she had every right to—"

"That has nothing to do with what happened."

"Still."

"Go home. See your kids."

"God knows, I want to. I need to do one more thing."

85

"Tell me who killed Mandy Wilks," Test said.

"I killed her," Abby Land said from across the table.

It had taken Test an hour to drive to the correctional facility. The public defender arrived twenty minutes later. Test had woken Blanc from her sleep and told her she had a way to get Abby Land's charges dropped or greatly reduced. Land had not killed Mandy Wilks despite all the hard evidence against her. Despite her own claims. Now, Blanc sat to Test's right, her black parka on the floor beside her, dressed in sweatpants and a Boston University hoodie.

"You're going to be tried as an adult," Test said, firing a look at Blanc: *Let me do this. For you and your client.* Blanc gave Test an approving blink.

"You'll do long hard time as an adult," Test said.

Abby Land shook her head, as if trying to escape invisible hands squeezing around her throat. "He tried to scare me before. Your *partner.* Even my so-called attorney here won't do her job right. Doesn't know jack shit. I'm out when I'm eighteen. *Out.*"

"You are going to be forty before you're out. Your life will be over. Is over. Who fed you that line of about two years?"

Land gnawed at her thumbnail, as if it she were working meat off the bone of a chicken wing. She was scared. Good. Maybe she was seeing reality. "No one fed me a line," she said.

"Boyd Pratt. Or his wife? Which one killed her? And why?"

Abby Land looked like she had just drunk gasoline.

"If you know," Blanc said. "For your sake, tell the detective."

"I know it was one of them," Test said. "It had to be. One of them killed Jamie Drake."

"I *told* you. I killed her. She had it coming. Thinking she was so perfect. Better than everyone else, better than me. Smarter than me. Always judging. The priss. Who's better now? Who's smarter? If she's so smart, how come she's dead?"

"Judging what?"

"It ain't your business just like it weren't hers. I'm old enough, I can do what I *want*."

"Is *this* what you *want*? Prison. Because you're going to do a lot of it. What you did, the brutality, combined with your lack of remorse—"

"Remorse. What's that?"

At first Test believed Land was being sarcastic. She wasn't. She didn't know the word. Blanc closed her eyes in disbelief.

"Regret," Test said.

"Why should I have regret when she was going to ruin—"

"Ruin what?"

"Nothing."

"You think your life isn't *ruined*? This place is the Double Black Diamond compared to hard time. You're going to maximum security in some place like Oklahoma. You want to end up in Oklahoma? Too far for friends to visit. You'll be forgotten in a month."

"I am *getting out of here in two years*," Land shouted.

The guard outside took a step toward the door.

Land stared at him bug-eyed, mocking, taunting.

"You don't have to protect them anymore," Test said.

"I'm not protecting shit."

"If you are, tell us, tell the detective. Help yourself, help me get you out of here," Blanc said. "I've informed you, you'll be tried as an adult."

"*They* can't protect *you* anymore," Test said. "Before the night is over, Victoria and Boyd Pratt are going to be arrested for the murder of Jamie Drake and another murder, perhaps three, in Canada. So. They also can't help or hurt you anymore. Either way, no reason to protect them."

"You're fuckin' with me," Land said.

"How can I be fucking with you if I'm trying to *keep you from doing hard time*?"

"Cuz that's what people *do*. They *fuck* with you. *Fuck* with me. That's all they ever done. Fuck with me. And *fuck* me. All my life." She said this as if she were a fifty-five-year-old woman and not a sixteen-year-old girl. She did not say it with anger—the steel and bite emptied from her voice now—but with a quiet defeat.

Her hands lay flat on the table, trembling.

"You don't have to be scared," Test said.

"The detective is right," Blanc said.

"I don't want to do hard time," Land said.

"You won't have to if you help yourself," Blanc said.

"Please don't let them make me. This isn't how it was supposed to happen. He *promised* me."

"*Who?*" Test and Blanc said simultaneously, each glancing at the other.

"Boyd."

"What did he promise?" Test said.

Blanc leaned in toward Land. "Tell her."

"I'd do two years and when I got out I'd be all set."

"All set?" Test said.

"Loaded. He was going to give me ten *thousand* dollars so I'd never have to worry about money again."

"He promised you that?" Test said.

"Who is this Pratt? Why did he tell you this?" Blanc said.

"I'm such a loser. Mandy was right. I'm a fuckin' loser." Land's eyes shimmered wetly.

"You can still get out in two years, honey," Test said, catching herself, feeling suddenly so horrible, so awful and sad. So homesick for her kids and husband. She felt as if she'd been away from them for years. "The D.A. can draw up new charges when you tell them the truth. That Boyd Pratt killed her and promised you money and an easy two-year ride to take the fall for him."

Abby Land could not stop her tears. Did not try. "I can't. Please don't let them. I don't want to go to Oklahoma."

"Then get it off your chest. Pratt can't hurt you or protect you now."

"I can't," she said.

"You can," Test said.

"This is your chance," Blanc said.

"I can't, I can't, I can't!" Land looked at Test. "I killed her. I killed her. *For* him."

Test sagged in her chair.

"Don't say another word," Blanc said.

"I see now how stupid I was," Land said, perking up with the delusion of hope in the face of futility. "I see. How stupid I am. I take it back. OK? I take it back," she said, as if this might bring Mandy Wilks back to life, make it all better.

Test rubbed her face in her hands. "Why?"

Land shrugged. "She deserved it. I mean. I thought she did. So perfect. And I was having such a good time for once, for the first time in my stupid life, with Boyd. Until Mandy found out about us. And about Jamie, too. The three of us. Jamie, me, and Boyd. We did some serious crazy shit together at his hotels. I mean, he let us stay in a *huge* fuckin' suite at the Double Black Diamond, for *free*. For a whole weekend. And in Montreal and Quebec. With important *business* men. There were some other chicks there, Euro trash, but we didn't care. I mean, as long as everyone was into it. I mean we had some serious crazy times. *Fun*. But then, Mandy was going to tell. Jamie. Stupid stupid Jamie. It's really her fault. She had all this stuff from the Double Black Diamond. Towels and shampoos and soaps. Notepads. And she brought them to school, was practically showing them off, and Mandy's locker was next to hers. Mandy asked about them and Jamie, stupid Jamie, she *told* her. Almost fuckin' everything. Like, bragged to her. She asked her to join the fun. Except Jamie was too dumb to know Mandy Wilks wasn't fun. Mandy didn't know *how* to have fun, how to party. And Mandy said we were losers. And she was going to tell."

"Who?" Test said, "Tell who?"

"I don't know. Adults. His wife. Definitely his stupid wife."

"And he told you to do it? Kill her?"

"If he told you, this is a whole different matter, Abby," Blanc said. "If he coerced or manipulated or threatened—"

"No, no, no, nothing like that," Land said. "He said I needed to convince her to shut up. She was a prissy know-it-all trouble-maker. Of course I agreed. But you can't shut a girl like her up. I came up with the idea. My car battery was shit, and I had one person jump-start me that day in the hotel lot already. And I knew Mandy would drive that road home after her new job. I knew it would be late and dark and no one around. It was perfect. I knew she'd stop, she was such a Goody Two-shoes."

"She'd stop to help jump-start you even though she hated you?" Test said.

"She didn't hate me. She pitied me. She treated me like her project. Like I was broken and needed fixin'. Like I needed to act a certain way. Act like her. All tra la la. Yeah, I'd *act* like her, if I *looked* like her. How hard would *that* be? So I knew she'd stop to help me jump-start my car. I knew it. And I was *right*."

"You planned it?" Test said.

"Don't answer that," Blanc insisted. "Do not answer that."

Land nodded.

"We're done here. Abby, you're done here," Blanc said.

Test felt gutted. "Why'd you keep her body in your car trunk so long? For days? You hit her with the tire iron as she bent into your trunk for battery cables and dumped her in, but—"

"Dump her? She *fell* in. I was just supposed to leave her at her car. I wasn't never supposed to *take* her. Why would I take her on purpose?"

"*Abby,*" Blanc said.

"If I wanna talk, I'll fuckin' talk," Land spat.

"Why leave her in the trunk for days?" Test said.

"I couldn't get her out. She was too heavy. I tried."

"So you left her?"

She shrugged. "I couldn't just ask someone to help me. Definitely not stupid Jamie after what she'd caused."

"What about Boyd?"

Blanc got up and opened the door. "Guard," she said and motioned.

"That's when he said even if I got caught it was no big deal," Land said. "If I kept shut up and didn't make mention of him. Our partying. I'd get out in two years after staying here, which he promised was a lot better digs than where I was living. He didn't lie 'bout that. You should see the TV. It's huge. I was freaking out still so he said he'd give me ten thousand bucks, too. So when I got out I wouldn't have no worries about money."

"He didn't offer to pay you beforehand?" Test said.

"Only after I fucked up. It was pretty good of him, even if he's a shit and lied about me doing hard time. I fucked up and he gives me ten grand? No one's ever given me squat. Never mind a *fortune*. Never mind because I fucked up. Whenever else I fucked up, someone would *fuck me* up."

"So it had nothing to do with Luke Montgomery?"

"No. I mean I hated how he fawned all over Mandy and I *could* have killed her for that. I was glad your partner thought he was the reason. It made Boyd feel safe, that you guys had a reason worked out. I was glad too. I mean, she was still in my trunk and I didn't know what to do and now we've got this warm thaw. If you guys hadn't busted me, I mean, she would've unfroze and started to smell pretty sick."

The guard entered the room.

"I ain't done," Land shouted at him.

"You are. She is," Blanc said.

"You can't decide!" Land shouted.

"So it was your idea and you did it for free?" Test said.

"Not for free. Money-wise, yeah. But. Fucked as it sounds, I did it cuz I loved him. Even if he is a perv. Or. Thought I did. Stupid. Stupid stupid *stupid*." She struck her temples with her balled fists.

Test stood up from her seat, put on her jacket.

"What you doin'?" Land said.

"Leaving."

"What? Wait. You can't *leave*. I got remorse," Land said. "That counts, don't it? That will help me, right? You gotta tell them how remorse I am."

Test walked out the door.

"Where you going!?" Abby Land screamed behind her, "What am I supposed to *do*!? What the fuck am I supposed to do *now*?"

86

Sonja Test arrived home at 11 P.M. expecting to crawl into bed beside her husband.

Instead, she found her husband and George and Elizabeth camped on the living room floor noshing on a bowl of popcorn and watching *Toy Story 3*.

"What on earth?" she said.

"Mama!" Elizabeth cried and leapt up from the floor, knocking the bowl over and scattering popcorn, nearly knocking over Test herself as she lunged for Test's legs and wrapped her arms around her.

Test collapsed on the couch with exhaustion as Elizabeth climbed in her lap and wrapped her arms around her mother's neck. "We've missed you! Where did you go!"

George picked a few pieces of popcorn off the floor and ate them as he climbed up next to Test. "She was working," he said.

"But where?" Elizabeth said. "Why? It's been dark so long!"

"She was helping people," Claude said, standing and stretching with a groan.

Test wasn't sure about that. Helping. It felt more and more she was simply cleaning up. Reacting instead of acting.

"Can I get you anything?" Claude asked her.

"Nothing."

Claude sat on the other side of her and she leaned into him.

God, her jaw and eyes ached with fatigue; even her eyelashes ached. Her head pounded as if squeezed in a vise. She tried to settle in, rid her mind of the images of Preacher in his chair, and of poor, sad, stupid Abby Land. And Mandy Wilks in the trunk of Abby's car. And—

The kids wrapped themselves more tightly against her to watch the video.

"I accepted the visiting artist position," Claude whispered in her ear.

"Shhh," Elizabeth said.

"Good," Sonja said and squeezed his hand.

"Shhh," George said.

"What'd they say about the fulltime position in the fall?" Sonja said.

"We don't have to talk about that now."

"Shhh," Elizabeth said.

"Tell me," Sonja said.

"It's available to me. To us," Claude said.

Sonja wondered if there were another way. To live her life. A way she could help more than she did now, where she was expected to refer to women and girls by their names, not be scolded when she did. A way to help the living instead of the dead. Perhaps become a domestic abuse advocate. Or work with disadvantaged girls who needed mentors, a woman to show them alternatives, to show them their worth, to show them not everyone wanted to fuck with them, fuck them up, or just plain fuck them. Girls who otherwise might not stand a chance. Girls like Abby Land.

But then, who would help the dead? Who would give them the dignity they deserved by calling them by their names and remembering they'd been alive, had lives, were humans who, even if not valued as much as they ought to have been in life, were valued now, at least, in death. And how could she ever leave this house? Her home?

She was too tired to think anymore about it tonight.

"And only if it worked for us," Claude whispered.

"Shhh," Elizabeth said but pressed closer, breathing heavily. She'd be snoring in a minute, Sonja knew.

Claude pulled Sonja in closer.

"I was thinking," Sonja whispered.

"Yeah?" Claude whispered.

"I *hear* you," George said, his voice drowsy.

"I was thinking I'd make a huge sweet potato casserole with extra brown sugar for Thanksgiving," Sonja whispered.

"Sounds good."

"That's it."

"That's what?"

"That's all I'm going to cook. A huge sweet potato casserole with extra brown sugar topping, served with four plastic spoons and four paper plates, out here on the coffee table while we watch movies in our pajamas. What do you think?"

"Perfect," Claude said as both George and Elizabeth began to snore, their bodies growing warm against Test who'd be snoring in another minute, too, if she stayed here on the couch with her family.

Which is exactly what she did.

87

Rachel sat at the kitchen table, listening to the wind in the eves. It sounded musical, like birdsong, though perhaps that was the Percocet at work. She plucked an ice cube from the cereal bowl of ice cubes Felix had put out for her with the same care and pride and love he would have shown if he'd prepared an exotic gourmet dish.

She sucked on the ice cube, letting the cold water trickle down her ravaged throat.

Felix and her father sat at the table with her.

No one spoke.

Rachel's voice was hoarse and it hurt to speak.

Besides, what was there to say?

She'd tried to sleep but was too tired and too tense.

She wished she could sleep. Her body begged for it, but her troubled mind played the foil.

Her father sipped a Labatt Blue from the bottle. Felix joined him, drinking from the bottle Rachel's father had cracked open for him. Rachel could tell Felix didn't have a taste for the Canadian pilsner, but he drank it anyway.

She hoped her father's phone would ring soon, a call to tell him Boyd Pratt had been arrested.

The couple was deranged. As Rachel understood from her father, the husband had a *thing* for young girls. A violent, psychosexual thing that entailed luring and grooming and manipulating girls younger than Rachel. Much younger. Like his wife had been when he'd met her.

Rachel was an exception, the wife had confessed, because Boyd liked risk. And did not like to be told what to do, by anyone. Especially a cop. Boyd had targeted her for who she was, the daughter of a nosy cop making trouble for him. What better challenge than to fuck with and try to fuck a nosy cop's daughter. It sickened Rachel.

How stupid she'd been.

How stupid she was.

No. Not stupid. Confused. An emotional and mental wreck from the Preacher business. Whoever had killed him had done the world a favor.

Sick with guilt, she looked at Felix, even though she'd, technically, done nothing wrong. All she'd done was talk to the guy. Taken a ride. Still. She did not want to live on technicalities. She'd betrayed Felix, that was the truth. She swore to herself she'd never do it again. She would never lie to him, never hide things from him again.

Drowsiness was creeping up on her.

She longed to sleep in her old bed, in her old bedroom.

Safe and sound.

Felix looked at her, smiled. He lifted the beer bottle, as if in cheers.

Her father raised his bottle toward her, too.

"I'm glad you're here," he said. "I'm glad you're safe."

Rachel let out a long sigh to stifle a sob.

"I bought a gun," she said. "A thirty-eight revolver."

Felix and Rachel's father stared at her.

"It's in my backpack," Rachel said.

Her father and Felix nodded.

"I thought you should know," she said. "I wanted you to know."

88

Sunday, November 13, 2011

The driver for CV Electric Utility Company tromped on his truck's brakes as the deer clambered out of the fog and brush and onto the dirt road in front of him.

The fog swam in the headlights.

No. Not a deer. A person.

A woman. Emaciated.

Hunched over and lurching gamely.

A woman who now collapsed in a heap on the road in front of him.

The driver jumped out of his truck and ran to kneel beside the woman.

"You're all right. You're going to be all right," he said, though he did not believe it.

Her face was swollen and bruised, her forehead busted and gashed, cheeks coated in blood. The blood old, crusted black. Like creosote in an old stovepipe.

No, he did not think she'd be all right.

His work cell had no bars. He hated to leave her even for a moment, not wanting her to die alone, but he needed to do it. He hurried back to his truck, got on his radio, and called it into his company dispatch to get on 911 and tell them to bust ass, fog or not.

He went back to the woman in the road. He did not dare move her, so stayed with her as she moaned and sobbed.

It was half an hour before the ambulance reached them.

When the Bloomfield deputy sheriff took over soon after, the driver took out a flashlight from his truck and looked more closely at the woods from which the woman had scrambled. It was hard to see anything, except fog.

It looked as though a car had gone off the road. It had flown over a steep bank, so it left no swath in the trees to see from the roadside, nothing to see from the road. He hiked down the bank, and followed the now visible swath into the woods. About fifty feet in, he spotted it, an old VW Bug, crashed into the trees.

The front end was demolished.

How she had ever survived the wreck was beyond him.

Some people, he thought, *are just plain survivors.*

89

Tuesday, November 15, 2011

One of Dana Clark's eyes was swollen shut, the other eye open but bloodied. The puckered skin along the black ragged zipper of stitches from between her eyes to the crown of her shaved skull was a hot, fierce red.

She was missing two teeth, but Rath only knew this because she smiled at him as her daughter led him into the living room of her home.

Dressed in a terrycloth bathrobe, Dana lay propped on pillows on her daughter's couch, her granddaughter snuggled in carefully next to her so as not to hurt her bruised ribs.

Dana gave her daughter a look and her granddaughter a pat on the thigh. Her daughter said, "Let's let Grammy talk to her friend," and the two left the room.

Dana sat up a bit, slipping her hands into her robe pockets. She brought out a tissue, dabbed at a scab under her nose.

"We were worried," Rath said. "I was."

"I'm all right now," she said and smiled, though Rath saw it pained her.

"How's the pain?" Rath said.

"I've known a lot worse."

Rath nodded. "You mentioned a man on the porch of the Wayside."

She looked confused as she slipped her hands back in her robe pockets. "I did?"

"When you were on the phone with your daughter."

"I don't remember being on the phone."

"A strange man. He had you worried."

"Oh?" She seemed to be thinking hard, trying to conjure up memory from the depths. "Maybe. It's. Cloudy."

"He had nothing to do with your accident?"

"How could he?"

"Maybe he frightened you and you drove off too fast. Or he followed you."

"No. It was the fog."

"You're certain?"

"How could he have anything to do with it?"

"I guess only you can answer that."

"You make it sound mysterious."

"It's the cop in me."

"You're a detective again, I hear?"

"Was. It doesn't suit me. I never wanted it to begin with, honestly, but it involved you and— After what happened before. We thought you'd been taken. There was a man, a Clay Sheldon. We thought he'd done something to you. He did time with Ned Preacher, a suspect in your attack. Sheldon had photos of you."

She sat up more, gritting her teeth and wheezing. "Photos?"

"Polaroids."

"Oh," Dana said in an exhale of breath. "Was it him then, who attacked me?"

"It was."

"And because I mentioned a man, you thought it was him who was on the store porch? And he'd—"

"Something like that."

"And where is he now?"

Rath could see she was scared.

"He was found in his bathtub in his motel unit yesterday. His wrists slit. What I can't get my head around is the coincidence."

"Coincidence?"

"We investigated your disappearance and another unconnected murder. A thread led us to him. And he had those Polaroids. Of you. From your attack. Like the one your daughter found. It was him. He was your attacker. Had to be."

Her eyes welled up, she took another tissue from her pocket and blew her nose, tucked her hand back in the pocket.

"The odds just seem, unbelievable," Rath said. "He was seen with a drunk woman who fit your description and we believe she was bleeding and that he'd hurt her or—"

"It wasn't me."

"Of course. Still, it's hard for me to make sense of it all."

"Stop trying. I have. I mean, you can't make sense of everything. Sometimes, there *is* no sense to be made. A coincidence is a coincidence. A horrific act happens for no reason good enough to answer *why?*"

She closed her good eye and seemed about to nod off, but the eye fluttered open again.

"I should let you rest," Rath said. He leaned over and kissed Dana's cheek lightly.

"I'm sorry," he said.

"For what?"

"For telling you he was dead. For your pain."

"I'm sorry for your pain, too."

90

On the way home, Rath stopped by Preacher's old place.

The night was dark. The duplex, too. No cars.

The fog persisted in the trees.

He barely noticed, had grown used to it the way one gets used to anything when it refuses to go away.

The neighbor woman had moved out. Who would possibly stay after what had happened? Who would possibly want to ever live here again? *They should burn the place down*, Rath thought. Start over. Or better yet, let the woods reclaim the plot.

He walked into the trees, the beam of his flashlight illuminating the fog.

He'd not been able to get here sooner. There had been police and media and the neighbor's family in and out for days.

Now, finally, in the night, he was here. Alone.

The birdhouse was gone.

"Fuck," he said in the dark. "Fuck."

He searched the ground with his flashlight.

There it was. The birdhouse.

It had fallen.
He opened its lid.
The trail camera was inside.
The SD card inside it.
He took them both and drove home.

91

After Frank Rath left, Dana took the letter out of her robe pocket. The pink letter soiled with blood.

Her daughter and granddaughter came into the room and Dana waved them off. "Give me a minute?" she said.

Alone again, she unfolded the letter and read it.

Dear Mr. Preacher,

Many have said you are a monster. An animal. A beast. The Lord knows this is not true. I know this is not true. No man is a monster. You are a man. A human. Made in his image. With the beast inside you. I followed your story. I learned you have found the Lord, and through him, found your release to freedom. I hope you have also found forgiveness and peace through Christ. As you enter the world from prison, you will still be seen as a beast by others. But not by me. If no one else forgives you, know I forgive you. Know I, though a woman,

know, as you do, how women can be. They are not free of
sin themselves. They lust. They tempt. I confess, I am not
without sin. Only love can rid you, or me, of the beast.
Know that Christ loves you. And that I love you too. My
love can rid you of the beast, if you'll have it. If you'll
have me. Will you? Will you have me? If so, bring this
flower I've given you, this rose, back to the end of your
road and place it on the rock. Then I will know you'll
have me. That you will receive me. Receive my love. Take
my love. I will come to you soon, if the flower is placed
on the rock. I will come for you.

　　I am Love.

She folded the letter and reached into her other pocket and
took out the Polaroid.

Not the one her daughter found that day.

The other one.

The one Clay Sheldon had taken a picture of and shown to her
on his phone that night on the Wayside porch.

It had pained Dana to lie to Frank Rath, but she'd done what
she needed to do. She remembered everything on the store porch
that night.

She remembered fighting and screaming and kicking at Sheldon, terror splitting her in two it seemed, a nightmare awakened.

Finally, he'd calmed her. Explained. About Ned Preacher being
his prison mate, about Ned Preacher being the Great Pretender,
not a lick of remorse for his crimes. The crimes he'd bragged about
inside. Not a drop of regret. As if he'd never committed them.
Never caused pain. Like the pain Sheldon's daughter had felt,
and the pain Sheldon had felt on behalf of his daughter. Preacher

had not committed the crime against Sheldon's daughter, but he bragged about much worse. Bragged.

It was what had happened to Sheldon's daughter that decided it for Dana, that and the dozens of photos Sheldon had shown her. Dozens of photos Preacher had kept hidden in a metal box in the woods, behind Dana's old house where Preacher had originally attacked her. Behind her *home*. Photos that Preacher had traded for a lousy old truck. A truck he planned to use to *get around in, once the dust settled*.

Preacher would deny the photos were his if Sheldon ever designed to use them against him. Preacher. Who'd killed that kind Frank Rath's sister and brother-in-law. And others. Girls. Preacher, who was out of prison. Alive and living. Without regret or remorse. Waiting to start again.

So close.

Too close.

She'd seen it in his eyes the night at his house. Seen what he had in mind for her.

After Sheldon found her at the Wayside, she and Sheldon had hidden her and her car in an old, abandoned barn in New Hampshire. She'd written the letter and mailed it to Preacher. Sheldon had driven past Forgotten Gorge Road and seen the rose out on the rock. A second letter, which she also now had in her robe pocket, was sent. The date set for a few days later, so Dana could prepare herself, and she and Sheldon could plan it perfectly.

The night of her *date*, she and Sheldon had crashed her car into the trees using a barbell to weigh down the gas pedal. Straight over the bank, on a curve, where the car would never be seen, even if there was no fog. She'd eaten almost nothing since that first night at the Wayside. Couldn't eat out of nervousness and fear and trauma. It was a good thing she hadn't. She'd appeared weaker when found, like a woman trapped in a car for days.

Preacher had not recognized her. Had looked her in the eye, the gaze of his dead black eyes crawling all over her body, and not known who she was. Not until she had undone her third button on her dress and he had begun to see her ruined and scarred flesh he'd carved.

After she'd done what she needed to do, Sheldon had picked her up on the road. Driven her to her crashed car and struck her ribs with a piece of firewood. As she'd sat in the seat, he'd cracked her forehead with a violent blow of a fiberglass ax handle, then taken her by the hair and cracked her forehead again, against the wheel.

She'd known worse pain.

The plan was to have her awaken from the blow and wander out onto the road and be rescued. But Sheldon had struck her so hard she'd been knocked out and too weak and concussed to move for a couple days. It was for the better. The wounds were older, crusted. She'd grown even weaker and thinner. She realized now if she'd stumbled out earlier, the wounds would have been too fresh. Perhaps raised suspicion about her crash, and who knew what else. It was a good thing poor Clay Sheldon had struck her so hard. It was a good thing the utility man had come along. She may have died if she'd gone much longer without water or attention. It was a miraculous coincidence. If that was what one chose to call it.

She'd not thought of that when she'd thought the original plan was perfect. She wondered what else she and Sheldon had overlooked, but she did not worry about being caught. Not now. Even if she were caught, she'd do it all over again.

Dana got up slowly from the couch and walked to the fireplace.

She stared into it, then tossed the photo and the two letters into the flames.

"What are you doing up?" her daughter said behind her, startling her.

The photo and letter curled on themselves and were gone.

"I was cold," Dana said.

Her daughter wrapped her arms around her from behind. "Just tell me next time and I'll turn up the heat."

"I'm fine now."

92

Rachel lay asleep in her room as Rath sat at his kitchen table with the envelope. He opened it and for a long time he did nothing but stare at the two strands of hair inside it: Preacher's and Rachel's.

He took both hairs out and placed them side by side on a blank piece of white paper. He connected his trail cam by USB cord to Rachel's laptop computer.

Thumbnail images from the SD card appeared on the screen. Several dozen.

A prompt appeared on the screen: Import or Delete Images?

He needed to erase evidence of himself from the card then mail it with the remaining images to the police. It was likely moot. No doubt Sheldon's image was on the SD card. Sheldon and Preacher had experienced a falling-out and Sheldon had done his deed.

Rath began to enlarge each photo as he selected them. Some of the photos were of birds. Others were of raccoons and skunks foraging at night. There were images of the neighbor coming and going. Images of Test and Larkin coming and going. Images of

Rath and Test and the troopers and forensics. Images of Preacher. Images of Rath setting up the trail camera, and of him from hunting and fishing trips when he'd used the SD card in his regular camera.

And still other images of someone else entering Preacher's house.

Rath sat staring at those images for a long time. Checked the time code.

The time right before the estimated time of death for Preacher. The same person left an hour later.

Rath took a drink of beer.

The woman in the pictures had her hat pulled down and a scarf around her chin, but it was her.

It came clear now.

Sheldon's tattoos of his daughter's name on his chest.

The pain of his daughter's death. Preacher's own crimes were of the same ilk as had been exacted on Sheldon's daughter. Remorseless, guiltless Preacher. Somehow, over sixteen years, Sheldon had forged a fake bond with Preacher. Gained Preacher's confidence. Perhaps feigned an affinity for such cruelty. Or been so desperate he'd lied and told Preacher he, Sheldon, had been the one to rape and kill his own daughter. One way or another, he'd won Preacher's trust and stolen or traded the truck for the Polaroids.

The gray hair in the tub may not have been Dana Clark's, but Dana had been the woman the motel manager had seen at the North Star. Had she gone there with Sheldon, distraught and sobbing from shock so she appeared drunk to the manager? Had she perhaps even fought Sheldon on the Wayside steps, enough to cut herself before he calmed her and convinced her he was not her attacker, but Preacher was, and that he, Sheldon, had a plan?

Rath could not figure the specifics. They didn't matter. He'd seen Dana Clark with her granddaughter and her daughter. She loved life. Her life. She'd done what she'd done because it was what she needed to do, to do more than survive, but to live.

She'd done what Rath had not dared to do.

But. It did not make what she'd done right, legal, or moral.

He of all people understood this.

She'd almost gotten away with it.

She'd left no proof behind and had the perfect alibi of being wrecked in the trees and fog at the time of Preacher's killing. As of yet, there was no evidence whatsoever to link Preacher and Dana Clark. No reason at all to suspect her, except for the images on the SD card and computer screen.

Rath thought about Preacher in the interview room. People got away with murder. How many went to their grave with a murder on their conscience? Most of them heinous, stupid people who somehow managed, in the only respect that mattered, to commit the perfect murder. Mean, merciless, cruel people who deserved to pay, yet didn't.

While girls like Jamie Drake and Lucille Forte and Mandy Wilks lay in their graves, and people like Dana Clark slipped up and now faced prison for the rest of her life if discovered.

There was nothing anyone could do to right that sad balance sheet.

Almost nothing.

Rath studied the photos of Dana Clark coming and going from Preacher's house.

He glanced at the hairs on the blank sheet of paper. Blew on them lightly. The hairs shivered, lifted on his breath, danced in the air, and were gone.

He looked at the photos of Dana Clark on the laptop screen until his vision blurred and the images of her seemed to be dissolving in a fog.

Then, he hit Delete and went down the hall, checked on his sleeping daughter, climbed into his bed, and slept like a man with no regrets.

ACKNOWLEDGMENTS

Thanks to all who've encouraged, improved, and championed my writing over the years. My lovely wife, Meridith. My daughter, Samantha, and son, Ethan, for their smiles, hugs, and joy, and for their love of books and stories. My mother. My sisters: Beth, Judy, and Susan. All of my nieces and nephews: Jaclyn, Jacob, Harrison, Emily, Bryanna, Eric, Willa, Boone, Hailey, and Poppy. Gary Martineau. Libby and Herb Levinson. Todd and Diane Levinson. Allyson Miller. Ben Wilson. Dan Myers. Dan Orseck. Tom Isham. Mark Saunders. Lailee Mendelson. Kimberly Cutter. Anya DeNiro. Rob O'Donovan. John Mero. Roger and Susan Bora. Jeff Racine. Mike and Janice Quartararo. Stephen and Carole Phillips. Eric Weissleder. Chris Champine. Andrea Diamond. Dave and Heidi Bouchard. Jim Lepage. Phil Monahan. David Huddle. Tony Magistrale. Bill and Mary Wilson. Jamie and Stephen Foreman. Bruce Coffin. Matthew Engels. Daniel Nogueira. Lucinda Jamison. Greg Cutler. Paul Doiron. David Joy. Steve Ulfelder. Roger Smith. Meg Gardiner. Hank Phillippi Ryan. Jake Hinkson. Lisa Turner. Drew Yanno. Tyler Mcmahon. Howard Mosher. Rona and Bob Long. A special thanks to my agent Philip Spitzer, and to Lukas Ortiz and Kim Lombardini. And to the wonderful and creative people at HarperCollins, especially my editor, Carrie Feron.

AUTHOR'S NOTE

Hello, readers. I often get asked where I get my ideas, or how the idea for the Canaan Crime series came to be. It's a long story. This is the short version. But I hope it explains in part how I came to write novels such as *The Silent Girls, Lie in Wait,* and *The Names of Dead Girls.*

I grew up in Vermont, and as a kid I was drawn to the desolate, beautiful, and bucolic woods of the northeast corner of the state known as the Northeast Kingdom, where Canada borders the north and the Connecticut River and New Hampshire border the east. I fished, hunted, camped, and explored the woods. They were full of wild mystery and majesty.

I saw the woods as an escape to a place of ultimate tranquility, where nothing bad happened.

I was wrong. Naive. There is no such place.

I read a lot of dark tales, even then. Perhaps it was the works by the likes of Poe, King, and Washington Irving that made me start to see the beauty as a mask for something more ominous. Or perhaps the woods and wilderness have always frightened humans, which is why we write about them and why they play such a large role in our psyches and our lore of dark tales. Tales like "Hansel and Gretel" come to mind. "Little Red Riding Hood." "The Legend of Sleepy Hollow." *The Blair Witch Project.* The woods in the Kingdom can grow dark in the day just from the density of the boreal forest, the cedars and spruce and hemlocks that hem in the rivers and swamps grow so thick and tall they blot out the sun. When dusk fell, or the skies darkened with storm clouds, or fog settled in thick as cobwebs, the woods took on a threatening, haunted air.

But it was a certain fishing trip with a cousin when something bad, and unforgettable, happened to me.

I was fourteen. I stood all of 5'6", weighed a whopping 115 pounds. Pipe-cleaner arms. Skin and bones. My cousin was seventeen. We'd taken his old Jeep CJ5 up to the most remote spot we could find to fish a hidden trout stream. The road was dirt, not a house in sight except for an old dilapidated shack that looked like a chicken coop backed up to an outhouse. There were no other houses for miles. We pulled the Jeep into a field by the stream and set up our tent, readying it for when we returned from fishing that evening. We'd found the spot just in time. The Jeep was overheating. We'd had to stop and fill the radiator a while back and we knew the Jeep likely would not have gotten us much farther and would likely not start again until it cooled over several hours.

I was fishing down in a ravine and came to the culvert that took the stream under the dirt road by the broken-down house. I climbed the bank to the road as my cousin continued to fish, out of earshot.

Up on the road, crossing to the other side, I saw two men lumbering toward me from the old house. One man was maybe thirty-five, the other maybe fifty-five. A father and son, I imagined. Unshaven and grizzled, they each wore greasy overalls and sported thick Coke-bottle glasses with florescent orange tape at the bridges of their noses. And they each carried a single-shot, break-action shotgun.

I said hello as they approached.

They said nothing.

Until they were upon me. Close.

Close enough for me to smell their reek of B.O.

Close enough for me to pick up the sense of something sinister vibrating off of them.

The son snarled, "That your fuckin' Jeep up there?"

I was about to say it was my cousin's, who was in the stream, out of sight, out of earshot.

I didn't get a chance. "Move it the fuck now," he hollered. He stepped closer. He and the father. Real close. In my face. So I could smell and feel their breath on me, and see the spittle foaming at the corner of their mouths. They had twenty and forty years on me, at least. Each had seventy-five pounds and a half foot on me. And each carried a shotgun. We stood in the middle of a dirt road in the middle of nowhere, miles from another house. No cars were going to be coming along. No one was coming along. It was me and them.

I looked back toward the creek, for my cousin.

"What the fuck din't you understand?" the son yelled. "Move your fucking Jeep now!"

I tried to tell them I couldn't. I didn't know how to drive. It wasn't my Jeep. My cousin would be up soon and we'd leave. We would. If we could. The Jeep might not start. It was overheating, and it might not start for hours.

Before I could say any of that, the son howled: "Move that

fucking Jeep. Who the fuck do you think you are parking in our field? Move it!"

My cousin was clambering up the bank now, oblivious. "Hey," he said. Then he saw how close the two men were to me. Their guns. My fear.

"That your fucking Jeep?" The son screamed. "Move it the fuck now. Get the fuck off our property. Who the fuck do you think you are?"

My cousin, shaken, tried to explain. To apologize.

The father handed his shotgun to the son. The son now held a shotgun in each hand and, his face a foot from mine, held them with one barrel beside my left ear and one beside my right.

"Move! Now!" he roared. And he fired a shotgun.

I went deaf. No ringing of the ears. No vacuum roar of silence. Just. Nothing. The men were yelling and my cousin was explaining, but I heard nothing. Just saw the son's jaw yawning open and snapping shut like the jaws of a wolf, his face red and contorted with rage, spittle flying.

We backed away.

Slowly. Instinctively. We did not dare put our backs to them.

My ears started to ring. They hurt with the ringing, as if a sharp sonic needle were piercing my eardrums.

"Walk slow," my cousin said. "Don't make 'em mad."

We backed up more.

The men stood in the road watching us, knowing no cars would be coming.

The son broke open the shotgun he'd fired. Gun smoke poured out of the breech. The empty shotgun shell ejected into the air and skittered in the dirt road.

The son took a loaded shotgun shell from his pocket, seated it in the shotgun, and snapped the shotgun shut.

"Why is he reloading?" I said.

We backed away until we were on the edge of fatal shotgun range, maybe fifty yards, then we turned and ran.

We ripped the tent up with all our gear inside and stuffed it in the Jeep. And, just like in a bad horror flick, when my cousin turned the key in the ignition, the engine did not turn over. Not at first. Finally, it did, and we drove back to the road and pulled out onto it, looking back to see the two men still standing there in the road. That is when I knew no one was safe anywhere.

Although I'd always loved dark stories and novels, that was the real genesis of the themes that would interest me in my writing.

Dark, desolate woods and landscape, suffused with beauty yet lurking with potential violence. An old story. Perhaps the oldest.

When one visits any region of sublime natural beauty, one is lulled into a sense of being safe, a dreamlike state that nothing bad could ever happen in a place so beautiful. As I wrote in *The Silent Girls*:

> Violence lurked here as it did the world over, most often exacted between known parties. Intimate, familial, and unspeakable. [Rath] had always wondered why people in rural areas, when interviewed after horrific violence, said, "This isn't supposed to happen here." As if violence had forgotten to keep itself within some prescribed geographic boundary.

This is the theme I took into this Canaan Crime series. The sense that acts of malevolence can strike anywhere, anytime. It allows me to examine the nature of good and evil. Of the very real repercussions of violence and crime, and the way small communities and individuals respond to such acts when those they know are victims of it. What do you do when the law is not enough to protect you? What would my cousin have done if I was shot? What would our families have done if we'd both been killed and the Jeep hidden in an old barn and our bodies in a shallow grave? No one knew where we were. We could easily have disappeared.

It also allows me to write novels steeped in suspense, dread, and tension, play with twists and revelations in a way most of us seek and enjoy as readers.

In the last ten years, several very violent and especially cruel and merciless murders have taken place in the Kingdom that outraged me as much as any other citizen. They broke hearts. They ruined lives and undermined that sense of safety that those of us who have never experienced violence or the threat of it often have. These crimes change the trajectory of the lives and psyches of survivors, of communities. I write about them to try to understand them from every angle, and because they are timeless. The landscape's beauty and mystery, its darkness, the old barns and abandoned skeletons of homes, old root cellars and dark attics make for a superb setting for psychological thrillers for these classic, chilling, suspenseful stories that are as old as humanity.

Two months ago, an eighty-one-year-old neighbor who lives a half mile away was murdered. She was stabbed to death when a break-in went wrong. Eighty-one years old. She'd lived a long, good life and raised a family in that house, and her life came to a terrifying end like that. For two months no one has been arrested. For two months the killer has remained at large.

How can this be? I wonder. Who does such a thing? Commits such an act? How can the killer still be out there, likely among us? One of us, yet not one of us. Not anymore. The killing separated the murderer from the rest of "us." We in this small town of 2,300 people are held in suspense, awaiting word of an arrest. It is the stuff of horror novels and tall tales. Lore. Except it is real. I go by my murdered neighbor's road at least four times a day to bring my daughter to kindergarten. Now. Today, as it turns out in a twist as write this, I learn that the murderer has just been arrested, at the recreation park two miles from my home where my wife and I bring our kids. He is one of us. Or was. He lived just a few miles from my house. Grew up here. He'd broken into the house and then "got scared and one thing led to another." I don't know how it can be. I hope he is put away for decades, not able to find release until he is infirm and unable to hurt anyone else. Except "justice" does not always work this way. Too often violent criminals, murderers, and especially sexual predators of women and children are released early to do harm again. It happens over and over. How many times have you seen a news report about a killer or rapist just being arrested, one who'd spent a lifetime in out of jail for the very same crimes only to be freed and victimize again? This, too, is part of my theme. Moral codes versus legal codes. Such events compel me to explore them, to write about them with all the darkness, suspense, mystery, dread, and outrage I can. To try to find an answer.

I plan to write many more of this series, and many stand-alones.

Crime and violence and murder will forever intrigue me, as it does so many of us, as we try to find a way to render the inexplicable explicable.

Thank you for reading.